The COMPLETE IDIOT'S GUIDE TO

Netscape Navigator with Windows® 95

by Joe Kraynak

A Division of Macmillan Publishing
201 W.103rd Street, Indianapolis, IN 46290 USA

To Marc Andreessen, Netscape founder, for demonstrating how easy it is to work your way through college.

©1996 Que® Corporation

All rights reserved. No part of this book shall be reproduced, stored in a retrieval system, or transmitted by any means, electronic, mechanical, photocopying, recording, or otherwise, without written permission from the publisher. No patent liability is assumed with respect to the use of the information contained herein. Although every precaution has been taken in the preparation of this book, the publisher and author assume no responsibility for errors or omissions. Neither is any liability assumed for damages resulting from the use of the information contained herein. For information, address Que, 201 W. 103rd Street, Indianapolis, IN 46290. You may reach Que's direct sales line by calling 1-800-428-5331.

International Standard Book Number: 0-7897-0680-6
Library of Congress Catalog Card Number: 95-72606

98 97 96   8 7 6 5 4 3 2 1

Interpretation of the printing code: the rightmost number of the first series of numbers is the year of the book's printing; the rightmost number of the second series of numbers is the number of the book's printing. For example, a printing code of 96-1 shows that the first printing of the book occurred in 1996.

Screen reproductions in this book were created by means of the program Collage Complete from Inner Media, Inc., Hollis, NH.

Printed in the United States of America

Publisher
Roland Elgey

Vice President and Publisher
Marie Butler-Knight

Editorial Services Director
Elizabeth Keaffaber

Publishing Manager
Barry Pruett

Managing Editor
Michael Cunningham

Development Editor
Seta Frantz

Technical Editor
Discovery Computing, Inc.

Production Editor
Phil Kitchel

Copy Editor
San Dee Phillips

Cover Designers
Dan Armstrong, Barbara Kordesh

Designer
Kim Scott

Illustrations
Judd Winick

Technical Specialist
Nadeem Muhammed

Indexer
Brad Herriman

Production Team
Steve Adams, Trey Frank, Jason Hand, Damon Jordan, Stephanie Layton, Michelle Lee, Julie Quinn, Bobbi Satterfield, Karen York

Contents at a Glance

Part 1: Getting Wired with Netscape Navigator   **1**

  1 The Top Ten Things You Need to Know   3
     Ten Steps to Navigator and the World Wide Web.

  2 Netscape Navigator and the World Wide Web   9
     Orientation day.

  3 Taking Netscape Beyond the Web   15
     More stuff you can do with Navigator.

  4 What You Need to Start   21
     The bare software and hardware essentials.

  5 Setting Up Your PPP or SLIP Connection in Windows 95   35
     Windows 95 takes on the Internet.

  6 Setting Up Your Internet Connection Using Windows 3.1   47
     Finding an Internet entrance ramp in Windows 3.1.

  7 Now, You Can Install Netscape Navigator   65
     Finally, you get to install the program.

  8 Day Trippin' on the Web   75
     Some quick trips behind the wheel of Navigator.

  9 What Could Possibly Go Wrong?   85
     Deciphering error messages and regaining your footing.

Part 2: Mastering Navigator   **91**

  10 Weaving Through the World Wide Web   93
     High-powered navigational tools.

  11 Revisiting Your Favorite Pages   105
     Marking your favorite Web pages with bookmarks.

  12 Going Multimedia with Helper Applications   117
     Playing sounds, pictures, and video clips.

  13 Saving and Printing Your Finds   129
     Hauling off truckloads of goodies.

  14 Corresponding with Electronic Mail   137
     Using Netscape Mail to send and receive missives.

  15 Customizing Navigator to Make It Your Own   153
     Customizing and detailing the Navigator Interface.

Part 3: Stretching the Web with Navigator   **165**

16 Grabbing Files with FTP   167
Copying files from the Internet to your computer.

17 Chatting Online with Other Users   177
Talking with other users by typing at your keyboard.

18 Gophering from Navigator   191
Graphical Gopher menus from Navigator.

19 Telnetting with Navigator (and a Little Help)   201
Using other people's computers from your keyboard.

20 Reading and Posting Newsgroup Messages   213
Special interest bulletin boards.

21 Other WAIS of Finding Information   223
Playing librarian on the Web.

22 Finding People on the Internet   233
Looking up lost friends and relatives.

23 Forging Your Own Hyperdocuments   239
Making Web pages of your own.

24 More Internet Sites Than You'll Ever Have Time to Visit   251
A list of cool (at least I think they're cool) Internet sites.

Speak Like a Geek: The Complete Archive   291
The glossary of Netscape and the World Wide Web.

Index   301
Finding (and refinding) information in this book.

Contents

Part 1: Getting Wired with Netscape Navigator — 1

1 The Top Ten Things You Need to Know — 3

1. Think of the World Wide Web As a Huge Multimedia Encyclopedia 3
2. Navigator Is Your Window to the World Wide Web 5
3. Is Your Computer Powerful Enough? 5
4. You Need a Couple Special Programs, Too 6
5. Here's Where You Get the Programs 7
6. You Have Everything—Now What? 7
7. Connecting for the First Time 7
8. Rolling Through the Web 7
9. Playing Photos, Sounds, and Video Clips 8
10. Exit, Stage Left 8

2 Netscape Navigator and the World Wide Web — 9

First, There Was the Internet 10
In the Beginning 10
Here's Where the Web Fits In 11
Tracking Down Information with URLs 13
Channel Surfing on the Web 13
The Least You Need to Know 14

3 Taking Netscape Beyond the Web — 15

Postage-Free Mail, Same-Day Delivery 16
Gophering Here and There 16
Snatching Files with FTP 17
Using Archie to Track Down a File 18
Swapping Information in Newsgroups 18
Poking Around on Other People's Computers 18
Chatting Incognito with Other Users 19
WAIS to Find Information 20
Fingering to Find Friends and Colleagues 20
The Least You Need to Know 20

4 What You Need to Start — 21

Does Your Computer Have What It Takes? 22
Getting Wired: Finding an Internet Connection 23
    A "Free" Permanent Connection 23
    Using an Internet $ervice Provider 23
    Shopping for an Internet Service Provider 24
    Get Your Credit Card Handy 26
Setting Up and Signing On 27
    No Sweat: Logging On with a Permanent Connection .. 27
    Logging on to a Service Provider 28
    What to Expect 31
    What Went Wrong? 32
    Logging Out and Hanging Up 33
The Least You Need to Know 33

5 Setting Up Your PPP or Slip Connection in Windows 95 — 35

Doing PPP or SLIP in Windows 95 36
Is Dial-Up Networking Even Installed? 36
Bondage 101: Binding Dial-Up Networking to TCP/IP 37
PPP Made Easy 38
You're Almost There: Creating an Icon to Dial 40
You Have a SLIP Account? Take Two Valiums 41
Does It Work? 43
    If Your Server Requires a Terminal Window... 44
    What Went Wrong? 45
The Least You Need To Know 46

6 Setting Up Your Internet Connection Using Windows 3.1 — 47

Make Your Service Provider Do It 48
If You Decide to Go It Alone... 48
Unzip Me 52
Setting Winsock on the Right Path 53
Now That You Have Trumpet Winsock... 54
A Sure Thing: Logging In Manually 57
Cheating Your Way Through a Login Script 59
Ugh! Writing Your Own Script 60
The Least You Need to Know 64

7 Now, You Can Install Netscape Navigator 65

Where Can You Find Navigator? 66
Snatching Navigator Off the Internet 66
    FTPing the Easy Way 67
    FTPing in the Old Days 70
    FTPing with a Web Browser 71
Installing Navigator 73
The Least You Need To Know 74

8 Day Trippin' on the Web 75

Ladies and Gentlemen, Start Your Engines 76
Hitting the Open Road 76
Does It Seem S...L...O...W? 77
Moseying Around the Navigator Screen 77
Working with Window Frames 79
Wandering the Web 79
Retracing Your Steps 80
I Clicked, But Nothing Happened 82
What About the Movie Clips? The Sound Clips? 82
Signing Off and Shutting Down 83
The Least You Need to Know 83

9 What Could Possibly Go Wrong? 85

Why the Web Is Soooo Buggy 86
Navigator Can't Find the Server 86
Navigator Can't Find the Document 88
Document Contains No Data 89
Less Frequent Problems 89
Finding Answers to Your Questions 90
The Least You Need To Know 90

Part 2: Mastering Navigator 91

10 Weaving Through the World Wide Web 93

Starting from Your Home (Page) 94
Navigational Tools Revisited 95
Touring the Web with URLs 96
    URLs Dissected 97
    Hitting the URL Trail 98

This Page Has No Links!	99
Juggling Two or More Web Documents	100
Searching for Topics: Indexes and Web Robots	101
Searching for Information on a Page	103
The Least You Need To Know	104

11 Revisiting Your Favorite Pages   105

Going Back in History (Lists)	106
Marking a Page with a Bookmark	107
Giving Your Bookmark List a Makeover	108
Renaming and Deleting Bookmarks	109
Shuffling Your Bookmarks	110
Grouping Bookmarks with Separators and Submenus	111
When You Add Bookmarks Later…	113
Ugh! Adding Bookmarks Manually	114
Creating and Saving Additional Bookmark Lists	114
Trading Bookmark Lists with Your Friends	115
The Least You Need To Know	116

12 Going Multimedia with Helper Applications   117

How Do Helper Applications Help?	118
Free and Inexpensive Programs That Fit the Bill	118
Downloading Helper Applications with Navigator	119
Decompressing and Installing the Software	121
Mapping Files to Their Helper Applications	122
Playing Multimedia Links	125
Do It! Cinema, Sounds, and Photos	125
Moving Pictures with Java	127
A Word About Sound and Video Quality	127
The Least You Need to Know	128

13 Saving and Printing Your Finds   129

Saving and Playing Clips and Pics	130
What About Hyperdocuments?	131
Taking a Peek at the Locals	133
Making Paper—Printing	134
Entering Your Page Preferences	134
Previewing Pages Before You Print	134
The Least You Need to Know	136

14 Corresponding with Electronic Mail — 137

You Have to Set It Up First 138
Writing (and Sending) an E-Mail Message 141
Finally, a Browser That Can Read Mail! 142
    Checking the Mail 143
    Responding to Messages 144
    Organizing Messages with Folders 145
    Selecting, Moving, Copying, and Deleting Messages ... 145
    Sorting Out Your Messages 147
    Compacting Folders to Save Space 147
Making an E-Mail Address "Book" 147
    Displaying Your Address Book as a Web Page 149
Behave Yourself: E-Mail Rules and Abbreviations 150
    :-) Emoticons: A Symbolic Internet Language 150
    Common Abbreviations, To Save Time 151
The Least You Need to Know 152

15 Customizing Navigator to Make It Your Own — 153

Turning Screen Things On and Off 154
Giving Navigator a Makeover 155
    A Peek at the Appearance Options 156
    Dressing Your Text in the Right Font 157
    Taking Your Crayolas to the Screen 158
    You Can Control Pictures, Too 159
Turning the Security Warnings On and Off 160
    Be Careful! 160
    Additional Security Options 161
Tinkering with Some Additional Settings 162
    Establishing a Strong Cache Flow 162
    You Gotta Have the Right Connections
    (But How Many?) 163
    A Word About the Proxies Tab 164
The Least You Need to Know 164

Part 3: Stretching the Web with Navigator — 165

16 Grabbing Files with FTP — 167

FTP: What's It All About? 168
    Connecting to FTP Sites 168

    FTP Sites That Anyone Can Use 168
    Using URLs to Access Specific Sites 170
    Stumbling Around in FTP Sites 170
    Viewing and Getting Files 171
    ZIP, TAR, and Other Compressed Files 172
    Using Archie to Sniff Out Files 172
    The Monster FTP Site List 175
    A Cool Trick 175
    The Least You Need to Know 176

17 Chatting Online with Other Users   177

    Where to Get Netscape's Chat Program 178
    Installing Netscape Chat 178
    Finding a Chatty Cove 179
    Connecting to a Chat Server with Netscape Chat 181
    More You Should Know About Conversations 184
    Person-to-Person Conversations 185
    Joining an Auditorium Discussion 186
    Sending and Receiving Web Pages 187
        Sending Web Pages to Discussion Participants 188
        Receiving and Viewing Web Pages Sent by Others 189
    Configuring Netscape Chat 189
    The Least You Need To Know 190

18 Gophering from Navigator   191

    Gopher and FTP: What's the Difference? 193
    Connecting to a Gopher Site 193
    Romping Around in a Gopher Server 194
    Searching Gopherspace with Veronica 195
        Searching with "And," "Or," "Not," and Wild Cards ... 196
        Narrowing a Search with Switches 197
    Making Bookmarks for Your Gopher Sites 198
    Searching a Single Server with Jughead 198
    Playing and Grabbing Files 199
    The Least You Need to Know 199

19 Telnetting with Navigator (and a Little Help)   201

    The Ins and Outs of Telnetting 202
    Whoa! You Need a Telnet Program First 202

Getting a Telnet Program for Cheap 202
Setting Telnet as a Helper Application 203
Running a Telnet Session 203
How Do I Connect? 204
I'm Supposed to Know My Terminal Type? 205
Greeting Your Telnet Host 205
What Do I Type? 206
HYTELNET, a Directory of Telnet Hosts 207
UNIX Primer 208
Bare Bone Basics 208
What's in This Directory, Anyway? 209
Changing Directories 209
Tracking Down Files 209
Taking a Peek at a Text File 209
Grabbing a File 209
Running a Program 210
Telnetting to an Archie Server 210
The Least You Need to Know 212

20 Reading and Posting Newsgroup Messages 213

Before You Can Read Newsgroups… 214
Connecting to a Newsgroup 215
Dissecting Newsgroup Addresses 216
Searching for Newsgroups 217
Reading Newsgroup Messages 218
Replying to Newsgroup Messages 220
Starting a New Discussion 221
Receiving and Sending Files in Newsgroups 221
The Least You Need to Know 222

21 Other WAIS of Finding Information 223

Cheating Your Way to WAIS 224
Composing Your Search Instructions 226
Now for the Complicated Stuff 227
Choosing a WAIS Proxy or Gateway 227
Performing a WAIS Search 227
The Least You Need to Know 230

22 Finding People on the Internet — 233
Fingering Your Friends 234
Other Things You Can Finger 235
Whois This Person? 236
Other Tools and Services for Finding Lost Souls 237
When All Else Fails, Write the Postmaster 237
The Least You Need to Know 237

23 Forging Your Own Hyperdocuments — 239
Crafting a Simple Home Page 240
Does It Work? 242
More Stuff You Can Stick in a Home Page 243
Inserting Inline Images and Sounds 244
Listing Things 245
The Philosophy of Logical Codes 246
Proper Form (for the Culturally Elite) 247
Cheating Your Way to HTML 247
Using HTML Authoring Tools 248
Learning More About HTML 249
The Least You Need to Know 250

24 More Internet Sites Than You'll Ever Have Time to Visit — 251
Quick Guide to Web Sites 251
The Arts, Fine and Otherwise 252
Books, Magazines, and Other Rags 255
Business, Not Pleasure 259
Computers, Hard and Soft 261
Education for Students and Teachers 264
Fun, Games, and Entertainment 266
Health and Fitness 269
Hobbies and Recreation 271
Internet News and Information 273
Investing Your Money 274
Job Hunting 275
Laws and Other Legal Stuff 277
Musical Notes 278

Movies and Videos	279
News, Real News	280
Philosophy and Religion	282
Politics and Government	284
Shopping Networks	285
Sports Scores and Schedules	286
Travel	288
Weather Reports and Maps	289
The Uncategorical Category	290

Speak Like a Geek: The Complete Archive   **291**

Index   **301**

Introduction: Picture This

You wake up and find yourself strapped into some souped-up virtual reality machine. You pop in a short stack of quarters, and perch your fingers over the controls. With the press of a button, a list pops up in front of your eyes, offering you everything from politics and pizza to Shakespeare and sex.

You punch in MOVIES, and call up a list of 50 movie sites covering everything from Tarantino to Sharon Stone. You whack the TARANTINO button, and see a complete list of his movies. You pick PULP FICTION and copy a clip from the movie to play later. You copy the script. You copy a picture of Tarantino, the man himself. Then, as quickly as you hit the site, you're gone. Backed out and on your way to nab some still shots of the alien autopsies from your favorite UFO site. You grab a few shots to use as Windows backgrounds, and you're outta there.

A couple hours later, your hard drive is packed full of sound clips, movie clips, scripts, pictures, and comics...just some stuff to keep you busy during the slow periods. You decide that you'd better do some work before noon; your boss wants you to come up with a savvy marketing strategy for a new product line. You don't even know what a marketing strategy is, so you click on BUSINESS and then on DUNN & BRADSTREET. Lucky guess—Dunn & Bradstreet offers a quick primer on developing a marketing strategy. You pull some sales figures and marketing numbers off another site and type up your report.

By three o'clock, you've e-mailed your marketing plan to the boss. You still have two hours to check out the movie clips and graphics you nabbed earlier. You lean back with your second bag of microwave popcorn and start playing.

You Want It...

This Flash Gordon/multimedia stuff isn't science fiction anymore. It's real. It's now. And it's here for anyone who has a computer, a modem, and a World Wide Web browser, such as Netscape Navigator.

With these few items and a bit of persistence, you can travel the world, accessing documents, video and sound clips, graphics, stock data, jokes, and any other information and media that are stored on computers connected to the Internet.

But You'd Have to Be a Genius!

Nah! You don't have to be a genius to wander the World Wide Web or use Netscape Navigator. You don't have to know how the Internet works, or even how the text, pretty pictures, sounds, and movie clips travel from computers all around the world to your computer. You have more important things to learn:

- Where to get the latest version of Netscape Navigator.
- How to connect to the Internet.
- How to install and run Netscape Navigator (or Navigator, for short).
- How to use Navigator to bounce around the World Wide Web.
- How to make a list of your favorite Web documents.
- How to get pictures and video clips...and look at them.
- How to get files from other computers.
- How to use Navigator to harness the power of other Internet features.

In this book, you'll be up and running with Navigator in six—count 'em, six—chapters. In the remaining chapters, you'll learn how to use Navigator to fly around in the Web and plunder its resources. You'll be surprised at how little you *need to know* in order to use Navigator...and how much you *can know* to cruise the Web like a master.

And You Are...?

In writing this book, I came up with a few generalizations about you. First, I figure you have some computer savvy. You know how to work with directories or folders, save and open files, and run programs. And you know the basics of using a modem. You may not sleep with your computer, but you feel pretty comfortable with it.

However, I could be wrong. If your knowledge of computers and modems is limited to what you've seen on *Good Morning, America,* maybe you should start with a more general

Introduction

computer book, first. I suggest *The Complete Idiot's Guide to PCs* (for general computer knowledge), and *The Complete Idiot's Guide to Modems & Online Services* (to brush up on modem basics).

And You Have a PC That's Running Windows?

Before you buy this book, make sure you have a PC-compatible computer that has Windows 95, Windows 3.1, or Windows 3.11 installed on it. There are other versions of Netscape Navigator (for Macs and for UNIX), but this book isn't going to cover those versions in great detail.

How We Do Things in This Part of the Country

There are several conventions in this book to make the book easier to use. Here's a list:

➤ Any text you type or items you select appear **bold**. For example, you click the **Start** button or type **Help!**.

➤ If you have to press two or more keys to enter a command, the keys are separated with plus signs. For example, you might press Ctrl+C to copy a selected item. To enter the command, hold down the first key while pressing the second one.

➤ Finally, any text you might see on your screen is shown in a funny-looking type like this: OK. For example, you might see a Login: prompt asking you to type your username.

> **By the Way...** These boxes contain notes, tips, warnings, and other information about the Web, the Internet, and Navigator. Some of these boxes contain only snide comments and quips.

If you want to understand more about the Internet, the World Wide Web, Navigator, and the commands you're told to enter, you'll find some background information in boxes. I put this sideline information in boxes so you can skip the gory details. But, just in case you're interested, look for the following icons:

> **Technical Twaddle** These boxes contain high-tech fluff that I promised not to inflict on you, but I would feel guilty if I didn't include it. you can skip this background fodder (technical twaddle) unless you're truly interested.

Common Trademark Courtesy

As a courtesy to all the computer and program manufacturers who have complicated our lives, we have decided to list their trademarks or service marks here (so you'll know who's responsible). In addition, if we suspected a term of being a trademark or service mark (you just can't trust anyone these days), we capitalized it. We at Que

xvii

cannot attest to the accuracy of this information, so don't expect any of this information to hold up in court.

Netscape Communications, Netscape, Mozilla (Netscape's old mascot), Netscape Chat, and Netsite are trademarks of Netscape Communications Corporation. (Although Navigator is a take-off of Mosaic, another Web Browser, Netscape Communications Corporation lives under the illusion that Navigator is an original idea.)

Microsoft Windows 95 is a registered trademark of Microsoft Corporation, and you can bet that you'll be sued if you try to use it.

John Ratzenberger (Cliff Claven on *Cheers*) is not a trademark and is not registered. John is the only guy from an old television show who would let us take a picture of him holding one of our books.

Part 1
Getting Wired with Netscape Navigator

The vast expanse of electronic data we call the World Wide Web is flowing through networks, cables, and satellites as we speak. You need to find some way to tap into this electronic flow and start pumping those resources into your computer.

Before you can start pumping, you need to get wired to the Internet and fire up Navigator. In this part, I'll show you just what to do. I'll give you a list of what you'll need to start, and where to gather the supplies. I'll show you how to connect to the Internet in Windows 95 and Windows 3.1, where to get the latest version of Navigator, and how to use it to plug into the World Wide Web. I'll even take you on a quick tour of the Web, giving you a little practice at the controls.

Chapter 1

The Top Ten Things You Need to Know

You've heard the hype—the promises of a global media network offering you a bottomless sea of information you can access with a simple click of a button. You dream of tapping into libraries around the world, of digging up dirt on politicians you despise, of hearing the latest recordings before they even reach the ears of your local deejay.

Now, you just want to connect and poke around a bit, to see for yourself if this Web thing lives up to its reputation. Well, here's your guide. The following list gives you a quick peek at the World Wide Web and Netscape Navigator (Navigator, for short). It tells you what you'll need to connect, what to expect when you get there, and how to get out when you've had enough. Don't expect a lot of details; this list is just a teaser to make you want to read the rest of the book.

1. Think of the World Wide Web As a Huge Multimedia Encyclopedia

If your computer has a CD-ROM drive, chances are that it came with an encyclopedia on CD (or you bought one of these multimedia encyclopedias). Maybe you have Grolier's or Compton's Encyclopedia, or Microsoft Encarta. If you don't have one of these encyclopedias on CD, here's a picture that's fairly representative of what one looks like.

If you don't have an Encyclopedia on CD, here's what one looks like.

Click here to hear a recorded speech.

Click here to view a related article.

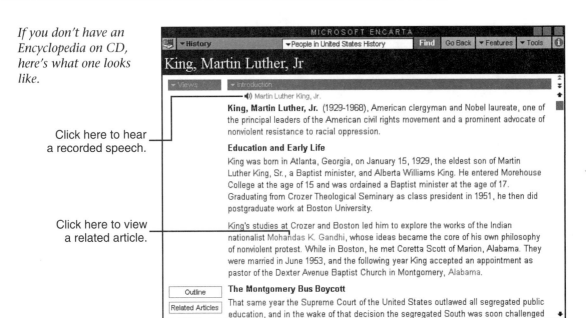

As the screen shows, these encyclopedias display articles about various topics. Each article usually contains highlighted text that you can click on to view an article about another *related topic*. For example, this article about Martin Luther King Jr. contains the highlighted text, "Mohandas K. Gandhi." You can display an article about Martin Luther King's role model simply by clicking on "Mohandas K. Gandhi." Notice that the article also contains an icon that you can click on to view a picture of Martin Luther King, and hear a portion of one of his most famous speeches.

Because these encyclopedias contain text, sounds, video clips, and pictures, they are commonly referred to as *hypermedia documents*. The "hyper" indicates that two or more articles are commonly linked (with icons or highlighted text), and "media" refers to the fact that the articles use different types of media (text, sounds, and video) to convey information.

The World Wide Web works in much the same way. You might pull up a general business page that contains highlighted text for "Starting Your Own Business" or "Stock Quotes." You simply click on the highlighted text or on an icon or button to display the specific information, play a video or audio clip, or take a look at a picture.

The only difference is that the pages you call up on the World Wide Web are not contained on a single CD. They are stored on computers all over the world. As you click on highlighted text (called *links*) and on icons, you might be travelling from Chicago to Milan to Tokyo!

2. Navigator Is Your Window to the World Wide Web

Although these hypermedia Web documents are there for anyone to tap into, you can't just connect to a Web document and start reading it. You need a program to convert the document (a collection of text and incomprehensible codes) into something your computer can understand and show on your screen.

This is where Navigator comes in. Navigator can read and interpret the codes that tell your computer how to display text, and indicate where other information (such as video clips and other Web documents) are located. Navigator displays the Web documents for you and handles the behind-the-scenes navigational tasks that make it possible for you to wander from one Web document to another.

Web Documents and Pages

I use the terms "Web document" and "Web page" interchangeably, because on the Web, a page is not necessarily a page. You might connect to a Web page that's 10 printed pages long, which is essentially a document. Other Web documents may consist of a series of single-page Web pages that are connected with icons or highlighted text.

3. Is Your Computer Powerful Enough?

I know, the salesperson at your local computer store said your computer could handle all your needs well into the 21st century. But that was before the big multimedia push of '94, and long before Windows 95 changed its name from Chicago. Now you're sitting on the beach with your puny 386SX, and your former friends are kicking sand in your face.

The point is that the Web is a multimedia document, and "multimedia" generally translates into "you need to upgrade your computer." Is your computer powerful enough to handle the Web? Here's what you need:

- An IBM PC or compatible with a 386SX processor and 4MB of RAM or better (preferably better). If you're running Navigator from Windows 95, you'd better have a 486 processor with 8MB of RAM.
- Microsoft Windows (Windows 95 or Windows 3.1). This book includes instructions on setting up and using Netscape Navigator for Windows 95 and Windows 3.1.
- A Super VGA (SVGA) monitor that is capable of displaying at least 256 colors. Anything less, and the pictures and video clips you try to play will look blobby.
- A 16-bit sound card, if you want to hear the sounds and voices of the Web. Some Web pages consist almost entirely of sound recordings, and you'll want to play them.
- A direct Internet connection (if you're fortunate enough to be on a network at your place of business). A direct connection is a cable that connects your network directly to the Internet.

OR

A 14,400 bps modem and an Internet service provider that offers SLIP (Serial Line Internet Protocol) or PPP (Point to Point Protocol) accounts. See Chapter 4 for details.

4. You Need a Couple Special Programs, Too

Once you make sure your computer can handle the Web, you need to acquire a couple programs. The first is a TCP/IP (tee-sea-pea-eye-pea) program. *TCP/IP*, which stands for *Transmission Control Protocol/Internet Protocol*, controls the data flow between your computer and the remote (Internet) computer. It works in the background, so once you get it set up and running, you can forget about it.

If you're still working in Windows 3.1, you'll need a separate TCP/IP program, which your Internet service provider should be able to send you. Windows 95 has built-in TCP/IP support, and you can establish a connection with your service provider by using Dial-Up Networking (a program that comes with Windows 95). In Chapter 5, you'll learn how to set up an Internet connection using Dial-Up Networking. In Chapter 6, you'll learn how to get and set up a TCP/IP program in Windows 3.1.

5. Here's Where You Get the Programs

If you have Windows 95, and you purchased the commercial version of Navigator at your local computer store, you have everything you need to start. If you haven't even thought about purchasing Navigator, don't despair. You can get the programs you need (the TCP/IP program and Navigator itself) from the Internet. You'll learn how to do all this in Chapters 6 and 7.

6. You Have Everything—Now What?

Most files you get off the Internet are squished into an electronic equivalent of little balls of aluminum foil. This makes the files smaller so they can roll through the phone lines faster. You have to unsquish (*decompress*) them to make them usable. You need a decompression program, which you can usually get from an online service or Internet site. Chapters 6 and 7 contain complete instructions on how to use a decompression program to make the files you've acquired useful.

7. Connecting for the First Time

When you install Navigator, the Netscape Navigator icon appears on your screen, tempting you to double-click on it. Don't. If you double-click on this icon, you'll get the Navigator screen alright, but you won't be connected to the Internet or the World Wide Web. The reason? Because you haven't dialed the phone yet.

To connect to the World Wide Web, you have to fire up your TCP/IP program and have it dial into your Internet service provider and establish a connection. Once your computer is "logged into" the Internet, then you can run Navigator and start pulling up Web pages.

8. Rolling Through the Web

Navigator has a couple high-tech navigation tools. Forget about them for now. All you need to know is that to display linked data, you click on an icon or a highlighted term, and wait for Navigator to make the necessary connections and "play" the data. If you get a message that Navigator can't make the connection, you've reached a dead end. Click **OK**, and then try a different term or icon.

In the upper left corner of the Navigator toolbar are two buttons you can click to move forward or back. With the links and these two buttons, you can move around the Web with sufficient ease (for now, anyway).

Part 1 ➤ *Getting Wired with Netscape Navigator*

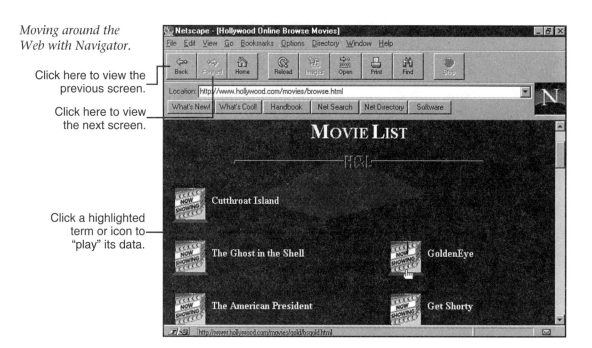

Moving around the Web with Navigator.

Click here to view the previous screen.

Click here to view the next screen.

Click a highlighted term or icon to "play" its data.

9. Playing Photos, Sounds, and Video Clips

Nobody hits the Web wanting only text. Every other Web page you bounce into will offer a picture, recording, or movie clip. The only trouble is that Navigator can't handle these multimedia links by itself. Navigator needs help; it needs other programs that can play the pictures, sounds, and video clips stored on the Web.

These programs, called *helper applications*, are available as freeware or shareware (programs you can try for free and pay for if you decide to keep them). You can usually copy these applications from an online service or another Internet server. (Chapter 12 tells you all you need to know.) Once you have your helper applications in place, you can play Web clips simply by clicking on them.

10. Exit, Stage Left

When you're done wandering around the World Wide Web (or when your hard disk is packed with all the goodies you copied), you should exit and disconnect. Exiting Navigator is easy. You simply open the **File** menu and click the **Exit** command. However, that doesn't hang up your phone or disconnect you from the service provider. In order to disconnect, you have to use your TCP/IP program. If you're in Windows 95, simply switch to the Dial-Up Networking program, and then click the **Disconnect** button. If you have some other TCP/IP program, change to it and enter the **Disconnect**, or **Hang-up** command.

Chapter 2

Netscape Navigator and the World Wide Web

By the End of This Chapter, You'll Be Able To...

➤ Define "World Wide Web" at your next cocktail party.

➤ Name the country where the World Wide Web started.

➤ Explain the concept of hyperlinks to a foreign exchange student.

➤ Write a complete sentence using only Internet acronyms.

Unless you've set up permanent residence in the New York subway, you probably know something about the Internet. If nothing else, you know it has nudie pictures you might want to keep your kids from seeing (but that *you* secretly want to look at).

All you really have to know about the Internet is that it consists of a collection of computers and networks that are connected. The World Wide Web is a part of the Internet, and it contains multimedia documents (pages) that are linked to each other. These documents contain text, sounds, video clips, maps, and, yes, nudie pictures. To view the Web documents, you need to connect to the Internet using a computer, modem (or network connection), and Web browser, such as Navigator.

In this chapter, you'll get more details about the Internet, the World Wide Web, and Navigator, so you can form a mental picture of what you're about to get yourself into.

First, There Was the Internet

Before anyone ever dreamed of spinning the World Wide Web, there was the Internet, a massive computer network connecting thousands of computers all over the world, including computers at universities, libraries, businesses, government agencies, and research facilities.

World Wide Web Pseudonyms The World Wide Web goes by several names: WWW, W3, The Web, and Da Web (in Chicago).

The Internet was originally a United States military communications tool (which explains why the Internet is so complicated). The idea was to create an indestructible communications network that would function even if one or more computers on the network were toasted. But when businesses discovered there was a place where people could find information and entertainment without being subjected to commercials, they naturally decided to get involved.

Currently, the Internet is a semi-commercial, semi-free wonderland of networked computers whose resources you can tap into. You can copy files from them, use their programs, send and receive electronic mail (*e-mail*), chat with other people by typing messages back and forth, get information about millions of topics, shop electronic malls, and even search for a job or a compatible mate.

In the Beginning

When the Internet first started to catch on, it didn't look very pretty. When you connected to your Internet service, you usually saw a menu like the one shown on the next page. You had to work through these generic menu systems to find what you wanted. As you'll see later, the World Wide Web and browsers (such as Navigator) gave the Internet a pretty face, just as Windows gave the PC a complete make-over.

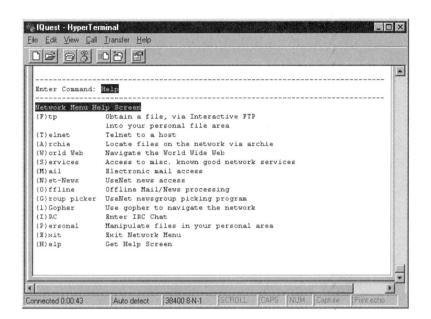

A simple Internet connection can provide you with a bare-bones menu.

Here's Where the Web Fits In

The World Wide Web is part of the Internet...sort of. Some computers on the Internet are designated to act as *Web servers*, and are given the illustrious mission of storing the multimedia documents that make up the Web. These servers are located all over the world, but together they act as a single entity.

What makes these Web documents unique is that most Web documents contain links to other documents, which might be on the same Web server or on a different Web server (down the block or overseas). You can hop around from document to document, from Web server to Web server, from continent to continent, simply by clicking on links.

Here's how it works. Whenever you connect to a Web server, it displays a *home page* that usually welcomes you and displays pictures and highlighted terms called *links*. Home pages contain several links for popular areas, topics, or terms. If you find a topic or area that interests you, click on its link. The server shovels the information over your Internet connection to your computer, and it appears on your screen. Usually, the screen you see contains additional links. You keep clicking till you find what you need...or reach a dead end. When you can go no further, you backtrack and follow another trail of links.

Part 1 ➤ *Getting Wired with Netscape Navigator*

The Web gives you a more graphical encounter with the Internet.

Click on a hyperlink to follow the trail

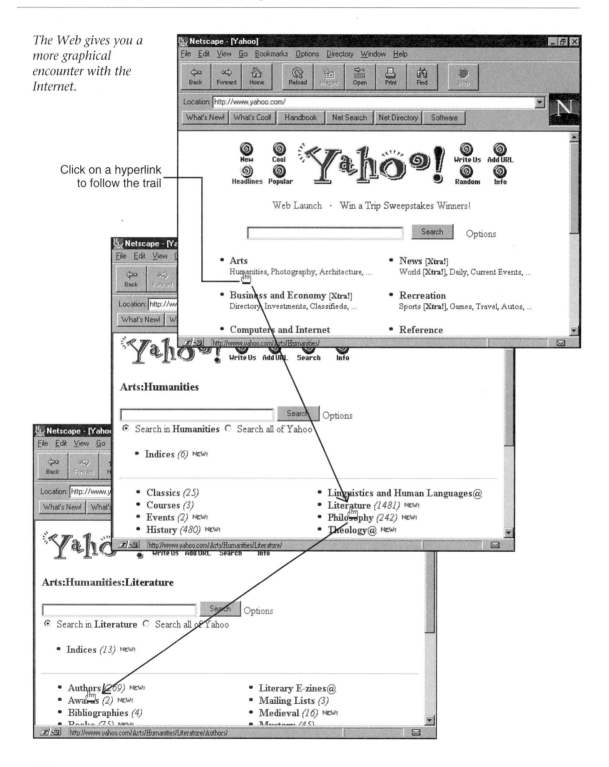

Hyperlinks

Hyperlinks (**links** for short) are icons, pictures, or highlighted chunks of text that connect two documents. For example, a document about pork might contain a link for sausage. If you click on the link, Navigator displays a document about how to make sausage. Sausage is the link, although it's not actually a sausage link.

How the Web Was Spun

The World Wide Web started in Geneva, Switzerland, where a group of bored Swiss physicists stitched together the first hypermedia documents. The idea was to make it easy for physicists from all over the world to share information. The idea got out of hand, and grew into the beast we now know as the **World Wide Web**.

Tracking Down Information with URLs

If you're wondering how the Web keeps track of all these servers and documents, the answer is by using URLs (pronounced "you-are-ellz"). *URL* stands for *Uniform Resource Locator* (or Unreliable Resource Location, depending on the URL). The Web uses URLs to specify the addresses of the various servers on the Internet—as well as the documents on each server. Here's a sample URL for the Federal Government's Web server:

http://www.whitehouse.gov

The **http** stands for *HyperText Transport Protocol*, which means this is a Web server; **www** stands for, you guessed it, *World Wide Web*; and the rest is pretty obvious. I'm not going to say more about URLs just yet. You'll get an earful in Chapter 10. For now, just be aware that URLs exist, and that the Web uses them to keep track of storage locations.

Channel Surfing on the Web

Although you can search for and find specific information on the World Wide Web, the Web is designed more for wandering. You'll find yourself clicking on link after link, just as you might click on the up and down channel buttons on your TV's remote control.

To give you a taste of the Web, here is a list of Web servers you might stumble across in your wanderings. I'm not giving addresses (URLs) here; this list is only intended to whet your appetite for Web exploration. For a list of Web servers and their URLs (so you can find them), see Chapter 24.

Worldwide Web Art Navigator contains a list of Internet sites where you can view and copy art.

The Internet Mall is an electronic shopping mall where you can shop for and order products ranging from PCs to flowers.

Wired is *Wired* Magazine's Web server. *Wired* is the hip cyberworld counterculture magazine.

Games Domain contains hyperlinks to other servers that offer games, tips, secrets, and other resources related to computer games.

The Internet Movie Database Browser allows you to search for movies by title, actor, or director.

The Least You Need to Know

I think I've succeeded in giving you as little background information as possible. If I failed, and you're overwhelmed with detail, scan the following list for the most important points:

➤ The Internet consists of thousands of big, powerful computers that are connected via cables and satellite.

➤ The World Wide Web is a hypermedia system that stores text, graphics, video clips, and audio clips on computers all over the world.

➤ To move around in the World Wide Web, you click on highlighted terms and icons called *links*.

➤ A Web server is a computer that stores and delivers Web documents on request.

Chapter 3

Taking Netscape Beyond the Web

By the End of This Chapter, You'll Be Able To...

➤ Send mail without using a postage stamp.

➤ Name two types of gophers.

➤ Tell the difference between a newspaper and a newsgroup.

➤ Translate three more Internet acronyms.

Now that you have this clear picture of the World Wide Web as a neat little microcosm of the Internet, I'll complicate things for you. While the Web is known for its hypermedia documents, it also provides easy access to other Internet features. For example, through the Web, you can use a tool called *FTP* (short for *File Transfer Protocol*) to *download* files (copy files from the Internet to your computer). Using the Web, you can also access special interest forums called *newsgroups*, and *Telnet* to some servers (use the server just as if you were sitting at its keyboard).

This chapter shows you some other Internet offerings you may encounter in your Web wanderings. However, because Netscape provides such a smooth transition from one Internet feature to another, you might not even notice which feature you're using as you bounce from one Internet site to another.

Postage-Free Mail, Same-Day Delivery

Fed up with the United States Postal service—you know, rising prices, poor service? Then send mail electronically, over the phone lines. The Internet allows you to send electronic mail to anyone who has an e-mail address (and that's a whole lot of people).

In the recent past, you had to have a separate e-mail program to send e-mail on the Internet. Now, you can send and receive e-mail directly from Netscape. Just enter the **New Mail Message** command, type the person's e-mail address, and then type your message. As soon as you click the **Send** button, your e-mail message starts bouncing around the Internet in search of its destination. Within minutes (or hours, if the Internet has lots of traffic), your message arrives. See Chapter 14 for details.

To send e-mail from Navigator, you simply type an e-mail address and your message.

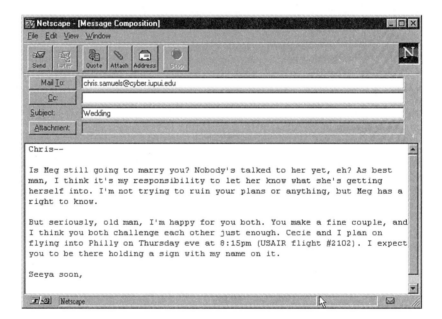

Gophering Here and There

In the early days of the Internet, everyone was trying to come up with some way to make the vast Internet resources easily accessible. Facing a long, cold Minnesota winter, some faculty and students at the University of Minnesota decided to put together a menu system for the Internet. They named this menu system "Gopher," after the university mascot—the Golden Gopher. Of course, Gopher also stands for "go-fer," which is what the menu system does; it "goes for" documents and files on the Internet.

Chapter 3 ➤ Taking Netscape Beyond the Web

You can use Gopher by itself, accessing it with a special Gopher program. When you connect to the Internet using Gopher, you encounter a basic menu system. When you select an item from the main menu (usually by clicking on it), you see a submenu. You continue to click on items until you find the file or document you want. See Chapter 18 for details.

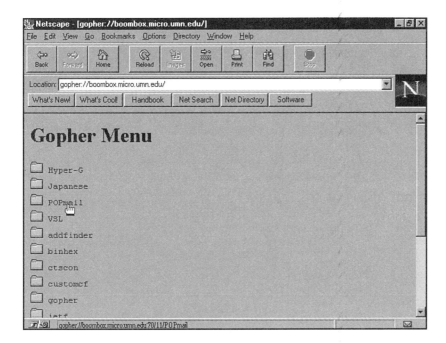

With Gopher, you work through a series of menus and submenus.

Snatching Files with FTP

Most computers on the Internet store files (and programs) that are free for the taking. You simply connect to the computer that has the file you want, change to the drive and directory that contains the file, and then copy the file to a directory or folder on your computer. Depending on the speed of your modem (and the size of the copied file), you can have the file in a matter of minutes (much faster and less expensive than if the file were sent on a disk by mail).

In order for this file transfer to work, both the sending and receiving computers must follow the same communication rules: *File Transfer Protocol* (or *FTP* for short). In the old days, you needed a special FTP program to grab Internet files, but now you can quickly download a file simply by clicking on its name in Navigator. In Chapter 16, you'll learn how to FTP (yes, you can use Internet acronyms as verbs).

Using Archie to Track Down a File

What if a friend tells you about a cool game she found on the Internet, or you read in a computer magazine about a helpful shareware program that you can snatch from the Internet? If you don't know the address of the computer that stores the file, and if you don't know which drive and directory the file is hiding in, you won't be able to access the file.

That's where Archie comes in. Archie is a program that can search for files on the Internet. As long as you know the name of the file (or a portion of its name), you can have Archie sniff it out and tell you where it's located. As you'll see in Chapter 16, the Web offers some search tools that make it much easier to perform an Archie search.

Archie, Veronica, and Jughead

If "Archie" conjures up images of comic book characters, it should. Archie (short for "archives") is one of the few Internet terms that is *not* an acronym. The developers named their file search tool after a comic book character. Veronica and Jughead are also search tools used on Gopher servers.

Swapping Information in Newsgroups

One of the most popular Internet features, *newsgroups* allow you to share information with people who share your interests and hobbies. You can find newsgroups that focus on everything from shoe fetishes to rock climbing. In newsgroups, members post messages to inform the group, state an opinion, share an interesting picture, offer help, ask a question, or just yank someone's chain. You can enter a newsgroup and simply read the postings, respond to a posting, or post your own message or question. Check out Chapter 20 for details.

Poking Around on Other People's Computers

When you're on the Internet, you're poking around on other people's computers. However, there are some computers on the Internet that allow your computer to act as a *terminal*. That is, you enter commands using your computer and keyboard, and the remote computer responds just as if you were using its keyboard. This process is called *Telnetting*, and you'll learn all about it in Chapter 19.

Chapter 3 ➤ Taking Netscape Beyond the Web

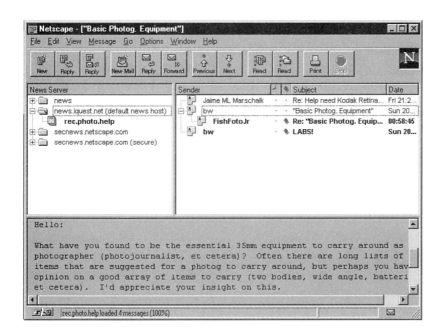

A newsgroup is like an electronic bulletin board.

Chatting Incognito with Other Users

People used to sit out on their porches and chat with passers-by, or tramp down to the neighborhood watering hole to trade war stories with the bartender and discuss politics with the locals.

The computer has changed all that. With modems, online services (such as America Online), and the Internet, people can now lock themselves in their basements and converse with anyone in the world. You simply enter a chat room and start typing. As you type, your messages pop up on the other users' screens, and their messages appear on yours. When you get tired of the conversation, you can just disappear and look for a more appealing one. In Chapter 17, you'll learn how to use Navigator (along with Netscape Chat) to converse on the Internet.

Thousands of Newsgroups
The Internet hosts thousands of newsgroups. Whatever your interests, hobbies, or psychoses, you can usually find a suitable newsgroup. Newsgroups are constantly being formed and destroyed. What keeps a newsgroup alive is the activity it inspires.

WAIS to Find Information

WAIS (pronounced "ways," and short for Wide Area Information Server) is an Internet tool that can help you find specific information. In the old days, you would connect to a WAIS server and find a list of 500 or more search categories ranging from cooking to United States politics. You pick a category and then enter a word or phrase that represents the desired information. The WAIS server would then search its index to find the articles that match your search.

The Web offers WAIS access, but what you'll encounter may vary depending on the WAIS server. On most WAIS servers, you can complete a simple search form to find what you need. On other, older, WAIS servers, you might still encounter the long list of categories and old-fashioned search tools. You'll learn more about WAIS in Chapter 21.

Fingering to Find Friends and Colleagues

Finger is a tool that lets you check whether the e-mail address you have for one of your friends or colleagues is accurate. With Finger, you enter a person's e-mail address, and the Internet displays information about that person, assuming the address is correct. This information might include the person's real name, address, phone number, and records of whether the person read the last hundred letters you sent. Finger can also tell you if the person even logged on.

The only trouble with Finger is that it doesn't do enough. You can't enter a person's real name (such as Joe Begovitz) and have Finger determine the person's e-mail address. There simply is no master list of all the users on the Internet, and many users choose to remain anonymous. However, Finger is useful for determining whether your mail is reaching the desired destination.

The Least You Need to Know

Think of the Web and Navigator as the Windows 95 of the Internet. In Windows 95, you don't have to worry about the DOS DIR or COPY command. You simply run Windows Explorer, and then drag files and folders where you want them.

With the Web and Navigator, you don't have to think about the complicated workings of the other Internet features. Don't get me wrong—you'll have full access to all the Internet offerings. You just won't have to jump through hoops to get at them. The Web and Navigator provide an almost seamless connection to these resources. All you have to do is point-and-click.

Chapter 4

What You Need to Start

By the End of This Chapter, You'll Be Able To...

➤ Figure out whether you need to buy any more computer equipment.

➤ Name two ways to connect to the Internet.

➤ Name one way you shouldn't connect to the Internet.

➤ Look at your first Internet screen without turning to stone.

Do you get the feeling that there's something I'm not telling you about the Web? So far, I've managed to laud its capability to ship cartloads of data from faraway lands to your computer. What I haven't mentioned is that this takes quite a bit of computing power, both for the remote computer and for your lowly desktop model. You need a fast modem, lots of memory, and a fairly speedy central processing unit. You also need the right Internet connection, a decent telecommunications application, and a couple more fringe items. In this chapter, you'll learn everything you need to know to connect to the Internet for the first time.

If you're already connected to the Internet, scan this chapter anyway. Your connection may not be the one you need to use Netscape, and your computer may be too feeble to shoulder the burden of multimedia documents. By knowing this up front, you can head off any minor frustrations.

Does Your Computer Have What It Takes?

Keeping up with the latest technology is tough. Until recently, my home computer had a 386SX 16MHz processor, a VGA monitor, 4 megabytes of RAM, no sound card, and a 2,400 bps modem. I couldn't even think of doing the Web on it. The documents would take forever to load, if they would load at all. The screen would take even longer to display images (which looked like tiny snow storms on my VGA monitor), and I couldn't play any sounds. If I wanted Web, I had to use my fancy computer at work.

Is *your* system up to the task? Check the following list to make sure:

- ➤ 386 computer with 4 megabytes of RAM. This is the very least. I recommend a 486 with 8 or more megabytes of RAM. When you open your first multimedia Web document, you'll see your system's memory dip by 2 or 3 megabytes. (Also, don't consume memory with complicated programs, such as Word or Excel, while you're jumping around the Web.)
- ➤ SVGA monitor. You can get by with a VGA monitor, but pictures and video clips will look grainy.
- ➤ Sound card (preferably a 16-bit sound card). For the full effect, you gotta play the sounds.
- ➤ Microsoft Windows 3.1 running in Enhanced mode (if you're using a PC). Windows 95 is even better, and it comes with the program you need to make your Internet connection.
- ➤ A direct Internet connection, if you are fortunate enough to have a network connection to a big fat computer that's on the Internet.

    OR

- ➤ A 14,400 bps modem and an Internet service provider that offers SLIP (Serial Line Internet Protocol) or PPP (Point-to-Point Protocol) accounts. Move on to the next section for details.

2,400 bps Doesn't Cut It

If you have a 2,400 bps modem, go buy a new one. The current standard is 14,400 bps, but get the fastest one you can afford. You won't regret it. 2,400 bps is way too slow to transfer the vast amounts of data stored in Web documents.

Getting Wired: Finding an Internet Connection

Now that you're back from the computer store, having slapped another four hundred dollars on your Visa card, you can start looking for an entrance ramp to the information superhighway. There are basically two ways to connect: using a network connection (if you are lucky enough to be networked to a server that's on the Internet), or using an Internet service provider. The following sections explain the two options.

A "Free" Permanent Connection

If you're a student at a major university or you're employed by a large corporation whose computers are networked, you may have an Internet connection without even knowing it.

This type of connection, called a *dedicated* or *permanent direct* connection, is the best type to have. Usually, you don't have to pay for the service—your school or corporation foots the bill. Also, communications run a lot faster, because they're not restricted by the speed of a modem; you're connected with high-speed network cables.

Are you connected? To find out, ask around. Check with the person in charge of technical support or information services. In a university, look for a computer lab or computer resource department. Before you decide to pay an Internet service provider, do everything in your power to get on the Internet for free.

Using an Internet Service Provider

Can't get it free? Then grab a fast modem and start hunting for a reputable (hopefully local) Internet service provider. The service provider has a huge computer connected to the Internet. For a monthly access fee, you can dial into this computer (using a modem) and connect to the Internet. This type of connection is slower and more expensive than a direct connection, but the cost is usually comparable to what you would pay for a commercial online service, such as CompuServe or America Online.

Make sure the service provides a PPP (Point-to-Point Protocol) or SLIP (Serial Line Internet Protocol) connection, *not* a terminal connection. A terminal connection allows you to connect to the Internet by using programs on the service provider's computer. PPP and SLIP give you a direct connection to the Internet, allowing your computer to act as though it is an integral part of the Internet. To access the Web with Netscape, you must have a PPP or SLIP connection.

Which Is Better, SLIP or PPP?

PPP is a better connection, especially if you're running under Windows 95. Windows 95 has a built-in TCP/IP program that can establish the connection between your computer and your service provider. If you have a PPP connection, setting up this program is relatively easy. With a SLIP connection, the process is a little more complicated.

Shopping for an Internet Service Provider

The most difficult part of choosing a service provider is finding two or three local providers to compare. You can't just flip to INTERNET in the phone book. And if you don't live in or near a major metropolitan area, you may not even *have* a local Internet service provider.

To get the names of service providers, try the nearest computer store and computer users group. Other computer users may already have done much of the shopping for you, and they're usually happy to recommend a reliable service (and slam unreliable ones).

When shopping for a service, your want to get the most Internet access for as little as possible. Given that obvious directive, look for the following offerings in a service provider:

➤ **Dial-in direct connection**—To use Netscape Navigator, you need a dial-in direct connection, *not* a terminal connection. A direct connection may be referred to as SLIP, PPP, or CSLIP.

➤ **Local access number**—The cost per minute for connecting to the Internet equals the phone charge plus the Internet service charge. By connecting locally, you reduce or eliminate the phone charge.

➤ **Toll-free (800 number) access**—No local service? Then try to find a service that has a 1-800 number. Although these services typically levy a surcharge for toll-free access, the charge is usually less than you would pay for the least expensive long-distance call.

➤ **Low (or no) startup fee**—Some service providers charge an initial startup fee ranging from $20 to $200. Ask the service to waive the startup fee. If the guy says, "Yeah, right," you can take that as a "No."

➤ **Low connect time charges**—You shouldn't have to spend more than three dollars an hour to connect. Look for a service that provides a low flat rate for a chunk of time; for example, $20 per month for 20 hours, and $4 an hour for additional connect time. Services may charge different day, evening, and weekend rates. They may also charge for a minimum number of hours.

- **Fast modem speeds**—Make sure the service supports transfer rates that match the speed of your modem. If you invested in a 28,800 bps modem, you shouldn't have to slow it down to meet the limits of your service.

- **Software included**—Many services provide all the software you need to connect to the service and access the various Internet features. Although this book shows you how to get all the software you need, the service might provide an easier method of getting the software and installing it.

- **Low-cost storage**—If you plan on storing lots of electronic mail and other files on the service provider's computer, find out how much it costs per megabyte per month. Most services won't charge you if you delete files from their computer *immediately* after copying them to your hard disk.

Free Introductory Service!

While you're looking for affordability, try to find a service that provides a free introductory offer. Use this service to gain some valuable experience on the Internet. If you like the service, keep it; otherwise, dump it and try another service.

As you look for the perfect service, keep an eye out for any hidden costs and service limitations. A service that looks less expensive on the surface may end up costing you more. In specific, avoid the following:

- **Dial-in terminal accounts**—A dial-in terminal account is a low-budget connection over which you cannot run Netscape Navigator. You need a dial-in direct connection.

- **E-mail only accounts**—Some people use only the Internet as a way to bypass the U.S. Postal Service. Because you want access to the World Wide Web, an e-mail only account won't do you much good.

- **Additional surcharges**—Some services offer low access rates, but then slap a surcharge on all calls. Be especially wary of services that offer 1-800 number ("toll-free") access. Although a call to an 800 number won't show up on your phone bill, it may show on the bill you get from your service provider.

- **Evening only access**—The Internet can be a busy place during business hours. If you plan on connecting during the Internet rush hour, make sure the service allows daytime access at an affordable rate.

- **Long delays**—If you get a service that doesn't have the computing power to keep up with customer demands, you may not be able to access the Internet whenever you want, and your connection may seem overly slow at times. The only way to know is to check with other people who use the service, or try the service for yourself.

Get Your Credit Card Handy

You found a service—now what? Grab your credit card, a pad of paper, and a pen, and head for the nearest phone. Before calling the prospective service provider, write down the type of computer you have (PC compatible), the operating system you're using (Windows 3.1 or Windows 95), and the highest speed of your modem. The person you call will usually ask for this information.

Now, call the service provider, and be ready to write fast. These computer people are fast talkers, and they usually assume you've been working with modems for half of your life, and programming for the other half. Here's the information you absolutely must get in order to connect:

- PPP or SLIP connection
- Phone number (for your modem to dial)
- Username (your name or abbreviation)
- Password (don't forget it)
- Terminal emulation (usually VT100 or VT52)
- Your e-mail address

Terminal Emulation

Terminal emulation is the way your computer and modem must act in order to connect to the service provider's computer. You'll learn how to set the terminal emulation later.

You'll need more information to set up your SLIP or PPP connection. The best way to obtain this information is to have the service provider e-mail it to you. However, if you can get the information over the phone, you can avoid connecting to your service provider with Windows Terminal (or HyperTerminal) and figuring out how to read your e-mail. If your service provider chooses to e-mail the information to you, go to the next section to learn how to connect to your service provider in Windows (so you can access your e-mail). If the service provider can give you the information over the phone, here's what you need to know:

- Domain Name Server
- Domain Name
- Your hostname
- News server
- Mail server

In addition to mailing you the information you need to connect to the Internet, many service providers will send you the files you need to gain full access to the Internet. Usually, the first e-mail you receive will contain instructions on how to copy the files to your computer and install the files. You'll learn how to connect to your service provider and nab your e-mail later in this chapter.

Home, Home on the Domain

The most important piece of information is the domain name server, which is a number such as 198.70.36.70. This odd looking number is the Internet address of your service provider's computer. Without it, no other computer on the Internet can send information to you.

Setting Up and Signing On

Now for the fun part. You get to connect to the Internet and see what's available. Don't get too excited. All you do at this point is connect to your service provider's computer. If your service provider sent instructions via e-mail, you can view those instructions to figure out what you need to do next. You're not setting up the PPP or SLIP connection you need to run Netscape; you'll do that in Chapter 5.

Note: Perform the following only if your service provider says that you must (to get instructions by e-mail or to copy the essential Internet files). If you purchased a program for connecting to the Internet, and if you already have all the files you need, don't waste your time connecting using Windows Terminal or HyperTerminal to connect to the Internet. You can also skip the rest of this chapter if you purchased Netscape Navigator Personal Edition (the commercial version of Navigator).

No Sweat: Logging On with a Permanent Connection

If you have a permanent connection, talk to the system administrator to find out whether you have Internet access, and to learn how to *logon* or *login* to the Internet. Usually, you logon by typing a unique username (preferably your own) and a password (ask the administrator for your password). Once you're connected to the central computer, you can use that computer just as if you were sitting at its keyboard. You don't need to set up any special software, turn on a modem, or perform any other technical feats.

Logging on to a Service Provider

To logon to a service, you need a modem and a special program called a *communications program*. Most modems come with a basic communications program that can do the job. Microsoft Windows also comes with a communications program, called Terminal (HyperTerminal, in Windows 95), that you can run from the Accessories group. Because the Windows Terminal is so popular and simple, I'll use it in the following steps. However, if you have a telecommunications program that you prefer to use, go ahead and use it (it's probably better than Windows Terminal).

Instead of telling you all the possible ways you can configure your communications program *before* dialing, let's take a more realistic approach. Dial first, and then if you have problems, read the section called "What Went Wrong" for some common solutions. (The following instructions assume that you've already set up your modem to work in Windows. If you haven't set up the modem, follow the instructions that came with your modem or Windows to set it up.) Once your modem is set up, take the following steps:

1. If you have an external modem, turn it on.

2. Run your communications program:

   In Windows 95, click the **Start** button, and then select **Programs**, **Accessories**, and **HyperTerminal**.

   In Windows 3.1, double-click the **Terminal** icon in the **Accessories** group.

3. Enter the **Phone Number** command:

   In Terminal, this command is on the **Settings** menu. A dialog box pops up prompting you to type a phone number.

   In HyperTerminal, double-click the **Hypertrm** icon, type a name for the connection, click an icon, and click **OK**. (This opens a dialog box, asking for the phone number of the remote computer.)

4. Type your service provider's phone number. If you have to dial a 9 to get an outside line, type **9** before the phone number. Don't forget to add **1**, then an area code for long-distance or 800 for toll-free calls. (In Windows 95, you may already have set up your modem to dial these numbers automatically.)

Chapter 4 ➤ *What You Need to Start*

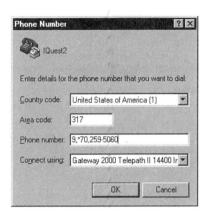

Enter the number you want to dial.

5. Click **OK**. (If you're working with HyperTerminal, skip to Step 11. If you're using Terminal in Windows 3.1, you have a few extra steps.)

6. Select the **Terminal Emulation** command. In Terminal, this command is on the **Settings** menu. (If you're using HyperTerminal, it is set up to automatically determine the terminal emulation type for you.)

7. Click on the terminal emulation setting that matches the one specified by your service provider, and then click **OK**.

Call Waiting Is Bad If you have call waiting, turn it off to prevent incoming calls from disrupting communications. Usually, you can turn off call waiting by typing ***70**, before the service provider's number. When you log out and enter the command to hang up, call waiting is automatically reactivated.

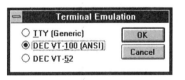

Select a terminal emulation, usually VT100.

8. Select the **Communications Settings** command. In Terminal, this command is on the **Settings** menu.

9. Click on the fastest baud rate listed, and then click **OK**. Most modems will automatically adjust to a slower baud rate if necessary, so pick the fastest baud rate. If you run into problems, you can try a slower baud rate later.

29

10. Enter the **Dial** command. In Terminal, this command is on the **Phone** menu. Your communications program dials the specified phone number and connects with the service provider's computer. A message should appear (such as **Login:** or **Username:**), prompting you to type your login name.

11. Type your login name *exactly* as the service provider specified, and press **Enter**. Login names are case sensitive; JSmith is not the same as jsmith. If you're not sure, try all lowercase. The service provider prompts you to enter your password.

12. Type your password and press **Enter**. The password may not appear on the screen as you type it, or it may appear as a series of asterisks.

Enter your username and password.

Enter your username here.

When you type your password, it probably won't show up on your screen.

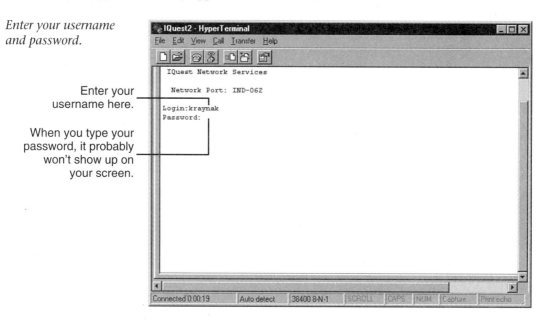

Twelve steps, and you're on the information superhighway, right? That's right, assuming the service provider was not too busy to answer your call, that your account was set up correctly, that the service provider isn't using alien telecommunication settings, and that your modem is properly set up (and turned on). If you're part of the majority, however, and you encountered problems, skip ahead to the "What Went Wrong?" section.

Chapter 4 ➤ *What You Need to Start*

What's with the Menu?

Using Terminal or HyperTerminal to connect to your service provider's computer gives you only a terminal connection to the Internet. At this point, you're using a menu program on the service provider's computer to connect to the Internet. You can't run Netscape through such a connection, although you can read any e-mail your service provider may have sent you. You eventually want to establish a PPP or SLIP connection, which you'll do in Chapter 5 (for Windows 95) or Chapter 6 (for Windows 3.1).

What to Expect

If you managed to connect trouble-free the first time, congratulations! You should now see an on-screen menu that allows you to start navigating the Internet. Most menus number the options or provide highlighted letters you can type to select the options. Go ahead and play around with the menu. This is the menu you'll use to get around the Internet till you set up your SLIP or PPP account and connect with Netscape.

If your service provider sent instructions via e-mail, use the menu that appears to select the **E-Mail** command. You can then read the e-mail and find out what to do next. Your service provider may also have placed some essential Internet program files on the system that you can copy to your computer. Because this procedure varies depending on your service provider, follow the service provider's instructions for downloading these files.

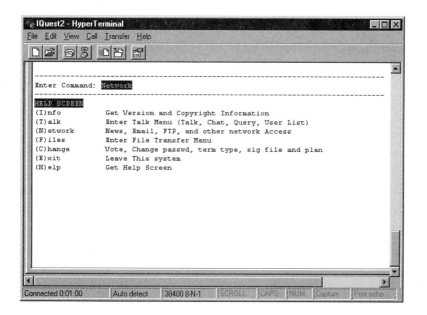

If you see a menu sort of like this one, everything is copacetic.

What Went Wrong?

Rarely do modem communications proceed error free the first time. Any minor problem or wrong setting can cause a major disruption in the communications between your computer and the service providers. The following list can help you solve the more common problems:

- **"Modem not responding" or "Cannot find modem."**—If nothing happens, or if your communications program displays a distress signal saying that it cannot find the modem, the COM port setting (the "outlet" that the modem uses) may be wrong. First, if you have an external modem, make sure the power is turned on. Then, enter the **Modem Settings** command, and make sure the correct COM port is selected (usually **COM 2**). Keep trying to dial with different COM port settings until the modem dials or you run out of COM port settings to try.

  If you have an internal modem, it may have tiny switches on the back that you can flip to give the modem a different COM port setting. Other modems have switches on the circuit board, which are more difficult to get at. Check your modem documentation to determine how to change the modem's COM port setting. Then, make sure the COM port setting in your communications program matches the COM port setting on your modem.

  Also, check your modem setup. In Windows 95, you can quickly check the setup by double-clicking the **Modems** icon in the **Control Panel**. Make sure Windows is set up to use your brand of modem. In Windows 3.1, check the settings in Terminal.

- **Busy signal**—You may not hear it, but if a message appears on-screen saying the lines are busy, the service provider is all tied up with incoming calls. Enter the **Hangup** or **Disconnect** command, and try again later...like at 2 a.m.

- **Voices from your modem**—You dialed the wrong number. Some poor sap on the other end answered and is wondering who's the jerk who woke him up and refuses to talk. Enter the Hangup or Disconnect command. Then, check the phone number you typed earlier, and pray that this guy doesn't have Caller ID.

- **On-screen garbage**—First, check the baud rate setting in your communications program. Make sure the setting matches the fastest setting that both your modem and the service provider can handle. Next, check the terminal emulation to make sure it conforms to the emulation required by the service provider (you may have to call the provider again).

  If neither solution works, call your service provider and find out the following settings: Data bits, Stop bit, Parity, and Flow control. You don't need to know what each setting does, just make sure your settings match those of your service provider. Most services use the following settings: Data bits, 8; Stop bit, 1; Parity, None; Flow control, Xon/Xoff.

- **Seeing double**—Both your computer and the service provider's computer are echoing back what you type. Try turning Local Echo off, so your computer will stop echoing echoing.

- **What you type is invisible**—Try turning **Local Echo** on.

- **Single line of text**—Turn on **Inbound CR/LF**. This tells your computer to place a carriage return after each line of text as it arrives.

- **Blank lines between text**—If you get blank lines between what you type, try turning off Outbound CR/LF. If you get blank lines between incoming text, turn off Inbound CR/LF.

If you still can't connect, call your service provider and describe the problem in detail. You pay your service charge, so demand service.

Windows 95 Modem Problems

Windows 95 has a built-in modem troubleshooter that can help you track down common modem problems and fix them. To run the Troubleshooter, click the **Start** button, select **Help**, click the **Index** tab, and search for **trouble**. Under **troubleshooting**, double-click **modem problems**.

Logging Out and Hanging Up

As long as you are connected to the service, you're using up valuable connect time. When you're done playing around, be sure to sign off and hang up. Most service provider menus have an Exit or Quit command. Keep choosing **Exit** or **Quit** until you see a message indicating that you have successfully logged out. Then, select the **Phone/Hangup** command in Terminal or **Call/Disconnect** in HyperTerminal.

The Least You Need to Know

You could devote an entire book to modems, communications programs, and Internet connections. In fact, people have done just that (check out *The Complete Idiot's Guide to Modems & Online Services* and *The Complete Idiot's Guide to the Internet*). However, you can also get by with very little knowledge. Just keep the following points in mind:

- You need a 14,400 bps modem or better.

- Get a permanent (network) connection, or a dial-in direct account.

- ➤ Don't get a dial-in terminal account.
- ➤ Find an inexpensive, local service provider.
- ➤ To sign on, you need to know a phone number to call, your username and password, and the terminal emulation type.

Chapter 5

Setting Up Your PPP or Slip Connection in Windows 95

By the End of This Chapter, You'll Be Able To...

➤ Understand why you need a SLIP or PPP connection in the first place.

➤ Cheat your way to a PPP connection using the Windows Help system.

➤ Set up a SLIP account in Windows 95...if you really have to.

➤ Figure out what went wrong if you still can't connect.

In the previous chapter, you used a basic communications program (Terminal) to connect to the Internet, but such a connection won't let you use Navigator. Why? Because when you connected, you were using the service provider's menu system to access the Internet. And this menu system is just too archaic. You want the flashy, user-friendly Internet interface that Netscape Navigator provides, and for that, you need a SLIP or PPP connection. Such a connection places your computer directly on the Internet, allowing you to use programs on your computer to control the way in which information is accessed and displayed.

But setting up a SLIP or PPP connection isn't easy. If you have Windows 95 and a PPP connection, the process is fairly straightforward. However, if you're still using Windows 3.1 (or 3.11), you have some work to do. You have to obtain a special TCP/IP (Transmission Control Protocol/Internet Protocol) program, and then set it up so it can manage the communications link between your computer and the Internet. In this chapter (and the next, for Windows 3.1 users), you'll learn all you need to know to establish the right connection.

Doing PPP or SLIP in Windows 95

If you have Windows 95, your service provider probably won't send you a configured TCP/IP program, because Windows 95 has a built-in program called Dial-Up Networking, which is a whole lot easier to work with. Although this program takes most of the pain out of TCP/IP, you still have to make sure you installed the program, and you have to enter a bunch of incomprehensible numbers and settings to make it work. But hey, that's the nature of dial-up networking.

To help, I broke the process down, so you wouldn't have too many steps to deal with at once. But I must warn you—this process is tedious at best, and it may cause you to go prematurely gray. The good news is that setting up a PPP or SLIP account in Windows 95 is still easier than doing it the old way.

Cheat Your Way to PPP

If you have a PPP account, the Windows Help system can lead you through the setup process. Start **Help**, click the **Index** tab, and type **Internet**. Double-click **connecting to** in the list of help topics, and then follow the on-screen instructions to set up your PPP account.

Is Dial-Up Networking Even Installed?

Before you can even think about connecting to the Internet in Windows 95, you have to make sure that the program you need is installed. Because Windows is a self-proclaimed disk hog, the Windows installation program may have omitted a couple programs, including Dial-Up Networking. To see if Dial-Up Networking is installed, double-click the **My Computer** icon. If you see the Dial-Up Networking icon, you're set; skip to the next section. Otherwise, take the following steps to install it:

1. Double-click the **Control Panel** icon in the My Computer window, and then double-click **Add/Remove Programs** icon.

Chapter 5 ➤ *Setting Up Your PPP or Slip Connection in Windows 95*

2. Click the **Windows Setup** tab.

3. In the Windows Components list, double-click **Communications**. This displays a list of the communications components.

4. Click the check box next to **Dial-Up Networking**, and then click **OK**.

5. Follow the on-screen instructions to complete the installation. You'll need your Windows 95 diskettes or CD, because the installation program will copy the necessary files to your hard drive. When you're done, you should have a Dial-Up Networking icon in the My Computer window.

Bondage 101: Binding Dial-Up Networking to TCP/IP

Once Dial-Up Networking is installed, you have to "bind" it to TCP/IP. That's just a fancy way of saying that you have to set up Dial-Up Networking to use the Internet communications protocol. Fortunately, this process is fairly simple. Here's what you do:

1. Display the Windows Control Panel by selecting **Start**, **Setting**, and **Control Panel** (if the Control Panel is not already sitting there on your screen), and then double-click the **Network** icon. This displays the Network Properties dialog box.

2. Look in the list of installed network components to see if TCP/IP is listed. If TCP/IP is not in the list, click the **Add** button, double-click **Protocol**, click **Microsoft**, click **TCP/IP**, and then click **OK**. This adds TCP/IP to the list of installed network components.

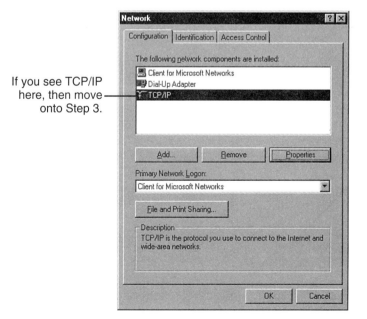

If you see TCP/IP here, then move onto Step 3.

TCP/IP must be installed.

37

3. Now for the bondage part. Click **Dial-Up Adapter** in the list of installed network components, and then click the **Properties** button.

4. Click the **Bindings** tab.

5. Make sure there is a check mark next to **TCP/IP**. If there is no check mark, click inside the check box.

6. Click **OK** to close the Dial-Up Adapter Properties dialog box, and then click **OK** to close the Network Properties dialog box.

7. If a dialog box appears telling you to restart your computer, follow the instructions to restart.

Are You on a Network?

Whenever you install TCP/IP, it is bound to all your adapters, including your network adapter. This can cause problems. If you don't use TCP/IP with your network card, follow the same steps given here to turn off TCP/IP for your network adapter. If you're not sure what to do, call your network administrator. You don't want to mess up your network connection when trying to establish an Internet connection.

PPP Made Easy

Now that you're bound, you can enter all the incomprehensible information that Dial-Up Networking needs to connect your computer to your service provider's computer. Dig out all the notes you took when you talked to your service provider. This includes the domain name, host name, and those funky numbers with all the periods. When you find your notes, take the following steps:

1. Run the Windows Control Panel (**Start**, **Settings**, **Control Panel**), and then double-click the **Network** icon. This displays the Network Properties dialog box you saw in the previous section.

2. Click **TCP/IP**, and then click the **Properties** button. The TCP/IP Properties dialog box appears. (If you have two TCP/IP entries, click the one that says **TCP/IP -> Dial-Up Adapter**.)

3. Click the **IP Address** tab (the most important tab of the bunch).

4. Assuming your service provider gave you an IP address, click **Specify an IP Address**, and then type your IP address and subnet mask into the specified text boxes, as shown in the next picture.

If your provider did not give you an IP address, call and ask for one. On the off chance that your service assigns an IP address automatically when you sign on, click **Obtain an IP address automatically**.

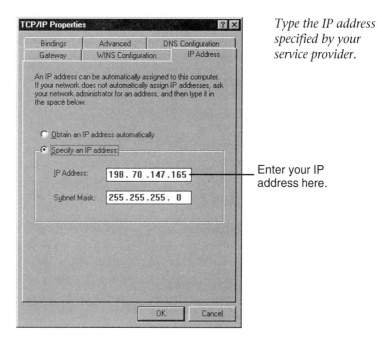

Type the IP address specified by your service provider.

Enter your IP address here.

5. Click the **Bindings** tab. If you see a **File and Printer Sharing** check box and it has a check mark in it, click inside the check box to remove the check mark.

6. Click the **DNS Configuration** tab, and enter any specific information from your service provider:

    Host is the name of your computer. This is usually the username that your service provider assigned to you.

    Domain represents the service provider's network. This tells the Internet which group of computers your computer is connected through.

> **Check This Out...**
>
> **Return to Sender** Communicating on the Internet without an IP address is like sending a letter with no return address. If the Internet doesn't know where you live, it can't transfer data to and from your computer.

Check This Out...

Domain Name

Domain names act as Internet addresses. For example, **microsoft.com** is the domain name of Microsoft Corporation. **microsoft** is the name of the organization, and **com** represents the type of organization (in this case COMmercial). You'll learn more than you want to know about domain names in Chapter 10.

7. If your service provider specified a gateway address, click the **Gateway** tab, type the gateway address, and click the **Add** button. (A *gateway* is a system that allows two incompatible networks to communicate.)

8. Click **OK** to save your changes, and then follow the on-screen instructions to reboot your computer (to put the settings into effect).

Keep these steps handy. If you have trouble connecting to the Internet later (like when you try to connect for the first time), repeat the steps to edit the DNS entry or one of the other entries that might be causing problems. Most connection errors are caused by a typo in the DNS entry or in your username or password (which you will enter later).

You're Almost There: Creating an Icon to Dial

If you've made it this far, you're more patient than I am. Fortunately, you're almost done. The last step is to create an icon in the Dial-Up Networking window that you can double-click to dial into your service provider's computer and establish the Internet connection you'll need to do the Web. Take the following steps:

1. Double-click the **My Computer** icon, and then double-click **Dial-Up Networking**. The Dial-Up Networking window appears. Unless you or someone else played with Dial-Up Networking before, you'll also see a wizard dialog box that will lead you through the process of setting up a new connection.

2. If you are not prompted to create an icon for a new connection, then double-click the **Make New Connection** icon. This starts a wizard that leads you through the process. This starts (surprise) the Make New Connection wizard.

3. Type a name for the connection in the **Type a name for the computer you are dialing** text box, and then click the **Next** button. (You might just type the name of your service provider, or type **Internet**.) The wizard prompts you to type the phone number of the service provider's computer.

4. Type the area code (if necessary) and the phone number your computer has to dial to connect to the service provider's computer.

If you have to dial a number (such as 9) to get an outside line, enter it, followed by a comma or two (for example, **9,555-5555**). If you need to disable call waiting, enter the code to turn it off (for example, **9,*70,555-5555**).

5. Click the **Next** button. The next dialog box that appears basically tells you that you're done.

6. Click the **Finish** button. An icon appears in the Dial-Up Networking window.

Terminal Window

With most Internet servers, Dial-Up Networking can connect behind the scenes. Other servers require Dial-Up Networking to display a terminal window. If your service provider or network administrator tells you that you need to display a terminal window, right-click on the icon you just created, and click **Properties**. Click the **Configure** button, and then click the **Options** tab. Click **Bring up terminal after dialing** and click **OK**.

If you have a PPP account, you now have an icon that will connect you with your service provider's computer...and with the Internet. All those who have a PPP account can skip ahead to the "Does It Work?" section later in this chapter. If you have a SLIP account, you still have some work ahead of you. Slip (no pun intended) into your waders and trudge through the following section.

You Have a SLIP Account? Take Two Valiums

If you have a SLIP connection through your service provider, the best advice is to dump it. Call your service provider, and change your connection type from SLIP to PPP. Then, set up Dial-Up Networking to establish a PPP connection, as explained earlier in this chapter. If you think that's too much trouble, wait until you see how much trouble it is to establish a SLIP connection with Dial-Up Networking.

The first problem you'll encounter is that the files you need to set up your SLIP account are only on the CD version of Windows 95. What's that? You have Windows 95 on diskettes? Sorry, pal, no SLIP for you. Call your service provider and switch your connection type to PPP, or skip to the next chapter to learn how to get and use a separate TCP/IP program.

If you do have the CD version of Windows 95, take the following steps to install the SLIP files:

1. Display the Windows Control Panel (**Start**, **Settings**, **Control Panel**), and double-click the **Add/Remove Programs** icon.

2. Insert the Windows 95 CD, click the **Windows Setup** tab, and then click the **Have Disk** button. The Install From Disk dialog box appears.

3. In the Copy manufacturer's files from text box, type the path to the SLIP files (this is usually **D:\ADMIN\APPTOOLS\DSCRIPT**), and then click **OK**. The Have Disk dialog box appears, showing the SLIP component you are about to install.

4. Make sure there is a check mark next to **SLIP and scripting for Dial-Up Networking** (click inside the check box to add the check mark, if necessary).

5. Click the **Install** button, and then click **OK** in the Add/Remove Programs dialog box.

Well, that was pretty easy. You're probably feeling pretty confident right now. Hate to tell you this, but you're a long way from done. Now, you have to set up your SLIP connection in Dial-Up Networking. You do this by changing the properties for the icon you created in Dial-Up Networking. Take the following steps:

1. Double-click the **Dial-Up Networking** icon (in My Computer), if the Dial-Up Networking window is not yet displayed. This runs Dial-Up Networking and displays the icon you created earlier.

2. Right-click the icon you created, and then click **Properties**. The properties dialog box for the connection you created appears.

3. Click the **Server Type** button. The Server Types dialog box appears.

4. Open the **Type of Dial-Up Server** drop-down list, and click the Internet account type you have:

    Slip: UNIX Connection if you have a SLIP account.

    CSLIP Connection With IP Header Compression if you have a CSLIP (Compressed SLIP) account.

5. If your service provider specified an IP address, click the **TCP/IP Settings** button. Then, click **Specify an IP Address** and type the IP address. (In most cases, you'll have to obtain this address when you sign on for the first time.) Click **OK**. This returns you to the Properties dialog box.

6. Click the **Configure** button, and then click the **Options** tab.

7. Click the **Bring up terminal after dialing** option.

8. Click **OK**. Your changes are saved.

Chapter 5 ➤ *Setting Up Your PPP or Slip Connection in Windows 95*

You are probably wondering about that **Bring up terminal** option is Step 7. Here's the story: with a SLIP account (and some networked PPP accounts), Dial-Up Networking cannot automatically establish a connection when you dial into your service provider's computer. Instead, it displays a terminal window that lets you enter commands. The service provider's computer will prompt you to enter your username and password, and then it will display your IP address. You'll have to jot down the address and then enter it as a TCP/IP setting. You'll learn how to do this in "Does It Work?" (the next section). Okay, pop another Valium, and let's move on.

Does It Work?

Once you have an icon, you can double-click it to connect to the Internet. When you double-click the icon, a dialog box appears as shown in the following screenshot, prompting you to type your username and password (supplied by your service provider). Type your username and password, and then click the **Connect** button. If you have a SLIP account (or a PPP account that requires you to use a terminal window), you don't have to enter your username and password; you'll do this after you connect in a terminal window.

Also, make sure there's a check mark in the Save Password check box. This saves your username and password, so you won't have to type it again the next time you logon.

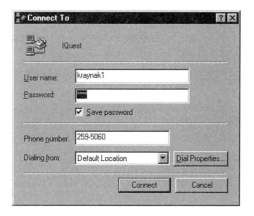

When you double-click the icon you just created, this dialog box appears.

If you have a PPP account that does not require you to use a terminal window, once you're connected, not much happens. You'll see a dialog box that shows you are connected and displays a clock showing how long you have been connected. You won't get a menu, as you did in Chapter 4. To use the Internet through your connection, you must run a specialized program, such as Navigator. For now, click the **Disconnect** button. You can connect again later, when you get Navigator up and running.

Part 1 ➤ *Getting Wired with Netscape Navigator*

When you're connected, this is all you'll see for now.

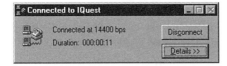

If you have a SLIP account (or a PPP account that requires a terminal window), you should see a terminal window asking you to enter your username (the name your service provider assigned to you). Skip to the next section to figure out what to do.

If Your Server Requires a Terminal Window...

With most PPP accounts, Dial-Up Networking enters all the commands and data required to establish the Internet connection. You can lean back in your chair and watch. With a SLIP connection and PPP connections that require a terminal window, you have to enter the commands and information yourself.

When you connect to your service provider's computer, you should see the Post Dial Terminal Screen dialog box. This dialog box allows the service provider's computer to display information on your screen asking for input. Here's what you do:

1. Type your username when prompted, and press **Enter**. Your service provider will now prompt you to type your password.

With some connections, you have to connect using the terminal dialog window.

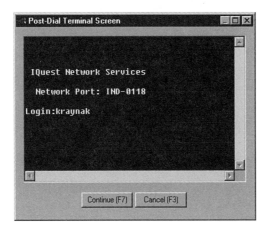

2. Type your password, and press **Enter**. Most service providers require only a username and password. However, your service provider may require you to enter additional information or agree to some terms.

3. Enter any other required information, as prompted. The service provider displays two IP addresses: the host IP address and your IP address.

4. Write down both IP addresses, and then click the **Continue (F7)** button.

5. In the SLIP Connection IP Address dialog box, type your IP address (the second address displayed), and then click **OK**. Assuming all goes as planned, you are now connected to the Internet.

Automating Your SLIP Connection

If you're given the same IP address each time you connect, you can save yourself some steps by entering that information for your connection. Right-click the connection icon, and click **Properties**. Click the **Server Type** button, click the **TCP/IP Settings** button, and then use the dialog box that appears to enter your IP address.

What Went Wrong?

If your connection proceeds smoothly the first time, lucky you. Most first attempts fail for some reason or another (these are computers, after all). If the connection fails, check the following:

➤ Did you type your username and password correctly? Try signing on again.

➤ Maybe your TCP/IP settings are wrong. To check them, display the Windows Control Panel, and double-click the **Network** icon. Click **TCP/IP**, and click the **Properties** button. Make sure you entered the settings exactly as your service provider specified.

➤ If the network TCP/IP settings are correct, make sure you have the same settings for your connection icon. Right-click the connection icon in Dial-Up Networking, and click **Properties**. Click the **Server Type** button, and click the **TCP/IP Settings** button. Make sure the IP address and domain server address are correct.

➤ If you're still having trouble, check your TCP/IP settings again. This time, click the IP Address tab, and select **Obtain an IP address automatically**. Some service providers are set up to assign the IP address when you connect.

➤ Go to the Windows Control Panel and check your modem setup. Make sure you've selected the correct modem, and that its settings are correct for connecting to the service provider.

➤ Try CSLIP instead of SLIP, or vice versa. If you're not sure whether you have a CSLIP or SLIP account, try connecting using the other server type. You can select a server type by right-clicking on the connection icon in Dial-Up Networking and then clicking **Properties**.

The Least You Need To Know

Setting up the initial Internet connection is the hardest part of doing the Web, or of doing anything else on the Internet. To avoid the agony, make sure you get a PPP account, and then let the Windows 95 Help system guide you through the process.

Sure, you'll suffer through a few headaches and error messages, but you'll suffer less than the poor saps in the next chapter who are still using Windows 3.1.

Chapter 6

Setting Up Your Internet Connection Using Windows 3.1

By the End of This Chapter, You'll Be Able To...

➤ Set up a SLIP or PPP connection in Windows 3.1 (if you really have to).

➤ Avoid all this complicated stuff by making your service provider do it for you.

➤ Use Windows Terminal to snatch the TCP/IP file you'll need to connect to the Internet.

➤ Do a bunch of technical things, which you can quickly forget once you're done.

I know, you're holding out on buying Windows 95 until they work out the bugs and all the other Windows 3.1 users in the world make the switch. Besides, you like the look and feel of your old Windows. Hey, it's okay. I like the look and feel of my old Windows, too. The only trouble is that with Windows 3.1, you have to come face to face with TCP/IP, and it's not a pretty sight.

In this chapter, you will encounter the behind-the-scenes activities of TCP/IP. You'll have to find a TCP/IP program for yourself, download it from the Internet, and then configure it to dial into your service provider's computer and establish a connection. The good news is that I'll show you a couple shortcuts that will alleviate most of the pain and discomfort of TCP/IP.

Make Your Service Provider Do It

When I first became involved in the Internet, my service provider sent me all the files I needed to connect, along with instructions on how to install the files. I received customized files that handled all the technical communications mumbo jumbo for me, so all I had to do to connect to the Internet was double-click on a funky icon. I didn't really have to know what was going on behind the curtains.

The moral of this story is that if you can avoid the complexities of TCP/IP software, do it. Call your service provider, explain that you don't want to deal with all this technical business, and ask for a configured TCP/IP program. Follow the instructions to install the program, and then skip ahead to the next chapter. That way, you avoid all the pain and frustration of TCP/IP, and you can spend more time playing with Netscape Navigator.

Netscape Navigator Personal Edition

If you wimped out and bought Navigator at your local computer store, you have the TCP/IP program you need to connect to your service provider. However, you still have to enter the settings to enable it to connect to your service provider's computer. Skip ahead to the section called, "Now That You Have Trumpet Winsock..." for instructions.

If You Decide to Go It Alone...

Windows 3.1 and 3.11 were firmly rooted before this Internet craze kicked in. Except for the puny Terminal program, these old versions of Windows offer no Internet support. You have to acquire a special program to handle a SLIP or PPP connection. Fortunately, you can purchase one of these programs at most computer stores. Ask for a Windows Socket program, TCP/IP, or Winsock; they'll know what you're talking about.

Another way you can get the program you need is to connect to the Internet, using Terminal (as explained in Chapter 4), and then use your service provider's computer to download a copy of Trumpet Winsock to your computer. This provides you with a shareware version of the program you need (shareware means you can try the program out and pay for it later—about $20).

Chapter 6 ➤ *Setting Up Your Internet Connection Using Windows 3.1*

Ch-Ch-Ch-Ch-Changes

Be flexible when copying files from the Internet. System administrators commonly reorganize the files on their computers and replace files with updated versions. If you can't find a file, check other directories, and look for files that have names similar (not necessarily identical) to the names I tell you to look for.

To download Trumpet Winsock, take the following steps:

1. Use Terminal to log in to your service provider, as explained in Chapter 4 in the section cleverly titled "Logging on to a Service Provider."

2. Perform one of the following steps:

    If you are at a prompt, type **ftp ftp.ncsa.uiuc.edu** and press **Enter**. A prompt appears, asking for your login name.

    If you are at a menu, use the menu to enter the FTP command (your service provider's menu system may require you to work through a series of submenus). When a prompt appears asking for the name of the FTP host, type **ftp.ncsa.uiuc.edu** and press **Enter**.

3. When asked to type your username, type **anonymous** and press **Enter**. A prompt appears, asking for your password.

4. Type your Internet e-mail address in the following form: *username@site.domain* (for example, jsmith@iway.com), and press **Enter**. You'll get a prompt that looks something like this: **rftp>**

5. Type **cd /Mosaic/Windows/sockets/Trumpet** and press **Enter**. **Important:** Type the command *exactly* as it is shown here. Use forward slashes to separate directory names, make sure there is a space after **cd**, and make sure the capitalization matches.

6. Type **ls** and press **Enter** to view a list of files in the current directory.

7. Type **bin** and press **Enter** to indicate that you want to perform a binary file transfer (as opposed to transferring a text file).

8. Type **get winsock.zip** (or the current name of the WinSock file) and press **Enter**. The host copies the file to your service provider's computer.

9. Type **quit** and press **Enter** to exit the host computer.

49

10. If you need PKZip (a program that decompresses the ZIP file you just downloaded, so you can use it), repeat steps 3–10 to download pkz204g.exe from one of the following sites:

   bitsy.mit.edu in the directory **/pub/dos/utils**
   ftp.cs.ualberta.ca in the directory **/pub/DOS**

Now the files are on your service provider's computer, not on your computer. Use your service provider's computer along with Terminal to download the files to your computer. The following steps lead you through a sample procedure. Your Internet service provider may have some other way of doing this:

1. Make a directory on your hard disk called **TEMP**, if you don't already have a TEMP directory. (You'll store your files temporarily in this directory.)

2. If you hung up on your service provider, sign on again.

3. Use the menu on your service provider's computer to go to the file transfer area, and then choose a file transfer protocol. You must select a protocol that matches something Windows Terminal supports: Kermit or XModem.

> **Techno Talk**
>
> **Proper Protocol**
>
> Whenever you transfer files, the sending and receiving computers must use the same protocol (sort of a file transfer language). Kermit and XModem are old protocols that allow you to transfer only one file at a time. ZModem is a newer, better protocol, which allows you to transfer multiple files. However, Windows 3.1 Terminal does not support ZModem file transfers.

4. Open Terminal's **Settings** menu, and click on **Binary Transfers**. In the dialog box that appears, select the protocol setting that matches the setting you entered for the service provider's computer.

5. Use the menu on the service provider's computer to go to the area where your personal files are stored. (When you downloaded the winsock.zip file, the remote computer sent the file to your Internet service provider's computer using the e-mail address you entered as a password. You now have to enter your personal file area to receive the file.)

Chapter 6 ➤ *Setting Up Your Internet Connection Using Windows 3.1*

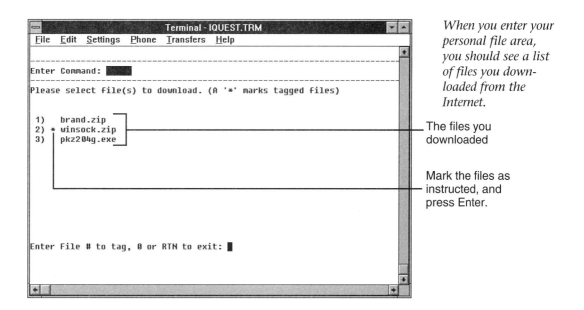

When you enter your personal file area, you should see a list of files you downloaded from the Internet.

— The files you downloaded

— Mark the files as instructed, and press Enter.

6. Use the commands as specified on your screen to mark and download the files to your computer (using XModem or Kermit, you can mark only one file at a time). In most cases, you mark a file by typing the number next to the file's name. At this point, the service provider's computer is ready to send the file. Now, you must enter the Receive command in Terminal.

7. Open the **Transfers** menu, and select **Receive Binary**. A dialog box appears, asking where you want the files placed on your computer.

8. Select the **TEMP** directory from the **Directories** list, and type **winsock.zip** in the **File Name** text box. Click **OK**. Your service provider works through Terminal to transfer the file(s) to your computer.

Type winsock.zip here.   Select the TEMP directory.

Terminal displays a dialog box, asking where you want the file(s) placed.

51

9. Wait until the transfer is complete, and then repeat steps 6 to 8 to download any additional files (including the PKZip file).

10. Don't forget to exit and hang up.

Unzip Me

The winsock.zip file you downloaded is squished (or *zipped*) so it would take up less disk space and roll through the phone lines faster. When you get it, you have to *unzip* the file (using a program called WinZip) before you can use WinSock.

How can you tell a file is zipped? Usually by looking at the end of the file name. Zipped files usually have the extension .ZIP. However, some zipped files travel incognito. For example, pkz204g.exe is a special *self-extracting* file, the Houdini of zipped files; it unzips itself.

If you haven't installed PKZip on your computer, do it now. Make a directory called **ZIP**, and move pkz204g.exe from the TEMP directory to the new ZIP directory. Change to that directory in File Manager, and then double-click **pkz204g.exe**. pkz204g.exe unzips itself, creating several files in the ZIP directory.

Run PKZip from Any Directory

Add the ZIP directory to the end of the path statement in your AUTOEXEC.BAT file. Your path statement might look something like this: PATH=C:\;C:\DOS;C:\WINDOWS;C:\ZIP. Then reboot your computer. Now you can run PKZip from any prompt.

Now that PKZip is installed, you can use it to unzip winsock.zip. First, make a directory called WINSOCK, and move winsock.zip to that directory. In File Manager, change to the WINSOCK directory, click **winsock.zip**, and then open the **File** menu and select **Run**. Click inside the **Command Line** text box to move the insertion point before winsock.zip. Now, type **c:\zip\pkunzip**, and press the **Spacebar**. The command in the Command Line text box should look like this:

   c:\zip\pkunzip winsock.zip

Press **Enter**, or click on the **OK** button. PKZip extracts all the files from winsock.zip that make up the Trumpet WinSock program. Now, make an icon for running WinSock from Windows:

1. Open Program Manager's **File** menu and select **New**.
2. Click the **Program Group** option, and click **OK**.
3. Type a name, such as **Internet**, in the Description text box to create a group window for your Internet programs, and then click **OK**.
4. Open the **File** menu again, and click **New**.
5. Make sure **Program Item** is selected, and then click **OK**. The New Program Item dialog box appears.
6. In the **Description** text box, type **Winsock**.
7. Click the **Browse** button, and use the dialog box that appears to change to the WINSOCK directory.
8. Click the **tcpman.exe** file, and click **OK**.
9. Click **OK**. You now have an icon you can use to run Winsock.

Setting Winsock on the Right Path

You can now run Trumpet Winsock, but you should place the WINSOCK directory in the PATH statement of your AUTOEXEC.BAT file, to ensure that your computer can find the necessary Winsock files. The easiest way to do this is to run the Windows System Editor. Open Program Manager's **File** menu and select **Run**. Type **sysedit** and press **Enter**.

You'll see the System Editor window shown here. Click inside the AUTOEXEC.BAT window. Move the insertion point to the end of the line that starts PATH= and type **;c:\winsock**, as shown in the figure. Open the **File** menu and select **Save**.

Place the WINSOCK directory in the PATH statement.

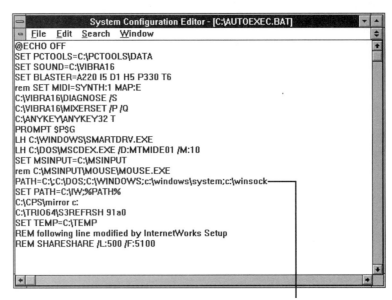

Type ;c:\winsock here.

Now That You Have Trumpet Winsock...

All that downloading and unzipping was just half the battle. You now have the tiger by its proverbial tail. It's on your computer, but in its current state, it is utterly useless. You now have to enter a bunch of settings that tell Winsock how to dial into and connect with your service provider's computer. Then, you have to write a sign-on script that automates the connection. First, the configuration part.

Double-click the Winsock icon you just created. The first time you run the beast, you get a dialog box showing you the shareware terms and conditions. Read this legal mumbo jumbo, and if you agree with it (do you have a choice?), click the **OK** button. Now, Winsock displays the dialog box, shown here, which prompts you to enter the connection settings. If the Trumpet Winsock Setup dialog box does not appear, open the **File** menu and select **Setup**.

Chapter 6 ➤ *Setting Up Your Internet Connection Using Windows 3.1*

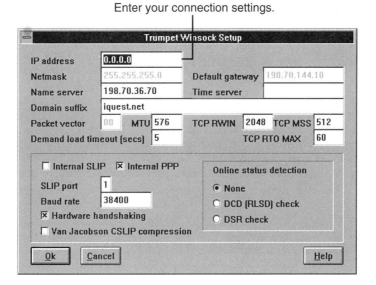

Enter your connection settings.

The first time's the hardest; Winsock asks for details.

Yes, this Setup dialog box asks for all sorts of incomprehensible entries. Instead of leading you through step-by-tedious step, here's a list of the option names along with samples of what you need to enter:

Internal SLIP or Internal PPP indicates the type of Internet account you have.

IP address (Internet Protocol address) is the address of your computer once you are connected to the Internet. It might look something like 189.190.123.122. This is a number you must obtain from your service provider. If your service provider supplies a different IP address each time you connect, leave this to 0.0.0.0 for now. Winsock will grab the address when you sign on and enter it for you.

Netmask is usually 255.255.255.0, but you can't change it here. If you have trouble connecting later, open the file named TRUMPWSK.INI (using the Windows Notepad), and type the Netmask number specified by your service provider next to **netmask=**.

Default gateway is initially 0.0.0.0 (nothing), but you can't change this one here, either. If you have trouble connecting later, ask your service provider for the default gateway, and then open the file named TRUMPWSK.INI (using the Windows Notepad). Then type the number specified by your service provider next to **gateway=**.

55

Name server (or Domain Name Server) is another number you must get from your service provider. The name server is a special computer that matches the names of computers (servers) on the Internet to their numbers, so Winsock can locate computers on the Internet. This number is very important.

Time server is another entry you can probably ignore. However, if your service provider specifies a Time server, enter it here.

Domain suffix is the part of your e-mail address after the @ sign. For example, if your e-mail address is jsmith@iway.com, you would enter **iway.com** here.

Packet vector is an advanced setting that tells your hardware how to deal with incoming data. Leave this setting alone, unless your network administrator tells you to enter something.

MTU (Maximum Transmission Unit) and the next few numbers control the way data is transmitted. You can usually establish a connection using the default entries. Later, as you learn more about TCP/IP (assuming you care to learn more), you can play with these numbers to increase the performance of your connection. Ignore them for now.

TCP RWIN (Transmission Control Protocol Receive Window) is another number you should ignore for now. It is usually four times the TCP MSS value (the next entry).

TCP MSS (Transmission Control Protocol Maximum Segment Size) is the final number in the list of numbers to ignore for now. It is usually 512 for a SLIP connection or 254 for a CSLIP connection.

Demand Load Timeout is the amount of time that Winsock remains loaded after the program that was using it is done. The default value (5 seconds) is okay.

SLIP Port is the COM port that your modem uses. This is usually 1 or 2.

Baud Rate is the maximum speed of your modem. If you have a 14,400 bps modem, try entering 19200. For a 28,800 bps modem, try 38400.

Hardware Handshake allows your modem and the remote computer to establish a connection (instead of allowing your programs to do it). In most cases, you should leave this on. If you have trouble connecting, try turning it off.

Van Jacobsen CSLIP Compression is a method for compressing and decompressing data as it is sent and received. Turn this on only if you have a CSLIP connection. If you have a SLIP connection, turn it off. For PPP connections, go ahead and turn this option on, although it is optional.

Online Status Detection specifies the method your modem uses to indicate its operating status to the remote computer. Leave this set to None unless your service provider gives you other instructions.

When you're done entering the requested information, click **OK**, exit Winsock, and then start it again. This time, you'll see a blank Winsock window.

A Sure Thing: Logging In Manually

Once you enter all the setup information, you should be able to log in manually with Winsock. This procedure is similar to the procedure you followed to log in with Terminal. You must perform these steps whenever you want to log in to the Internet to use Netscape Navigator or any of your other Internet programs. To log in, take the following steps:

1. Start Winsock by double-clicking the **Winsock** icon.

2. Open the **Dialler** menu, and select **Manual Login**.

3. Type **atz** and press **Enter** to reset your modem.

4. Type the command to dial your modem, followed by the phone number of your service provider's computer, and press **Enter**. For example, type **atdt5551234** and press **Enter**. If you have to dial a number (such as 9) to get an outside line, enter it, followed by a comma or two (for example, atdt9,555-5555). If you need to disable call waiting, enter the code to turn it off (for example, atdt9,*70,555-5555).

   Winsock dials the specified number, and connects to the service provider's computer, which asks you to enter your login name.

4. Type your username (or login name), and press **Enter**. The service provider now prompts you to enter your password.

5. Type your password and press **Enter**. A brief message or prompt usually appears followed by some strange characters.

6. Press the **Esc** key. Now, the service provider should display your IP address. If you left the IP address in the Setup dialog box as 0.0.0.0, Winsock should insert the IP address for you.

> **Check This Out...**
>
> **What's with the Commas?** A comma tells the modem to wait a moment. This allows a dial tone to sound before the modem dials any more numbers. Rarely, you might need to use more than one comma.

Watch the screen for clues on how to proceed.

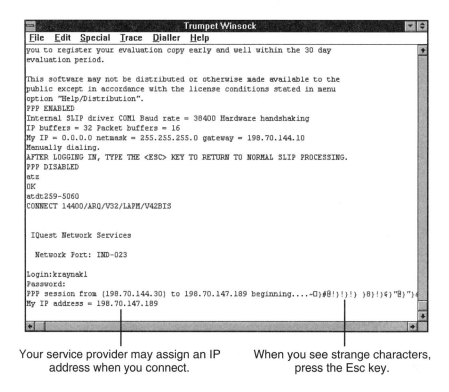

Your service provider may assign an IP address when you connect.

When you see strange characters, press the Esc key.

7. Open the **File** menu and select **Setup**, to make sure the IP address that's displayed matches the IP address in the Setup dialog box.

8. Take one of the following steps:

   If the IP addresses match, click the **Cancel** button.

   If the IP addresses do not match, type the IP address displayed by your service provider into the IP address text box, and click **OK**.

Assuming that everything proceeded according to plan, you are now connected. You can run Navigator (and other Internet programs) over the connection. However, if the connection failed, check your setup again (File/Setup). Make sure your IP address is correct. If your service provider assigns a new IP address each time you sign on, enter 0.0.0.0 in the IP Address text box. Otherwise, Winsock cannot automatically enter the correct IP address for you.

To cancel the connection, open the **Dialler** menu and select **Bye**.

Chapter 6 ➤ *Setting Up Your Internet Connection Using Windows 3.1*

Cheating Your Way Through a Login Script

Logging in to your service provider's computer manually usually works, but you can save time by writing a script that logs in for you. The trouble is that these scripts are difficult to write. Fortunately, Winsock comes with a login script, which, with a few modifications, just might do the job. (You might also obtain a script from your service provider.)

The first time you run the Login script, you're asked to enter the phone number to dial, your username, and your password. This information is then added to the TRUMPWSK file, so the script enters them for you later. To run the Login script for the first time, take the following steps:

1. Double-click the **Winsock** icon to run Trumpet Winsock. Winsock runs and displays its opening window.

2. Open the **Dialler** menu and click **Login**. The first time you run the Login script, a dialog box appears, prompting you to type the number you want to dial.

3. Type the number you must dial to connect to the service provider's computer. If you have to dial a number (such as 9) to get an outside line, enter it, followed by a comma or two (for example, 9,,555-5555). If you need to disable call waiting, enter the code to turn it off (for example, 9,,*70,,555-5555).

4. Click **OK**. Another dialog box appears, prompting you to enter your username.

5. Type your username, and click the **OK** button. The next dialog box prompts you to enter your password.

6. Type your password, and click the **OK** button. Winsock dials the specified number and attempts to connect to your service provider's computer.

If you see the message Script Aborted, the script has a problem that is preventing it from connecting your modem to the remote computer. Usually, this problem is caused with one of the *variables* in the script. (A variable allows you to modify the script to customize it for the way your service provider handles logins.) For example, if your service provider might for your username by displaying Login:, but the script expects to see Username:. By changing the variable Username: to Login:, you enable the script to recognize your service provider's way of doing things.

To fix the problem, you must edit the script. Open the **Dialler** menu and select **Edit Scripts**. In the dialog box that appears, click **login.cmd**, and click the **OK** button. This opens the Login script in Windows Notepad.

Scroll down until you see the area that contains the variables, as shown below. Edit the variables, so they match the prompts used by your service provider. For example, you might have to replace "sername:" with "ogin:". In case you're wondering...the first character is omitted from some words, because the words may or may not be capitalized. By omitting the first character, the script avoids problems with capitalization.

If your script aborts prematurely, check the variables.

```
                         Notepad - LOGIN.CMD
File  Edit  Search  Help
    end
  end
  if ![load $username]
    if [username "Enter your login username"]
      save $username
    end
  end
  if ![load $password]
    if [password "Enter your login password"]
      save $password
    end
  end
  $modemsetup = "&c1&k3"
  $prompt = ">"
  $userprompt = "ogin:"
  $passprompt = "assword:"
  $slipcmd = "cslip"
  $addrtarg = "our address is"
  $pppcmd = "ppp"
  $pppready = "PPP."
  %attempts = 10
```

The variables allow you to quickly customize the script for your service provider.

Check the other variables, such as "assword," and enter any changes as needed. Then, enter the **File/Save** command. If you still have trouble, read on to learn more about the language of scripts. Or, better yet, call your service provider, and ask for a customized Login script for Trumpet Winsock.

Changing the Phone Number or Password

If you need to change the phone number, your login name, or your password, open Winsock's **Dialler** menu and select **Setup**. This displays the three dialog boxes you saw when you first ran the Login script, allowing you to enter any changes.

Ugh! Writing Your Own Script

At this point, you're probably calling around to your local computer stores to see if they have a copy of Windows 95 in stock. If I'm wrong, and you've made it this far, you're more persistent than most. If you're still having trouble with your Login script, try using a simplified script. Rename the login.cmd file (try calling it login.old), and then create your own login.cmd file using Notepad.

Chapter 6 ➤ Setting Up Your Internet Connection Using Windows 3.1

Following is a sample script, just so you'll know what you're getting yourself into. This script is designed to connect to a service provider using a SLIP account. This is only a sample. You might have to adjust some of the commands, as specified by your service provider, to get it to work:

```
# initialize modem
#
output atz\13
input 10 OK\n
#
# set modem to indicate DCD
#
#output at&c1
#input 10 OK\n
#
# send phone number
#
output atdt259-5060\13
#
# my other number
#
#output atdt241644\13
#
# now we are connected.
#
input 30 CONNECT
#
# wait till it's safe to send because some modem's hang up
# if you transmit during the connection phase
#
wait 30 dcd
#
# now prod the terminal server
#
#output \13
#
# wait for the username prompt
#
input 30 login:
#username Enter your username
#output \u\13
#
```

61

```
output jsmith\13
#
# and the password
#
input 30 Password:
#password Enter your password
#output \p\13
#
output oglio\13
#
# we are now logged in
#
# jump into slip mode
#
#output slip\13
#
# wait for the address string
#
input 30 to
#
# parse address
#
address 30
#input 30 \n
#
# we are now connected, logged in and in slip mode.
#
#display \n
#display Connected.  Your IP address is \i.\n
#
#  ping a well known host locally...  our slip server won't work
#  for a while
#
#exec pingw 131.217.10.1
#
# now we are finished.
#
```

Your head is spinning. Your brain hurts. You're breaking out in hives. What does it all mean? Here's a blow-by-blow description of the essential commands. The lines in the script that are not listed here are not commands, for example **#set modem to indicate**

Chapter 6 ➤ *Setting Up Your Internet Connection Using Windows 3.1*

DCD is a description of what the next command does. As you write a script, you may want to include these lines as notes to yourself, although they are not essential.

And, in case you're wondering about the pound signs (#) at the beginning of some of the command lines, # prevents a command line from being read. This allows you to place notes and other information in the script without affecting its execution.

Okay, here are the script commands:

Command	Translation
initialize modem	Start the modem.
output atz\13	Reset the modem. ATZ is a common modem command that clears any other commands from the modem. \13 is a code that says "press Enter."
input 10 OK\n	Wait 10 seconds to make sure the modem is responding.
#output at&c1	Turn on the modem's Data Carrier Detect feature.
#input 10 OK\n	Wait 10 seconds again for the modem to respond.
output atdt555-5555\13	Dial 555-5555. This tells your modem to dial the phone number of the service provider's computer. Replace 555-5555 with the number your service provider gave you. If you have to dial a number (such as 9) to get an outside line, enter it, followed by a comma (for example, atdt9,555-5555\13). If you need to disable call waiting, enter the code to turn it off (for example, atdt9,*70,555-5555\13).
output atdt555-5454\13	If the previous number is busy, dial this number.
input 30 CONNECT	Wait at least 30 seconds for the modem to send the command indicating that the connection has been established.
wait 30 dcd	Wait for a Data Carrier Detect signal from the modem.
#output \13	Press Enter to get the service provider's attention. Not all service providers require this, so you may be able to eliminate this line.
input 30 login:	Wait up to 30 seconds for the login: prompt. If your service provider displays a username: prompt instead, type **input 30 username:** in place of this command line.

continues

continued

Command	Translation
output jsmith\13	Enter the username required to log in to the system. Replace jsmith with your username or login name. (The lines previous to this #username Enter your username #output \u\13 offer another way to log in. If you want Winsock to prompt you to enter your username, then use these two lines instead of the line shown at the left.)
input 30 Password:	Wait up to 30 seconds for the password: prompt.
output oglio\13	Enter the password required to log in to the system. Replace oglio with the password you use. (Again, the lines previous to this #password Enter your password #output \p\13 offer another way to enter a password.
input 30 to	Wait for an address. Your service provider will supply an IP address at this point.
address 30	Store the IP address for future reference. This gives Winsock the address it needs to establish the Internet connection.

After you create a script, run it to see if it works. To run the script, double-click the **Winsock** icon, open the **Dialler** menu, and select the script's name (usually **Login**). Watch the screen carefully to see what happens next. If the script aborts before dialing, check the commands up to and including the command that dials the phone number. If the script hangs when logging you in, you have a problem with the Login or Password command. Use your noggin to track down the problem and correct it.

The Least You Need to Know

TCP/IP settings and script writing are the stuff that programmers are made for. No ordinary person should have to go through the pain and agony of understanding these settings and commands only to use them once. So, get someone else to do it for you. If your service provider refuses to help or to at least supply you with a customized Login script, dump the service provider and find a new one. If you have any hacker friends who owe you a favor, give them a call.

Chapter 7

Now, You Can Install Netscape Navigator

By the End of This Chapter, You'll Be Able To...

➤ Know an FTP program when you see one.

➤ Grab the latest version of Navigator off the Internet...FOR FREE!

➤ Put Navigator on your hard drive.

➤ Fire up Navigator for the first time.

The hard part's over. You survived the preliminaries. You can connect to the Internet at will using your TCP/IP program. But all you have to look at are a bunch of funky hieroglyphics and strange numbers. Hardly the multimedia extravaganza I promised in Chapter 1. You now have to snatch a copy of Navigator and get it up and running. But where do you get Navigator, and, more importantly, how do you stick it on your computer?

In this chapter, you'll learn where Navigator hangs out, which version you should use, and where to score the latest, greatest version. I'll even show you how to install it...and run it. By the end of this chapter, you'll be Web-bound!

Where Can You Find Navigator?

Navigator is the Gideon Bible of Web browsers. You can find it everywhere—at your local computer store, on the inside back covers of some Netscape Navigator books, and even on the Internet. I expect that soon you'll be able to pick up a copy at the airport by making a small donation to a robed man with a shaved head. Sari...er...Sorry for my political incorrectness.

But seriously, where can you get a copy of Navigator, and which version should you get? Here's a list to help you decide:

➤ **Commercial version (a.k.a. Netscape Navigator Personal Edition)**—You can pick up Navigator wherever fine software is sold, for about fifty bucks. This gives you a licensed version, just in case the software police ever raid your home office. It also comes with its own TCP/IP program, so you don't have to do the downloading dance you performed in Chapter 6.

➤ **Latest Shareware version**—Netscape Communications Corporation has an Internet site that offers the latest version of Navigator (as of the writing of this book, version 2.0). You can connect to this site and download Navigator as explained later in this chapter. If you're a student, educational institution, beta tester, or are otherwise impoverished, you can use this version for free. Otherwise, you have to send a check to Navigator and register the program.

➤ **The 16-bit version**—This is the old version of Navigator. If you have Windows 3.1, this is the version you want. It is designed to work under a 16-bit operating system, which is what Windows 3.1 is all about. If you have Windows 95, make sure you get the 32-bit version.

➤ **A book version**—Several books that compete with this book (MY book) include a version of Navigator. To appeal to the lowest common denominator, the 16-bit version of Navigator is usually the version you get. You can use this version of Navigator to download the 32-bit version from Netscape's Internet site, so if you have the 16-bit version, don't trash it yet.

Snatching Navigator Off the Internet

If you bought the latest version of Navigator or grabbed it off your computer at work, you can skip this part. However, if you don't have Navigator, or if you have an old version (pre-version 2.0), then you should use your Internet connection to download (copy) the file to your computer.

When you download a file from the Internet, you use something called *FTP (File Transfer Protocol)*, which you may have encountered earlier in this book. This FTP thing is just a file transfer standard that ensures the sending and receiving computers are speaking the same language.

Chapter 7 ➤ *Now, You Can Install Netscape Navigator*

As with most Internet procedures, you can FTP in a number of ways. The easiest way is to use a special FTP program (if you have one). The next simplest way to FTP is to use a Web browser (such as Mosaic or an old version of Navigator). If you have neither of these tools, you can use Windows Terminal or HyperTerminal (it's tough, but you may not have a choice). The following sections explain the various FTP procedures.

> **Check This Out...**
>
> **Don't Be Choosy** If your service provider gives you a copy of a Web browser (any Web browser), take it. You can use just about any Web browser to FTP from the Internet, and it's a whole lot easier than using Windows Terminal.

FTPing the Easy Way

Poke around in your program groups to see if you have a Windows FTP program (your service provider may have slipped you an FTP program). One of the more popular Windows FTP programs is called *Ws_ftp*. If you have it, your job is going to be a lot easier. In fact, transferring files with a Windows FTP program is almost as easy as copying and moving files using the Windows Explorer or File Manager. Here's what you do:

1. Make a directory or folder on your hard disk called **TEMP**, if you don't already have one. (You'll store your files temporarily in this directory or folder.)

2. Run your FTP program. (You may have to run your TCP/IP program to connect to your service provider before you can run the FTP program.)

3. Enter the **Connect** command, and type **ftp.netscape.com** in the **Host Name** text box. (This is the address of the remote FTP site where you'll get your files.)

4. Type **anonymous** in the **User ID** text box.

5. In the **Password** text box, type your e-mail address. For example, you might type **jsmith@iway.com**.

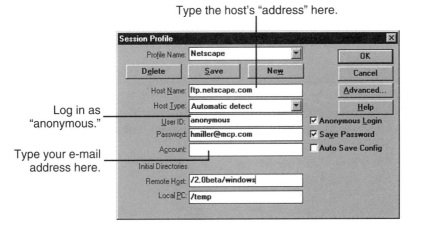

Enter your connect information up front.

67

6. Click the **OK** or **Connect** button. If all goes right, the FTP program connects you to the remote server.

7. Select **Binary** as the Transfer option.

8. Use the **Remote System** list to find the file you need: **n32e20b3.exe** (the filename may differ slightly). Try this one of these directories: **/2.0b3/windows** or **/netscape/windows**.

   If you have Windows 95, make sure you get the file that has "32" in its name (meaning it is the 32-bit version). If you're still using Windows 3.1, make sure you get the file with "16" in its name.

   The "20" represents the version number (version 2.0).

   The "b" stands for beta, meaning this is a test release of the program. If the finished version of the program is out by the time you read this (fat chance), the b might be missing.

> **Poke Around**
>
> At the time this book was published, the Netscape Navigator file was in the /2.0b3/windows directory. Some joker may have moved the files since then. If you don't find the files in one directory, switch to another directory that looks promising.

9. If you can't connect to Netscape's main FTP site, try any of the following sites:

   ftp://ftp2.netscape.com
   ftp://ftp3.netscape.com
   ftp://ftp4.netscape.com
   ftp://ftp5.netscape.com
   ftp://wuarchive.wustl.edu/packages/www/Netscape/netscape1.1/
   ftp://ftp.cps.cmich.edu/pub/netscape/
   ftp://ftp.utdallas.edu/pub/netscape/netscape1.1/
   ftp://unicron.unomaha.edu/pub/netscape/netscape1.1/
   ftp://server.berkeley.edu/pub/netscape/
   ftp://SunSITE.unc.edu/pub/packages/infosystems/WWW/clients/Netscape/
   ftp://ftp.orst.edu/pub/packages/netscape/

Chapter 7 ➤ *Now, You Can Install Netscape Navigator*

9. Use the Local System to change to the TEMP directory on your hard disk.
10. Click the name of the Netscape Navigator file to highlight it.
11. Click the arrow button to copy the files from the host computer to your PC.

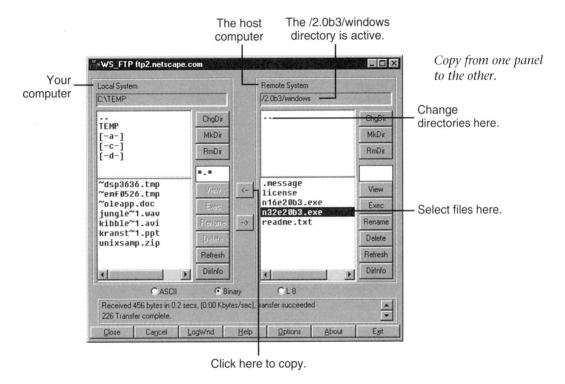

12. Wait until the copying is complete.
13. Exit your FTP program.
14. Disconnect from your service provider.

Now you have a self-extracting zip file (a compressed file) on your computer. This file contains all the files that comprise Navigator. Skip ahead to one of the "Installing" sections later in this chapter for instructions on how to proceed.

FTPing in the Old Days

If you connect to the Internet and get this...

You can FTP from here, but it won't be easy.

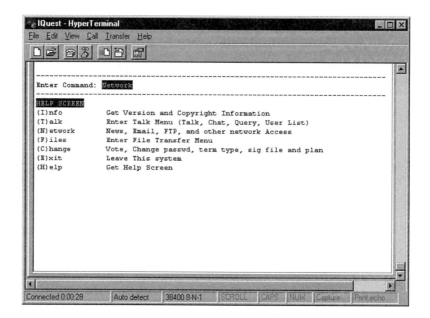

...then you're not using your TCP/IP software to connect, and you can't transfer files directly from a remote server to your computer. You are using your Internet connection as a *terminal account* (which, by the way, won't work for Navigator). However, you can use this type of connection to FTP. This is a two-step process. First, you download the files from the remote server to your service provider's computer. Then, you download the files from the service provider's computer to your computer.

You may already have done this FTP dance in Chapter 6 to get your TCP/IP program. Well, now you're going to have to do it again. Flip back to Chapter 6, and skip to the section called "If You Decide to Go It Alone..." Follow the step-by-step instructions to connect to the following FTP site:

ftp.netscape.com

Login as:

anonymous

When asked for a password, type your e-mail address as shown in the following example:

jsmith@iway.com

Then, enter the following **change directory** command (remember to use forward slashes, use the correct case, and insert a space after **cd**):

cd /2.0b3/windows

If you receive a message saying that this directory does not exist, type **ls** and press **Enter** to view a list of directories that do exist. Then, use the **cd** command to change to a directory that looks as though it might contain the Netscape Navigator file you need.

Next, enter the following command to list the files in that directory:

ls

And specify that you want to perform a binary transfer by entering:

bin

Finally, enter the command to get the file (if the file name differs, type the correct name instead of the one in the example below; if you have Windows 3.1, make sure you get the 16-bit version):

get n32e20b3.exe

This places the file on your service provider's computer. Follow the steps given in Chapter 6 to transfer the file to your computer.

FTPing with a Web Browser

You learn all about using Navigator to FTP in Chapter 16, but you have to get Navigator before you can use Navigator to get Navigator. (Sorry, I studied metaphysics in college.) However, if you have a Web browser (Mosaic, InternetWorks, an old version of Navigator), you can use the browser to quickly download the latest version of Navigator. Here's what you do:

1. Run Winsock, or whatever TCP/IP program you're using, and login to your service provider. (You can't use a Web browser until you're connected to the Internet.)

2. Look for a URL or Location text box or command. Most Web browsers display such a text box at the top of the Window, but others might require you to select the URL or Location command (usually from the File menu).

3. Drag over any text that might be in the URL or Location text box, type **ftp://ftp.netscape.com** and press **Enter**. After a moment, you should be connected to Netscape Corporation's FTP site.

4. Click the **/2.0b3** link, and then click the **/windows** link. This opens the **/2.0b3/windows** directory, which contains a link for the Netscape file you must download: **n32e20b3.exe** (the file name may differ slightly).

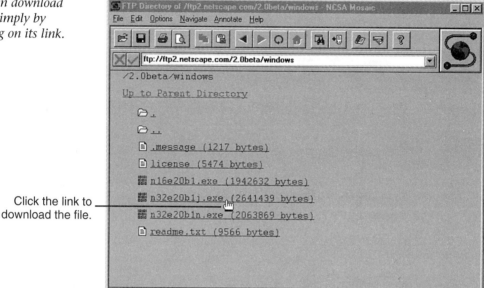

You can download a file simply by clicking on its link.

Click the link to download the file.

5. Take the required steps to download the file using your Web browser. The steps vary depending on the browser you're using:

    With an old version of Navigator, simply click the link, and then follow the dialog boxes to nab the file.

    With Mosaic, hold down the **Shift** key while clicking on the link, and then follow the dialog boxes to complete the task.

6. Wait until the file transfer is complete.

7. Close your Web browser, and then disconnect from your service provider by using your TCP/IP program.

Chapter 7 ➤ *Now, You Can Install Netscape Navigator*

Installing Navigator

Installing Navigator is a no-brainer. The file you just nabbed is a self-extracting zip file, so all you have to do to unzip it is run the program file. Simply run Windows Explorer (or File Manager, if you're using Windows 3.1), change to the folder that contains the file you just downloaded (Netscape), and then double-click the file. Windows opens a DOS window, showing you the extraction process in action.

After the extraction process is complete, you can close the DOS window. You now have all the necessary Navigator files on your hard drive, including the most important file of all: setup.exe. In Windows Explorer or File Manager, double-click the **setup** icon. This runs the Navigator Installation program. Just follow the on-screen instructions to install Navigator.

> **Check This Out...**
>
> **If You Purchased Navigator...** If you have Navigator on disks, insert the first disk into drive A or B. Use Windows Explorer or File Manager to change to the floppy disk drive that contains the disk. Then, double-click the SETUP file. Follow the on-screen instructions to complete the operation.

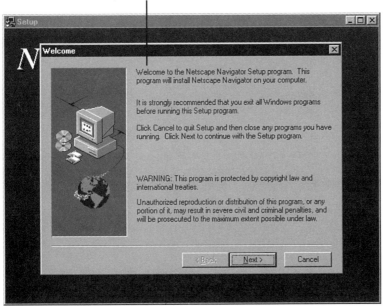

Follow the on-screen instructions to complete the installation.

The Navigator Installation program installs Navigator for you.

73

When you're done, you should have a Netscape Navigator icon on the Windows Start menu and on the desktop (in Windows 95), or (if you're using Windows 3.1) in the Netscape program group.

You'll be tempted to double-click the icon now (or choose it from the Start menu in Windows 95). Go ahead, live a little. What you'll get is the Netscape window, but you won't see a Web page yet. You haven't told Navigator where to go, and if your TCP/IP program isn't running, then you're not even connected to the Internet. But all this is the topic of the next chapter, so let's get to it.

The Least You Need To Know

Now that Navigator's installed, you don't need to know much more. However, you should check the Netscape's Web site every couple months or so to see if it has an updated version of Navigator. Simply run your TCP/IP program to connect to the Internet, run Navigator, and then open the **Directory** menu and select **Netscape's Home**.

This displays Netscape's home page (the main Web page), which displays news about and links to Netscape Communications Corporation's product line. Simply follow the links to download the latest version of Navigator.

Chapter 8

Day Trippin' on the Web

By the End of This Chapter, You'll Be Able To...

➤ Name the parts of a Navigator screen.

➤ Define *home* page and go to a home page in a foreign country.

➤ Use hyperlinks to get lost in the Web.

➤ Find your way back to where you started.

Your dog just brought you the leash. Your spouse is nagging you to come upstairs and eat. Your kids are pounding on the den door. You've been at this Navigator thing too long, and you still haven't dipped your pinky into the ocean of Web.

You've waited long enough.

Now it's time to fire up Navigator and frolic in the Web. In this chapter, you'll stare into the bright light of the Web. You'll learn how to start Navigator, pull up a Web page, skip around with links, and even return home. I promise to get you thoroughly lost, and I promise that you'll like it.

Ladies and Gentlemen, Start Your Engines

It's tempting to just double-click the Netscape Navigator icon. Don't. If you do, Navigator appears alright, but you can't drive it anywhere, because you're not yet connected to the Internet. Starting Navigator now is like firing up a new Ferrari in the showroom; you have no way to take it out on the open road.

So, before you can run Navigator, run your TCP/IP program.

➤ If you're in Windows 95, double-click **My Computer**, double-click **Dial-Up Networking**, and then double-click the icon you created in Chapter 5. Use the dialog box that appears, to connect to the Internet.

Tip: Hold down the right mouse button while dragging the icon you created from the Dial-Up Networking window to the Windows desktop. Release the mouse button, and then click **Create Shortcut(s) Here**. This places a copy of the icon on the Windows desktop.

➤ If you're in Windows 3.1, double-click your **TCP/IP** or **Winsock** icon, and then perform the required steps to login to your service provider.

Once you're connected, minimize the window—DON'T close it. Closing the window essentially hangs up the phone—or worse, it can keep the connection open, running up your Internet bill.

Okay, you're connected, right? *Now* you can double-click the **Netscape Navigator** icon (or choose it from the Windows 95 Start menu). The Netscape opening screen appears, and Navigator automatically connects to the Netscape home page.

Hitting the Open Road

To go anywhere on the Web, you first have to enter the "address" of the destination Web page. This address is called a URL, and fortunately, the URL for Netscape's home page (the starter page) is in the **Location** text box at the top of the screen. In other words, the Location text box shows the address of the currently displayed Web page.

This page is the incarnation of boredom. If you want to have some fun, go to the Yahoo Home Page. Click inside the **Location** text box, type **http://www.yahoo.com** and press **Enter**. You don't have to know all about URLs to type one. Just type it exactly as shown, and press **Enter**. You'll learn all about URLs in Chapter 10.

You might notice that the name of the text box that has the URL in it changes back and forth from Location to Go To. Whenever Navigator successfully loads a Web page, the text box is called Location. Whenever you type a URL into the text box, and whenever Navigator is in the process of loading the page, the text box is called Go To.

Chapter 8 ➤ *Day Trippin' on the Web*

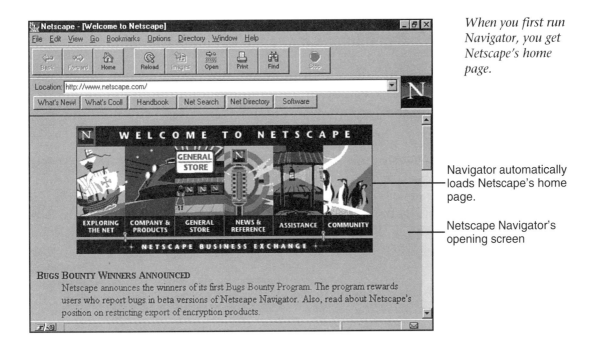

When you first run Navigator, you get Netscape's home page.

Navigator automatically loads Netscape's home page.

Netscape Navigator's opening screen

Does It Seem S...L...O...W?

Hyperdocuments can be packed with pictures called *inline images* (no relation to inline skates). These buggers take forever to transfer over the phone lines and can slow your Navigator sessions down to a crawl. There is, however, a trick to speeding up Navigator. Open the **Options** menu and select **Auto Load Images**. In the next hyperdocument you load, standard icons will appear in place of the images. To view a single image, you can click it. To view all images on the page, click the **Images** button (below Navigator's menu bar).

You can always switch back to having all the images displayed by opening the **Options** menu again, and clicking on **Auto Load Images**. However, as you wander the Web, you'll get to where you're going a whole lot quicker by turning Auto Load Images off. When you find the page you were looking for, click the **Images** button.

Moseying Around the Navigator Screen

The overall Navigator screen should look pretty familiar...like all Windows applications, Navigator is in a standard window. It has a menu bar, a toolbar, scroll bars, controls for resizing and closing the window, and a status bar at the bottom that displays informative messages.

Check This Out...

What's This Button For?

You can quickly find out the name of any button in the toolbar. Just rest the mouse pointer on the button in question. A box appears, showing the button's name, and the status bar (at the bottom of the Netscape window) displays the button's role in life.

What makes this window so different are its contents. Notice that the page displayed in the next figure has one or more underlined, highlighted words or phrases. These are *links* that point to other pages or Web sites. Click a link, and Navigator loads the appropriate page, no matter where that page is stored (on the current server or on a server in Alaska, Sweden, or anywhere else). Links can come in all shapes and sizes; they can be text, icons, or even small graphics, but they all work the same way.

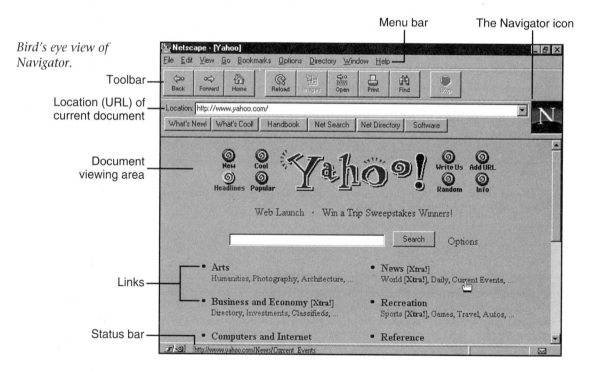

Bird's eye view of Navigator.

One other unique element on the Navigator screen is the big **N** with the flying comets. Look on the right side of Navigator window. This little eye-catcher isn't just for decoration. Comets fly across the **N** as your connection transfers data. This shows you when Navigator is busy fetching information for you.

Chapter 8 ➤ Day Trippin' on the Web

Working with Window Frames

Occasionally, you'll come across a Web page that splits your Navigator window into two frames: an upper and lower frame. Each frame has its own scroll bar, so you can view two or more Web pages at the same time, as shown here. Frames are especially useful for helping you move around in a long Web document. For example, one of the panes may contain an outline of the document. Whenever you click on a link in the outline, the other frame displays the page that contains detailed information about the topic.

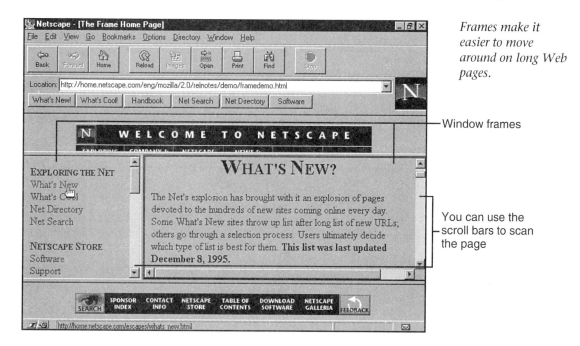

Frames make it easier to move around on long Web pages.

You can't turn these frames on or off from your end. They're built into the Web page, and they tell Navigator to split the window in two. You can change the relative size and dimensions of the frames by dragging the borders that separate them. You can also move from one page to another by clicking on a link in any of the frames.

Wandering the Web

Your first inclination is to click a link. Go ahead, live a little. Click away, and wander the Web. Your first time on the Web should be an exploration. You don't know where you're going, you don't really care, and the worst that can happen is that you'll get an error message or two. Don't let the error messages discourage you. Just click the **OK** button and try a different link. In Chapter 9, I'll explain some of the more common error messages—and let you know whether you can do anything about them.

As you're clicking away, you may notice that whenever you move your mouse pointer over a link, the pointer turns into a hand with a pointing finger. When the hand appears, look inside the *status bar*, and you'll see the location and directory for that link. This is one of those overly cryptic URLs (Uniform Resource Locators) I mentioned in Chapter 3. You can pretty much ignore URLs when you're wandering. Like street addresses, URLs are useful only when you know (or care) where you're going. See Chapter 10 if you have a specific URL you want to explore.

What's a Link?

Every **link** consists of three parts. First, there's the part you see (the text, icon, or picture). The link also has two parts you don't see: a *reference* to the linked data, and an *anchor* (which allows you to activate the link). Whenever you move the mouse pointer over an anchor, the mouse pointer turns into a hand pointer, showing that you can now activate the link.

Navigator likes displaying URLs, even though they mean absolutely nothing to human-type people. There's even a URL text box (called Location or Go To) below the toolbar that shows the URL of the currently displayed document. As you already have seen, you can type a URL in this text box, to go somewhere in a hurry. But if you're just wandering, you can safely ignore the URL.

Retracing Your Steps

Navigator has all sorts of advanced navigational tools that enable you to find places you've visited and hot spots you want to revisit. You'll learn all about how to use these tools in Chapter 10. For the current day trip, navigate with the four buttons in the toolbar: Back, Forward, Home, and Reload. These buttons appear on the left end of the toolbar.

When you first sign on, the Forward and Back buttons are grayed, meaning you can't use them. After all, you haven't gone anywhere yet, so you can't go forward or back. When you start to click links, you go forward, so Navigator activates the **Back** button, allowing you to return from whence you came. This is useful if the Web happens to ditch you in any of its many dead ends. If you back up too far, you can use the **Forward** button to move ahead one screen.

Chapter 8 ➤ *Day Trippin' on the Web*

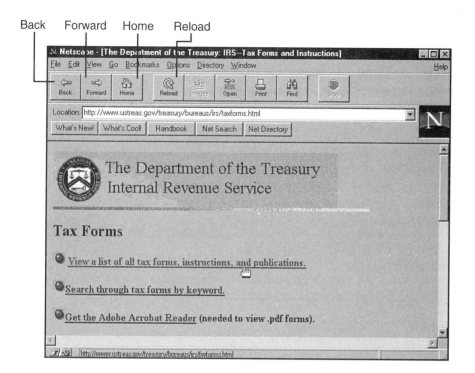

Use these buttons to retrace your steps.

If you end up in the Emerald City, just click your heels together and...sorry, wrong book. If you want to get back to where you started, click the **Home** button to return to the first Home page. You can then depart again on a new journey, trying another path.

That leaves us with one last button, the Reload button. If your screen goes bonkers and displays half the page or some other oddity, click the **Reload** button to try again. Remember, all these signals are flying around in phone lines and network cables, and sometimes, they get crossed.

Skipping Back

As you go back, you may notice that previously loaded documents load more quickly. That's because Navigator stashes (or, more formally, *caches*, which rhymes with "stashes") up to two documents in memory. Navigator also displays the links for sites you've visited in a different color, to help you return to a site or avoid it.

81

I Clicked, But Nothing Happened

Hey, it happens. You click a link, wait a few seconds...nothing. No error message, no grinding sounds, nothing that would indicate trouble. Try clicking on the link again, but this time, watch the flying comets and the status bar. Assuming all is going according to plan, you should see the following series of messages in the status bar:

Connect: Looking up host: <host URL>
Connect: Connecting host: <host URL>
Connect: Host contacted. Waiting for reply...
Transferring data
Document: Received <so many> of <so many> bytes
Document: Done

...and the comets should fly.

Sometimes, however, the status bar goes blank and the comets freeze. This means trouble—and unless you get an error message, Navigator isn't about to tell you that there's trouble.

The best thing to do at this point is cut your losses. The Web server you're trying to connect to might be down or the place is packed with interested users. If the comets are still flying, click the **Stop** button (in the toolbar), and then try another link. If Navigator is locked up, wait to see whether your computer will rectify the situation on its own. If Navigator still refuses to budge, you may have to exit (see the "Signing Off and Shutting Down" section) and start over.

What About the Movie Clips? The Sound Clips?

Although Navigator can display pictures and play some sounds on its own, the larger graphics—as well as movie and sound clips—require special *helper applications*. When you click a link for one of these clips, Navigator transfers the file to your computer, launches the helper application, loads the linked file into it, and starts to play the movie or sound clip. If you don't have the right helper applications, or Navigator can't find them, you get a dialog box asking you to pick an application.

Navigator may not be able to play a link you clicked on.

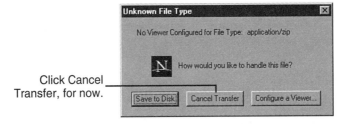

Click Cancel Transfer, for now.

For now, wander the Web without trying any of the special links. After you sign off, read Chapter 12 to learn how to download, install, and configure helper applications to work with Navigator.

Signing Off and Shutting Down

When you're done meandering the superhighway, open the **File** menu and select **Exit** or **Quit**. Navigator closes the document and disappears but might not disconnect you from your service provider. If your TCP/IP program is still running, switch to it and disconnect or hang up.

The Least You Need to Know

This chapter was meant to be "The Least You Need to Know About Using Navigator," so including a Least You Need to Know section seems a bit redundant. However, there are a few points that are more important than others, and here they are:

- Before running Navigator, run your TCP/IP software.
- To speed up Navigator, open the **Options** menu and select **Auto Load Images** to turn off this feature.
- To view linked information, click the desired link, and wait for Navigator to get the data. You may have to wait a long time.
- When you first encounter the Web, have some fun, get lost, and don't take the error messages too seriously.
- Use the **Back** and **Forward** buttons to move back one screen or ahead to the next screen.

Chapter 9

What Could Possibly Go Wrong?

By the End of This Chapter, You'll Be Able To...

➤ Translate an error message into plain English.

➤ Determine what caused the error.

➤ Find out the answer to the question, "Was it me?"

➤ Sidestep most connection problems.

When I first ventured into the Web, I received all sorts of error messages:

> Failed DNS Lookup.
> Connection timed out.
> Unable to Locate Document

I began to wonder. Was I doing something wrong? Did I inadvertently try to access classified Pentagon documents? Is my Internet service provider trying to tell me something?

You'll get many of these error messages. I guarantee it. Just realize that it's usually *not* you, and you can't do much about most error messages. The purpose of this chapter is to desensitize you to these messages, and help you fix any problems that you can solve on your end. As for problems that are out of your control, why worry?

Why the Web Is Soooo Buggy

It's amazing that the World Wide Web works as smoothly as it does. Think about it: People all over the world have stitched together documents that refer to other documents on other computers all over the world. Now, say somebody deletes one of the documents or moves it to another directory. Maybe the link you click on has a typo, sending you to a page that doesn't exist. Or perhaps the network administrator on one of the Web servers decides to close down the network for maintenance. Any of these scenarios contains the formula for producing an error message.

But the Web is not the only thing under construction. The copy of Navigator you downloaded in Chapter 7 might also have a few bugs. Sure, it's a good program, and it'll get you around the Web, but the programmers who are developing Navigator are constantly tweaking it to make it run more efficiently. Until the program is perfected, you, too, will likely encounter at least one of these bugs.

And that's not all. Now add your own human error into the equation. You might mistype a URL, try to skip around the Web too fast for it to keep up, or try to view a link before you've installed the proper helper application. When you take all these variables into account, you begin to realize how amazing it is that you can navigate the Web at all.

Navigator Can't Find the Server

If you spend an hour on the Web and you *don't* get this error message, you're probably doing something wrong. This reigning king of Web error messages is ambiguous; it can have any of several meanings. First, it might mean that the DNS (Domain Name Server) is having trouble matching the domain name of the server you're trying to access to its IP (Internet Protocol) number. Huh? (That's what I say. Look at the Techno Talk, if you're interested in learning about the DNS.)

When Navigator can't find a server, it displays this dialog box.

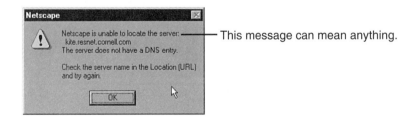

This message can mean anything.

The Trouble with DNS

All servers on the Internet have a **domain name**—for example, www.yahoo.com, which is sort of understandable. Each server also has a unique IP (Internet Protocol) number, such as **128.252.135.4**, which is almost impossible for any person with an average IQ to remember. A special server, called a *DNS (Domain Name Server)*, matches the domain name to the IP number to find the server that has the requested data. As you innocently click on hyperlinks, the DNS is matching domain names and IP numbers to make sure you get where you're supposed to be.

More commonly, this error message *really* means that maybe you mistyped the URL of the desired server (or the person who created the Web page mistyped the URL for the link you clicked on). Try any of the following tactics to pull up the desired Web page:

➤ Did you remember to run your TCP/IP program before running Navigator? If you forgot, Navigator can't find the page, because it's not even connected to the Internet. Establish your Internet connection, and try again.

➤ If you typed the URL (in the Location or Go To text box), check your typing. One minor typo (an uppercase letter that should be lowercase, a slash mark that points the wrong way, or even a misplaced period) can cause the problem. Retype the URL and press **Enter**.

➤ If you received the error after clicking on a link, the URL behind the link may have a typo. Rest the mouse pointer on the problem link, and look at the URL in the status bar. If you see an obvious typo, retype the URL in the Location or Netsite text box, and press **Enter**.

Common Courtesy

If you find a Web page that has a link referring to a page that doesn't exist or that has a typo in it, let the Webmaster (the creator of the page) know about it. At the bottom of most Web pages is the Webmaster's e-mail address. Click on the e-mail address, and then use the dialog box that appears, to notify the Webmaster of the problem.

Part 1 ➤ *Getting Wired with Netscape Navigator*

➤ Finally, this error message might mean that you lost your connection with the service provider. In other words, your TCP/IP program hung up on you. Try some other links to make sure you're connected. If you keep getting this message no matter which link you click on, you've probably been disconnected. Go back to your TCP/IP program, and log in again.

Navigator Can't Find the Document

Say you type a long URL or click on a link for a long URL that looks something like this...

http://www.channel1.com/users/ambrosin/amy.html

...and you get a screen that looks something like this...

Web pages may move or disappear from a site.

The Web page you tried to go to is unavailable.

...then you're connected to the right Web server, but somebody moved or deleted the Web page you're trying to pull up. Try chopping the end off the right side of the URL, and enter the shortened URL into the Location or Netsite text box. For instance, in the example above, you would enter

http://www.channel1.com/users/ambrosin

Chapter 9 ➤ *What Could Possibly Go Wrong?*

If you still have trouble connecting, try chopping another portion off the right side of the URL (for example, /ambrosin). You can chop all the way down to the domain name (for example, www.channel1.com). This gets you in the general vicinity of the Web page you're looking for. You can then click on links to search for the specific Web page.

Think of it like this: You get into a cab, and give the cabbie the address of your in-law's house. The cabbie drives around for awhile, trying to find the house. As you watch the meter spin, you finally realize that you wrote down the wrong address, so you say, "Just drop me off at Fifth and Vermouth." The cabbie drops you off at the specified intersection, where you can then use landmarks to find the house.

On the Web, if you can connect to the server that contains the Web page you want, you can usually use links to poke around on the server and find a specific page. Just be patient and alert.

Document Contains No Data

Another ambiguous error message, this one usually means that the end is chopped off the URL. URLs typically end with a file name, telling Navigator which page, graphic, video, or sound file to open. For example, **http://home.netscape.com/newsref/ref/index.html** opens a Web page document file called index.html. Sometimes, if the file name is chopped off (as in **http://home.netscape.com/newsref/ref/**), Navigator might tell you that the document contains no data.

Because you do not know the name of the file, you can't just type it into the URL and press Enter. Instead, try chopping more off the right side of the URL. Typed the chopped URL into the **Location** or **Go To** text box, and press **Enter**. Most Web servers display their home page whenever you connect to the server. You can then click on the links on this page to find a specific page.

Of course, this error message might also mean that the page you pulled up really is blank. However, Web people rarely stick blank pages on the Web. It's just not fun (or annoying enough) to inspire such an act.

Less Frequent Problems

Most of the problems you'll encounter in your Web wanderings are caused by some discrepancy between the URL you entered and the actual URL of the page you're trying to load. However, there are a few less common, more mysterious error messages:

> ➤ **403 Forbidden**   You've been locked out. You tried to load a Web page that someone doesn't want you to look at.

- **Connection Refused by Host** This just means that the site is probably too busy to let you in. Try again later.

- **Too Many Users** Standing room only; the Web site you're trying to get into is too crowded. You can't get the page now, but you might have some luck later (like at 3 a.m.).

- **TCP Error** This is some sort of network problem, which you can't do much about. Try connecting again later.

- **NNTP Server Error** NNTP (Network News Transport Protocol) is the language used to send and receive data for newsgroups. The problem here is that you are probably trying to connect to a newsgroup before selecting a newsgroup server. See Chapter 20 for details on how to select a Newsgroup server.

Finding Answers to Your Questions

If you're getting error messages that aren't covered here, or you have questions about other aspects of Navigator, go to the Web for additional information. The programmers at Netscape put together a bug list and a *FAQ (Frequently Asked Questions)* list. The bug list covers known problems in the program. The FAQ (pronounced "fack") list gives answers to the most commonly asked questions about Navigator.

Navigator makes it easy to access Navigator help on the Web. Simply open the Help menu, and click on the type of help you need. **Handbook** displays the documentation for using Navigator. **Release Notes** displays a list of bugs that were fixed with this release of Navigator, and a list of known bugs that have not yet been fixed. And **Frequently Asked Questions** displays a list of commonly asked questions about Navigator, along with the answers.

The Least You Need To Know

As you cruise the Internet with Navigator, you're going to hit some potholes and drive into a good share of dead ends. Don't let it get to you. If you hit a snag when you're wandering for fun, simply click on the **Stop** button and try a different link. If there's a page that you just have to access, keep trying.

Also, remember that you can take any of several paths to a page. If the URL you have doesn't work, try reentering a shorter version of the URL. Eventually, you'll clear the roadblock and be able to resume your expeditions.

Part 2
Mastering Navigator

Anyone can fire up Navigator, plunge into the Web, and click link after link in a trail of frenzy, but only masters of the Web and Navigator can get where they're going in a hurry. If you're interested in government, maybe you want to visit the White House. Or maybe you're a movie buff, and you want to see trailers for the latest Hollywood flick. Or perhaps you just need a recipe for tonight's dinner. Whatever the case, this wandering business isn't going to get you where you want to be.

In this part, you're going to learn how to take control of the Navigator and the Web. You'll learn how to find information; return to your favorite places; copy, save, and play movie and sound clips; configure Navigator to make it look and act the way you want it to; and even use Netscape Mail to send and receive mail without ever leaving your desk! By the end of this part, you'll know everything you need to know to master the Web.

Chapter 10

Weaving Through the World Wide Web

By the End of This Chapter, You'll Be Able To...

➤ Pick a page that will open automatically when you run Navigator.

➤ Use a URL to "dial into" a specific hyperdocument.

➤ Pick a page from a list of pages you visited.

➤ Describe what a Web robot does to someone who cares.

Wandering the Web is as stimulating as wandering through downtown Chicago. You find museums, shops, and cultural havens tucked into the most unlikely places. However, you'll eventually want to visit a specific site on the Web, to do research, or find a cool picture or game that one of your friends has told you about.

When you need to get somewhere in a hurry, links may not be the most efficient way to reach your destination. They'll just pull you deeper into the Web, and take you off on some fruitless journey. In this chapter, you'll learn how to take control of the Web. You'll learn how to go to specific Web sites, how to search for information, and quickly backtrack when you get stuck.

Part 2 ➤ *Mastering Navigator*

Starting from Your Home (Page)

Whenever you start Navigator, it loads Netscape Corporation's Home Page (a clever advertising scheme). Chances are that you *don't* want to start here. You can tell Navigator to load a different page when it starts, or load a blank page (so you can start from scratch). This page is called your *starting page*.

Ideally, this should be a page on your service provider's computer (or on your own computer), and it should contain links to your favorite Web documents. But you might not know the URL of your service provider's home page, and you probably haven't created your own home page yet (you'll do that in Chapter 23). So for now, try setting up Navigator to load the Yahoo Home Page, a page with thousands of links to interesting pages. Here's what you do:

1. Open the **Options** menu and select **General Preferences**. This opens the Preferences dialog box.

2. Click the **Appearance** tab. Next to **Start With** are the options for loading a specific page when Navigator starts.

3. Click **Home Page Location**. This tells Navigator to load a specific page at startup, rather than loading a blank page.

4. Drag over the URL in the Start With text box, and then type **http://www.yahoo.com**.

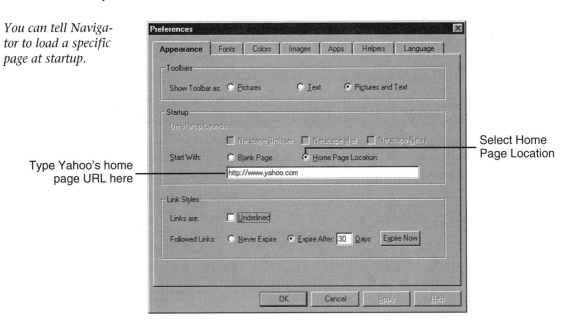

You can tell Navigator to load a specific page at startup.

Type Yahoo's home page URL here

Select Home Page Location

5. Click **OK** to save your change. Now, whenever you start Navigator, it will load the Yahoo home page, and you can use the links there to begin your wanderings.

If, in your Web wanderings, you find a different Web page that you want to use as your home page (or if Yahoo moves its home page), simply repeat these steps. To save time, you can copy the URL from the Location or Go to text box by clicking inside the text box (to select the text) and pressing **Ctrl+C**. Then, display the Preferences dialog box, drag over the URL in the Start With text box, and press **Ctrl+V**. This inserts the URL you copied into the text box.

Navigational Tools Revisited

You wandered the Web in Chapter 8. Maybe you clicked on one or two links, clicked on the Back button to return to a site, and used the Home button to restart your journey. In case you missed that class, here's a brief review of some of the tools you used, in addition to a couple you haven't used:

> **Check This Out...**
>
> **Home Page**
> A home page is sort of like one of those maps you find at a mall entrance. It's the first page that greets you when you connect to a Web site, and it usually contains links to all the other Web documents at that site.

Links are icons or highlighted text that you can click when you want to view additional information. Each link points to another Web document or to a graphic image, movie clip, sound clip, or some other file.

Red Links show links that you have already visited, so you can quickly revisit a site, or avoid retracing your steps.

Back button returns to the previous Web document, if you moved forward.

Forward button displays the next document, if you clicked the Back button.

Home button reloads the first page you saw when you signed on.

Reload button reloads the currently displayed document, in the event that the document became frazzled during the transfer.

Go menu lists the last few sites you visited (near the bottom of the menu). To quickly return to a site, open the **Go** menu and click the desired site.

History list lets you return to a place you previously visited. The history list doubles as the Location text box. To the right of this text box is an arrow button. If you click the button, a drop-down list appears, showing the URLs for the Web pages you've visited. Click a URL to load its page. You'll learn more about history lists in Chapter 11.

Part 2 ➤ *Mastering Navigator*

Know your navigational tools.

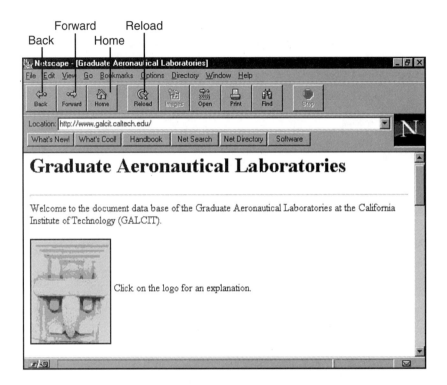

Although most of the navigational tools are conveniently placed on the button bar, you can also select them from the menus. The **Go** menu contains the **Back**, **Forward**, **Home**, and **Stop Loading** commands, and the **View** menu contains the **Reload** command. In addition, you can right-click inside the main viewing area to display a shortcut menu that offers many of the same commands, plus a few you haven't seen.

Touring the Web with URLs

So far, you've managed to avoid all the behind-the-scenes wizardry that enables you to jump from document to document. You click a link, and you're swept away to Switzerland. Three links later, and you're in a recipe database. You might start to wonder what's going on behind the scenes. More importantly, you might wonder how you can take more control of your wanderings.

The secret is to use *URLs (Uniform Resource Locators)*. URLs are addresses that specify the locations of the thousands of documents that make up the Web. Each link you select, each starting point you choose, has a corresponding URL that kicks you out to the linked document.

What does this have to do with you? You'll learn later in this chapter how to enter URLs to load specific hyperdocuments...assuming, of course, you know the document's URL.

URLs Dissected

Each URL indicates the type of server, the server's unique *domain* (name), the directory in which the hyperdocument is stored, and the document's name. Let's look at a sample URL to see how it's made. Here's the URL for a Web page that deals with the Beat Generation author, Jack Kerouac:

> http://www.charm.net/~brooklyn/People/JackKerouac.html

Let's dissect it. First, there's **http**. This stands for *HyperText Transfer Protocol*, which is a set of rules that govern the exchange of data on the Web. Every URL for Web servers starts with http. If you see a URL that starts with different letters (for example **ftp** or **gopher**), the URL is for a different type of server: Gopher (**gopher**), FTP (**ftp**), WAIS (**wais**), USENET (**news**), or Telnet (**telnet**).

The next part of the URL (**www.charm.net**) is called the *domain name*. Each computer on the Internet has a unique domain name that distinguishes it from other computers on the Internet. That way, when the phone rings, all the computers don't answer at the same time. Domain names usually provide some vague indication of the establishment that runs the server. For example, guess who runs this one: **www.whitehouse.gov**. As you work with URLs, look for these common abbreviations: **www** (World Wide Web), **edu** (educational), **pub** (public), **gov** (government), and **net** (network).

Next comes the directory path (**/~brooklyn/People**) that shows the location of the file. Following that is the name of the document (**JackKerouac.html**). The **.html** is a file name extension that stands for *HyperText Markup Language*, a simple set of commands that tells Navigator (or whatever Web browser you're using) how to display the document. You'll get to work with HTML when you create your own home page in Chapter 23.

To complicate matters, some URLs do not end in a document name. For example, **http://www.yahoo.com**, does not specify a directory or a file name. However, when you connect to the Yahoo Web server, it automatically loads the Yahoo home page by default. Many Web servers are set up to automatically load a home page.

Absolute and Relative References

URL references can be *absolute* or *relative*. Absolute references specify the complete trail to the file, including the server's domain name, and a complete directory path. Relative references may give only the file name or the path and file name, assuming that you are logged in to the correct server and are in the right directory.

Hitting the URL Trail

Opening an HTML document is like...well...opening a document. You enter the **File/Open Location** command, type the directory path and file name of the document, and then click **OK**. The only difference in opening an HTML document is that the "directory path" is a URL.

Practice entering URLs by taking the following guided tour of the Web:

1. Open the **File** menu and select **Open Location** (or click the **Open** button, or press **Ctrl+L**). The Open Location dialog box appears, prompting you to type the URL of the page you want to load.

The Open URL dialog box lets you type the location and name of a document.

2. Type the following URL: **http://ballet.cit.gu.edu.au/Movies/**. (Always type a URL exactly as shown. If you type **movies** instead of **Movies**, the domain name server won't know which page you want.)

3. Click the **Open** button. Assuming all goes as planned, you should now see The Internet Movie Database Browser at Griffith University in Australia.

Bypass the Open Location Dialog Box

A quicker way to enter a URL is to click inside the Location text box, type the URL, and press **Enter**. When you click inside the text box, the existing entry is highlighted, and **Location** changes to **Go to**. As you start typing, the characters you type replace the existing entry.

Chapter 10 ➤ *Weaving Through the World Wide Web*

The Internet Movie Database Browser.

4. Repeat steps 1–4 for the following URLs:

> http://www.clark.net/pub/journalism/awesome.html   Displays the Awesome list of World Wide Web sites.
>
> http://www.nasa.gov/   Connects you to NASA's (yes, the space program people's) Web server.
>
> http://www.w3.org/hypertext/DataSources/bySubject/Overview.html   Displays The WWW Virtual Library, an index of topics ranging from Aboriginal Studies to Zoos.
>
> http://www.bgsu.edu:80/~jzawodn/ufo/   Connects you with the UFO page.

This Page Has No Links!

Occasionally, you'll come across a Web page that does not use the standard blue text links. Instead, the page displays a Web navigational tool called a *map*, which uses graphics instead of text for its links. The following figure is a map on the Forrest Gump home page.

Part 2 ➤ *Mastering Navigator*

Maps contain graphic links.

This map acts as a navigational tool.

Click an area of the map to go there.

If you rest the mouse pointer on an area of the map, you can see its URL in the status bar.

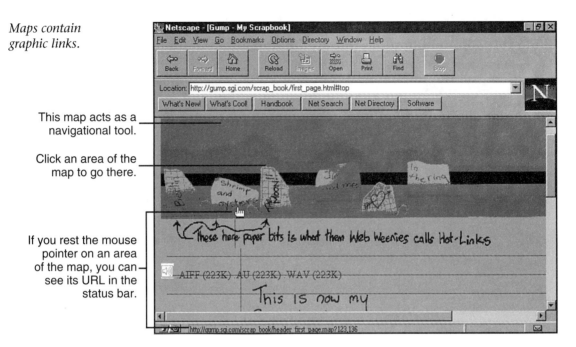

If you happen upon a map, but you're not sure what it is, roll the mouse pointer to different areas of the map, while keeping an eye on the status bar. The URL displayed in the status bar changes as you move the mouse pointer over different areas. If you click an area, Navigator loads the corresponding Web page.

Sometimes, a simple graphic might look like a map. Don't let it fool you. If the URL in the status bar remains the same no matter which part of the picture you point to, the graphic is merely a picture, not a map.

Juggling Two or More Web Documents

You're surfin' now, but if you really want to hang ten on the Web, you can load several Web documents. Navigator is set up to allow you to open several Web documents at the same time...each in its own separate window.

To open another Navigator window, open the **File** menu and select **New Web Browser**. A new window opens, showing the contents of the first document you opened after starting Navigator. You can now use this window to open another Web document, by clicking on links, or by entering the URL of the document you want to open. To change from one window to another, open the **Window** menu, and click the name of the window you want to go to (they're listed at the bottom of the menu). (You can also switch windows by pressing **Alt+Tab** or using the Windows 95 Taskbar.)

You can arrange the Windows by resizing or moving them, minimizing one window while you work in the other one, or using Windows to arrange the Windows for you. In Windows 95, you can quickly arrange windows by right-clicking on a blank area of the Taskbar and selecting **Cascade**, **Tile Horizontally**, or **Tile Vertically**. In Windows 3.1, these same commands are on the Program Manager's Window menu.

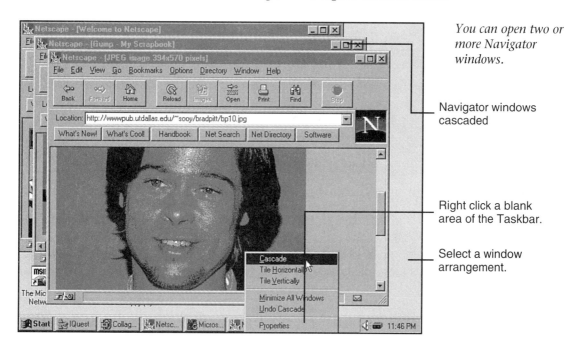

You can open two or more Navigator windows.

Navigator windows cascaded

Right click a blank area of the Taskbar.

Select a window arrangement.

Searching for Topics: Indexes and Web Robots

Although the Web allows for freewheeling, it does have several sites that can help you find specific information. These sites store indexes (also called directories and catalogues) of topics arranged in alphabetical order. You simply click the desired topic to go to its corresponding URL. Some sites also offer *forms* that you can fill out to search for specific topics in an index.

> **Check This Out...**
>
> **Right Click a Link**
> Right-click a link inside the current Web document, and then select **New window with the link**. This opens the Web document that the link points to and displays the document in a separate window.

To use an index or search form, you simply enter the **File/Open Location** command, type the URL of the index or search tool, and then click **OK**. Try WebCrawler, one of the more popular tools for searching the Web. Enter the following URL:

> http://www.webcrawler.com/

This displays a document called a *form* into which you can enter search instructions. Type the topic you want to search for in the text box (case doesn't matter). If you want to find those pages that have all the search words you entered, open the Find pages with drop-down list, and select **all**. Open the **return ____ results** drop-down list, and select the number of Web pages you want the search to present (10, 25, or 100); the larger the number, the longer the search will take. Click the **Search** button to start the search. The search displays a list of links to all the pages that match your search instruction; click a link to display its page.

If WebCrawler can't find a match, it displays a message telling you so. Try searching again, but this time, use fewer words in your search, or open the Find pages with drop-down list, and select **any**. Click the **Search** button to perform the search. If WebCrawler found more pages than you chose to display, a button appears, such as **Get the next 25 results**. Click the button to view additional pages.

Remember, if you click a link that displays a page you don't want, you can click the **Back** button to go back to the list of pages that WebCrawler found. You can then click another link to try a different page.

If WebCrawler doesn't provide the expected (or desired) results, try another type of search tool. Here's a list to help you start:

> CUSI: **http://www.eecs.nwu.edu/susi/cusi.html**
>
> Lycos: **http://www.lycos.com/**
>
> NIKOS: **http://www.rns.com/cgi-bin/nomad**
>
> Yahoo: **http://www.yahoo.com**

In addition, a company called Nexor provides a long list of Web search tools. To view this list, enter the following URL:

> **http://info.webcrawler.com/mak/projects/robots/active.html**

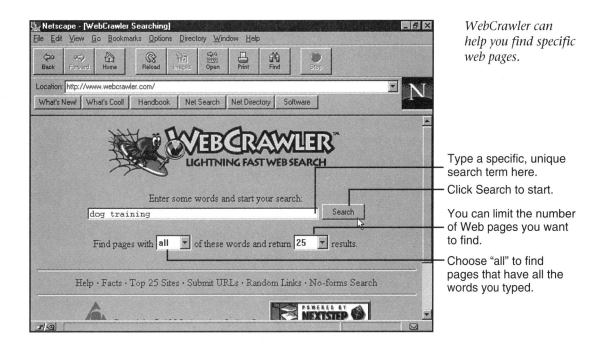

WebCrawler can help you find specific web pages.

Searching for Information on a Page

Some Web documents look like the neighborhood landfill. The Webmaster did a mind dump, and you're buried in text. You have no clue where to look for the information you want. Fortunately, Navigator has a search tool you can use to look for words or phrases.

To use the tool, open the **Edit** menu and select **Find** (or press **Ctrl+F**, or click the **Find** button in the toolbar). Type the text you want to search for in the **Find What** text box, and then click the **Find Next** button. Navigator scrolls the screen to bring first occurrence of the search text into view. You can click the **Find Next** button again (or press **F3**) to scroll to subsequent terms. Click **Cancel** when you're done.

> **Check This Out...**
>
> **Search for Unique Terms**
> Because there is so much information to index, Web robots refuse to index certain common terms, such as New York Times, University, WWW, Web, and so on. So, don't even bother searching for such terms. Try to enter search instructions that are both specific and unique.

The Least You Need To Know

Now that you know how to go places with URLs, you can skip to the back of this book for a list of nifty Web sites you can visit. While you're entering URLs and cruising, keep the following in mind:

➤ At the bottom of the **Go** menu is a list of the sites you most recently visited.

➤ Another way to go to recently visited sites is to open the Location drop-down list and then click the site's URL.

➤ There are three ways to enter a URL: type it in the Location text box and press **Enter**; click the **Open** button in the toolbar; or open the **File** menu and select **Open Location**.

➤ Type a URL *exactly* as it appears, or it won't take you where you want to go.

➤ "If you don't know where you are goin', you will probably not wind up there." —Forrest Gump

Chapter 11

Revisiting Your Favorite Pages

By the End of This Chapter, You'll Be Able To...

- ➤ Jump back to a page you just visited.
- ➤ Slap a bookmark on a page, so you can quickly return to it.
- ➤ Create a list of hot Web pages.
- ➤ Swap Web page lists with your friends.

You just clicked on a trail of 35 links trying to find the Elle MacPherson home page. You racked up an hour in Internet connect-time charges. But now your eyes are getting droopy, and you don't have the energy to look at the 120 pictures of Elle you found. What do you do? Even if you could remember how to get back to this page, you wouldn't have the energy or desire to repeat the trip. Well, maybe you would…for Elle. Or Brad Pitt.

In this chapter, you'll learn how to go back to pages you've visited by selecting them from the history list and by creating bookmarks for your favorite pages. As a bonus, you'll also learn how to transform a list of bookmarks into a Web page, and how to trade bookmark lists with your friends, family, and colleagues.

Going Back in History (Lists)

As you blithely click links and enter URLs, Navigator keeps track of the URLs for the pages you visited. Navigator tracks up to 10 pages from the last time you used Navigator, and it tracks scads more during the current session. It adds each URL to a *history list*. When you use the Back and Forward buttons, you are actually moving up and down the history list to return to the documents you viewed.

But what happens when you visit 10 sites and want to return to the fifth one? Clicking on the Back button five times is hardly the fastest way to return. To zip back, select the desired URL from the history list. The easiest way to do this is to open the **Location** drop-down list; then click the URL for the page you want to view, as shown here.

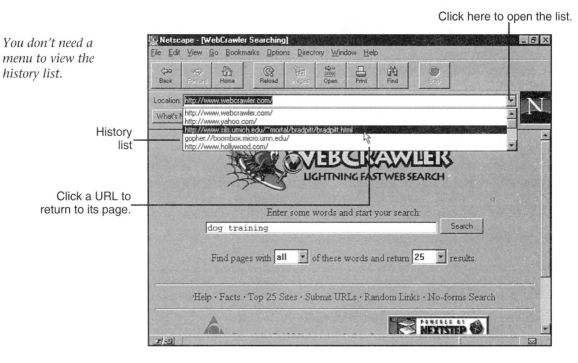

Click here to open the list.

You don't need a menu to view the history list.

History list

Click a URL to return to its page.

You can also get at the history list in a dialog box. To view the history list this way, open the **Window** menu and select **History** (or just press **Ctrl+H**). This displays the History dialog box. To return to a page, click its URL in the history list, and then click the **Go to** button. Ignore the Create Bookmark button for now; you'll learn what it does later in this chapter.

Another way to revisit a page is to open the **Go** menu, and select the page from the bottom of the menu. Unlike the Location drop-down list (which displays only URLs), the

Go menu displays the actual page names, so they might make more sense to you. The History list gives you the best of both systems, displaying the page name and URL.

Make a Shortcut

In Windows 95, you can make shortcuts to your favorite Web pages. (Shortcuts are icons that sit on the Windows desktop.) To create a shortcut, right-click on the link for which you want to make a shortcut, and then click **Internet Shortcut** to display the Create Internet Shortcut dialog box. Type a name for the shortcut in the Description text box, and click **OK**.

Marking a Page with a Bookmark

You have this gargantuan book—over a million pages—and you find a page that has an interesting picture, or a mind-altering quote. You want to remember this page, and you'll probably want to return to it someday. What do you do? Create a bookmark for the page. A *bookmark* is an entry that you can select (from the Bookmark menu) to quickly return to a page you visited.

You can quickly create bookmarks for any page that's displayed, and for any URL you have (even if you haven't yet visited the page). All the bookmarks are dumped at the bottom of the Bookmarks menu, but you can group the bookmarks, place them on submenus, and even juggle them to place them in some order that you can follow.

To create a bookmark for a page that's displayed, take the following steps:

1. Open the page for which you want to create a bookmark.
2. Watch the flying comets and the status bar to make sure the document has been completely transferred. If the document is in the process of being transferred, you can't mark it.
3. Open the **Bookmarks** menu and click **Add Bookmark** (or press **Ctrl+D**).

The bookmark is added to the bottom of the Bookmarks menu. When you add a bookmark in this way, the page name appears on the Bookmarks menu, and the URL remains behind the scenes. However, if nobody gave the page a title, the page's URL may appear on the menu. In either case, you can quickly revisit a page you've marked by opening the Bookmarks menu and clicking on the name of the page, or on its URL.

You can click a bookmark to quickly load a page.

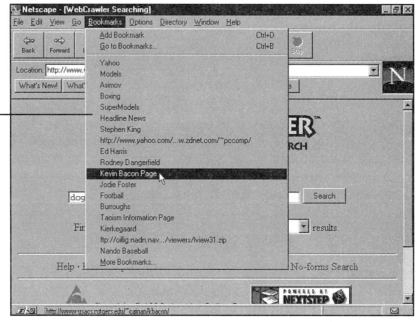

Bookmarks appear at the bottom of the Bookmarks menu.

If you have more bookmarks than will fit on the Bookmarks menu, you'll see the **More Bookmarks...** option at the bottom of the menu. Click this option, and a window appears showing all your bookmarks. You can double-click a bookmark to go to it.

Bookmarking a Link

If you see a link that you might like to visit later, you can create a bookmark for it without opening its page. Right-click the link to display a shortcut menu, and then click **Add Bookmark for this Link**. The only trouble with this method is that it adds only a URL (not the page name) to the Bookmarks menu.

Giving Your Bookmark List a Makeover

As you add bookmarks, they're dumped at the bottom of the Bookmarks menu and stuck with whatever name or complicated URL the Webmaster decided to use. As time passes, your Bookmarks menu becomes cluttered with all sorts of incomprehensible names and URLs listed in no logical order.

Chapter 11 ➤ *Revisiting Your Favorite Pages*

The good news is that you can take control of your bookmarks. In the following sections, you'll learn how to rename bookmarks, place them in logical groups, delete bookmarks you no longer need, and even create your own bookmark submenus. By the time you're done with these sections, you'll have a leaner, more efficient Bookmarks menu—one that even Al Gore would be proud of.

But before we get into the nitty-gritty of remolding your Bookmarks menu, let's display the screen you use to edit the Bookmarks menu. Open the **Bookmarks** menu, and click **Go to Bookmarks** (or press **Ctrl+B**). The Bookmarks window appears, showing the existing structure of your bookmarks.

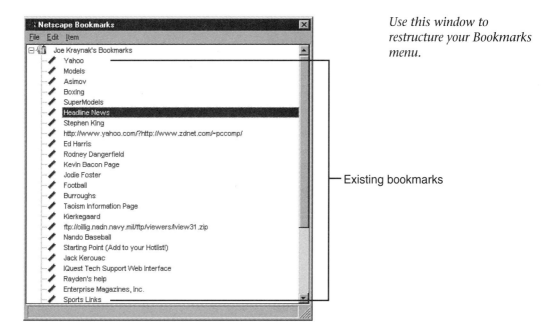

Use this window to restructure your Bookmarks menu.

Existing bookmarks

Renaming and Deleting Bookmarks

The first step in restructuring your Bookmarks menu is to give your bookmarks names that you can easily recognize. This is especially important if you have raw URLs on your menu. The easiest way to rename a bookmark is to right-click it and choose **Properties**. This displays the Bookmark Properties dialog box, with the Name entry highlighted. Type a new name for the bookmark, and click **OK**.

One word of caution: Don't change the Location (URL) entry. This is the URL that works behind the scenes to load the specific page. You can change the name of the bookmark, but changing the URL entry is the same as changing an address on a letter. If you give this bookmark the wrong address, Navigator won't be able to find the page.

You can give your bookmarks more recognizable names.

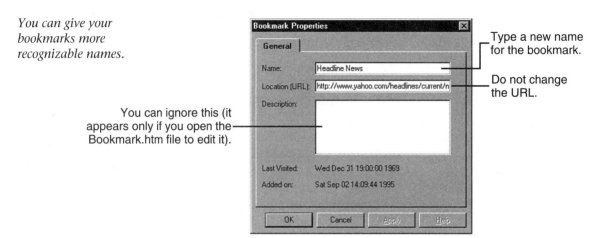

If your bookmark list is cluttered with bookmarks you no longer use, delete them. Simply click the bookmark, and then press the **Del** key (or select **Delete** from the **Edit** menu).

Shuffling Your Bookmarks

Once you rename any bookmarks that need it, think about rearranging your bookmarks. For example, you might want to place the bookmarks for all the sports pages together, and stick the bookmarks for entertainment sites next to each other.

To move a bookmark, click it, and then drag it up or down in the list. As you drag over other items in the list, they appear highlighted. Release the mouse button to insert the bookmark you're moving directly below the highlighted item.

Moving Bookmarks in the Old Days

If dragging the bookmarks is too easy for you, there's a more standard (and much more monotonous) way of moving bookmarks. The process consists of cutting and pasting the bookmarks using the **Edit** menu. I'm not about to encourage this method, so I'll let you figure it out for yourself.

Chapter 11 ➤ *Revisiting Your Favorite Pages*

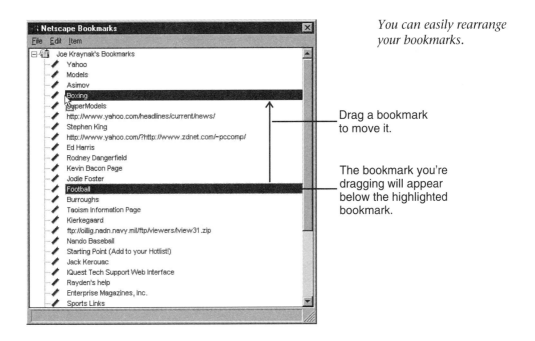

You can easily rearrange your bookmarks.

Drag a bookmark to move it.

The bookmark you're dragging will appear below the highlighted bookmark.

Grouping Bookmarks with Separators and Submenus

You've cleaned up your Bookmarks menu, deleted the fluff, and assigned names to faceless URLs. What more could you want? Well, if your list is still too long to fit on the Bookmarks menu, you might want to create some submenus and add separators to place your bookmarks in logical groups.

Separators are the lines that divide options on a menu into groups. If you open Navigator's File menu, you'll see three separators: one before the Open Location option, one before the Page Setup option, and one before the Close option. You can add separators to your Bookmarks menu. In the Bookmarks window, click the bookmark below which you want to insert the separator; then open the **Item** menu and click **Insert Separator**.

Separators are great if you have only about ten to fifteen bookmarks, but if you have many more than that, you should consider creating submenus for related bookmarks. For example, you can create a submenu called Business that includes bookmarks for all your business-related Web pages. To create a submenu and place bookmarks on it, take the following steps:

1. Open the **Navigator Bookmarks** window, and click the bookmark below which you want the submenu to appear.

111

2. Open the **Item** menu and click **Insert Folder**. The Bookmark Properties dialog box appears, prompting you to name the submenu.

3. Type a name for the submenu, and press **Enter** (or click **OK**). A folder appears in the list of bookmarks. You can now drag bookmarks into this folder to place them on the submenu.

4. Click one of the bookmarks you want to add to this submenu, and then **Ctrl+click** any additional bookmarks you want to add. The selected bookmarks appear highlighted.

   You can select a group of neighboring bookmarks by clicking the first one in the group and then **Shift+clicking** on the last one.

5. Move the mouse pointer over any one of the selected bookmarks, and drag it over the name of the submenu you created. The submenu appears highlighted.

6. Release the mouse button. The bookmarks are now listed below the submenu name.

7. Repeat these steps to create additional submenus.

8. If you end up creating a submenu of a submenu, you can move the submenu up one level in the tree by dragging it to the top of the tree. This moves the submenu and all its bookmarks.

Use submenus to group related bookmarks.

Bookmarks appear under the submenu you created.

When you are done editing your bookmark list, open the **File** menu and select **Close**, or click the **Close** button in the upper right corner of the window. Your Bookmarks menu is immediately updated to reflect your changes. To open a submenu, simply open the **Bookmarks** menu, and rest the mouse pointer on the submenu's name. You can then click a bookmark to select it.

> **Techno Talk**
>
> ### Your Bookmark List Is a Web Page!
>
> Congratulations, you just created your first HTML (Web) document. You don't believe me? In the Navigator Bookmarks window, open the **File** menu and click **Open File**. Use the dialog box that appears to open the file named **Bookmark.htm** (in Windows 95, the file is in the Program **Files/Netscape/Navigator/Program** folder). You can also set the Bookmark.htm file as your starting Web page, as explained in Chapter 10.

When You Add Bookmarks Later...

If you add bookmarks later, the bookmarks are placed at the bottom of the Bookmarks menu. You can move them to one of your submenus by displaying the Navigator Bookmarks window again and dragging the bookmark(s) over the submenu name.

Another way to add bookmarks to a submenu is to tell Navigator on which submenu you want the bookmarks placed. Open the **Bookmarks** menu and click **Go to Bookmarks**. Click on the name of the submenu to which you want new bookmarks added. Now, open the **Item** menu and click on **Set to New Bookmarks Menu Folder**. Now, whenever you display a Web page and then enter the **Bookmarks/Add Bookmark** command, the bookmark is added to the specified submenu, instead of to the bottom of the Bookmarks menu.

If you plan on using the bookmarks on a particular submenu exclusively during a current Web session, you can tell Navigator to display only that submenus bookmarks on the Bookmarks menu. To do this, open the **Bookmarks** menu and select **Go to Bookmarks**. Click on the name of the submenu whose bookmarks you want to appear on the **Bookmarks** menu. Now, open the **Item** menu, and click on **Set to Bookmark Menu Folder**. To return the Bookmarks menu to its original condition (displaying all bookmarks and submenu names, select **Bookmarks/Go to Bookmarks**, click on the folder at the top of the bookmarks list, open the **Item** menu, and click on **Set to Bookmark Menu Folder**.

Ugh! Adding Bookmarks Manually

By far, the easiest way to add a bookmark is to pull up a Web page, open the **Bookmarks** menu, and click **Add Bookmark**. If you're a masochist, however, you might like adding bookmarks yourself—by typing them in.

To insert a bookmark, first open the **Bookmarks** menu and click **Go to Bookmarks**. This opens the Navigator Bookmarks window. Click the bookmark (or submenu name) below which you want the bookmark to appear. Then, open the **Item** menu, and click **Insert Bookmark**. A dialog box appears, prompting you to enter the name and location (URL) of the page. Type the page's name (or the name you want to give it), and then tab to the Location (URL) text box and type the URL for the page. Click **OK**.

> **Check This Out...**
>
> **The Page Moved!**
>
> If some joker on the Web moves a page, you may have to change the URL for one of your bookmarks. This is easy enough; click the bookmark; then open the **Item** menu and click **Properties**. This displays the dialog box showing the bookmark's name and location. You can then edit the item, as necessary.

Creating and Saving Additional Bookmark Lists

As you know, the bookmark list you created is a Web document file called bookmark.htm, but you can save the list under another name. For example, if you have hundreds of bookmarks, you might want to save them in separate files—one for entertainment, one for business, and one for research. Then, you can choose which bookmark file you want to use.

To save a bookmark file under another name, display the Navigator Bookmarks window (**Bookmarks/Go to Bookmarks**). Open the **File** menu, and select **Save As**. Type a name for the bookmark file (you can leave off the extension), and click **OK**.

To specify which bookmark file you want to use (so its bookmarks will appear on the Bookmarks menu), open the **Bookmarks** menu, and select **Go to Bookmarks**. Open the **File** menu and click on **Open**. Use the Open bookmarks file dialog box to select the drive, folder, and name of the bookmark file you want to use. Click **Open**. This opens the specified bookmark file. Now, when you close the Netscape Bookmarks window, the specified bookmark file is made active; its bookmarks appear on the Bookmarks menu.

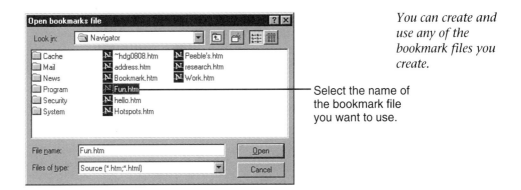

You can create and use any of the bookmark files you create.

Select the name of the bookmark file you want to use.

Trading Bookmark Lists with Your Friends

If you're reading all the little boxed tips throughout this chapter, you know that a bookmark list doubles as a Web page, which goes by the name of Bookmark.html or Bookmark.htm. You can open it in Navigator, and it even looks like a Web page. Because a bookmark is structured as a Web page, you can trade your bookmark lists with your friends and colleagues. You can send your bookmark file to a friend, who can then import it into her bookmark list. Or you can import a bookmark list you received from a friend. (You can also tell Navigator to use a specific bookmark file, as explained in the previous section.)

The Bookmark.html or Bookmark.htm file is in the NETSCAPE/NAVIGATOR directory, which is under the PROGRAM FILES folder in Windows 95. You can copy the file to a floppy disk or send it via e-mail. If you receive a bookmark file, you can add its bookmarks to your Bookmarks menu by performing the following steps:

1. Make sure the bookmark file is on your hard disk or on a floppy disk inside one of your floppy disk drives.

2. Open Navigator's **Bookmarks** menu and click **Go to Bookmarks**. This displays the Navigator Bookmarks window.

3. Open the **File** menu and select **Import**. The Import File as Bookmarks dialog box appears, prompting you to select the bookmark file you want to import.

4. Change to the drive and folder that contains the bookmark file.

5. Click the name of the bookmark file you want to import, and then click the **Open** button. The bookmarks are appended (tacked on) to the end of your bookmarks list.

Here's a great tip that makes this book well worth the money you paid for it: You've created a Web page, so consider using it as your starting page. Open the **Options** menu,

115

click **General Preferences**, and click the **Appearance** tab. Make sure **Home Page Location** is selected, and then type the path to your bookmark file in the text box. For example, type

> file:///C|/Program Files/Netscape/Navigator/Bookmark.htm

Notice that the "URL" starts with "file," indicating that the page is stored on your computer. There are three forward slashes after **file:**, followed by the drive letter and the pipe symbol (|), *not* a colon. Click **OK**.

Can't Get It to Work?

If you have trouble typing that **file:///C|** stuff, enter Navigator's **File/Open File** command. Use the dialog box that appears to find and open the Bookmark.html file. Navigator opens the file, and displays its URL in the Location text box. Click inside the text box, and press **Ctrl+C** to copy the URL. Then, click inside the Home Page Location text box, and press **Ctrl+V** to insert the copied URL.

The Least You Need To Know

Okay, I admit that this chapter probably contains about three times as much information about bookmarks as you really wanted. However, if you performed all the procedures in this chapter (including tips), you'll save yourself a lot of time you'd spend searching for cool pages you've already loaded.

Just keep in mind that you can add bookmarks to your Bookmarks menu by opening the page, clicking **Bookmarks**, and then selecting **Add Bookmark**. If you care to fiddle with your Bookmarks menu (no one says you have to), open the **Bookmarks** menu, and click **Go to Bookmarks**.

Chapter 12

Going Multimedia with Helper Applications

By the End of This Chapter, You'll Be Able To...

➤ In 25 words or less, explain what a helper application does.

➤ Find and download a sound player, movie player, and picture viewer.

➤ Use Navigator to download the files you need. (You get a sneak preview of Chapter 16.)

➤ Get your helper applications up and running.

➤ "Play" any multimedia link simply by clicking on it.

Navigator can take you around the world, connecting to computers in any of the contiguous and noncontiguous states, and with computers in foreign lands. It can play most audio files, and it can display some pictures. But if you click a link for a movie or picture file, and you get this...

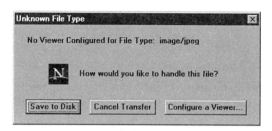

...then Navigator needs help. You see, Navigator is a Web browser, designed to "play" Web pages—pages with text and funky codes that make links appear blue. Navigator isn't designed to play audio or video clips, and although it can handle inline images (tiny graphics) and other small graphics files, it isn't a full-fledged drawing program, either.

To play the multimedia files that really bring the Web to life, Navigator needs help—it needs special programs called *helper applications*. In this chapter, you'll learn how to get helper applications off the Internet, install them, and set them up so that Navigator can use them.

How Do Helper Applications Help?

Helper applications are programs that perform the specialized jobs that Navigator by itself is unfit to manage. Whenever you click a link that Navigator can't play, Navigator loads the file to disk, and then summons (spawns) the helper application associated with that file. The helper application loads the file and plays it.

Sound simple? It's absolutely brainless, assuming you have everything set up correctly. Of course, setting up everything to run correctly takes some effort. You have to get and install the helper applications, and then tell Navigator which application goes with each type of file you might want to play.

Helper Applications Also known as *external viewers*, helper applications are programs that play the Web's multimedia files, including photos, sounds, and video clips. Typically, these programs run quickly and use little memory.

Free and Inexpensive Programs That Fit the Bill

Sounds, pictures, and movies. Those are the three common types of multimedia files you'll come across on the Web, and you need a helper application for each one. You need an *audio player* to play sounds files (files that typically end in .AU or .WAV), a *GIF or JPEG Viewer* to display photos and graphics (.GIF and .JPG files), an *MPEG Viewer* to play video clips (.MPG or .MP2 files), and (rarely) a PostScript viewer to view specially formatted documents.

Chapter 12 ➤ *Going Multimedia with Helper Applications*

The following table lists common helper applications. You'll learn a quick way to download these files in the next section.

Common Helper Applications

Application	Plays	File Name
GhostView	PostScript documents	gview10.zip
LView	Photos/graphics	lview31.zip
MPEG	Video clips	mpegw32g.zip
AVIPRO	Video Clips	avipro2.exe
WHAM (requires sound board)	Sound clips	wham133.zip
WPlany (no sound board required)	Sound clips	wplny.zip

Don't worry too much about nabbing an audio player. Most sound files you find on the Web end in .AU or .WAV. Navigator comes with an audio player that can handle the .AU files, and Windows Sound Recorder can handle .WAV files. These two programs (along with a couple woofers and tweeters) should be able to handle all your audio needs. You can probably skip the PostScript viewer, too; you'll rarely trip over a PostScript file in your wanderings.

Downloading Helper Applications with Navigator

Where do you get these helper applications? You have two options. You can use your FTP program to download the files (I'll tell you where to look in a minute). The other option is to use Navigator. That's right, you can FTP from Navigator! I tried to keep this secret till Chapter 16, but FTPing from Navigator is such an easy way to get helper applications, that I just couldn't wait. So, here's what you do to get your viewers the easy way:

> **Check This Out...**
>
> **The File Names You See May Differ**
> Remember, the file names given here might change as the programmers update these programs. When you connect to an FTP site in the next section, look for file names that are similar to the names given here. Don't expect an exact match.

1. Establish your Internet connection (using your TCP/IP program or Windows 95 Dial-Up Networking), and run Navigator.

119

2. Open the **Directory** menu, and click **Netscape's Home**. This loads Netscape Corporation's home page, which contains a link for common helper applications.

3. Scroll down the page, and look for a link called "Helper Applications." You can use the **Find** button, as explained in Chapter 10 to search for the text "Helper Application."

4. Click the **Helper Apps** link (it's in the Assistance column). This displays a jumping-off point for more information about helper applications.

5. Look for a heading called **Archive Sites**, and click **Windows**. This displays a list of Windows-compatible helper applications grouped by category.

6. Click the link for the helper application you want. One of the following will happen:

    ➤ If you're lucky, the link points directly to the helper application you need, and Navigator tries to connect to the server where the file is stored and download the file. You'll see a dialog box saying that Navigator doesn't know what to do with the file. If this happens, go to step 6.

    ➤ If you're somewhat lucky, you'll be transported to an FTP site and offered a list of files to choose from. Click the link for the file you want. You should now get the dialog box telling you that Navigator doesn't know how to handle the file.

    ➤ If your luck has run out, and the site is too busy, you'll receive an error message. Try one of the other sites listed at the end of this set of steps.

7. Click the **Save to Disk** button. A dialog box appears, prompting you to select the drive and folder (directory) where you want the file saved.

8. Use the dialog box to select the drive and folder in which you want to save the downloaded file, and then click **OK**. A dialog box appears, showing you the progress of the download.

9. Wait until the file is transferred to your computer (when the progress dialog box disappears).

10. Repeat these steps to download additional helper application files. If you were transported to an FTP site, you may have to use the **Back** button to go back to the Netscape page that has the links to the helper applications. (It's a good idea to save each helper application file in its own directory.)

I'm not going to assume that everything proceeded as planned. If you couldn't connect to the computer that holds those precious helper application files, you have two options.

Chapter 12 ➤ *Going Multimedia with Helper Applications*

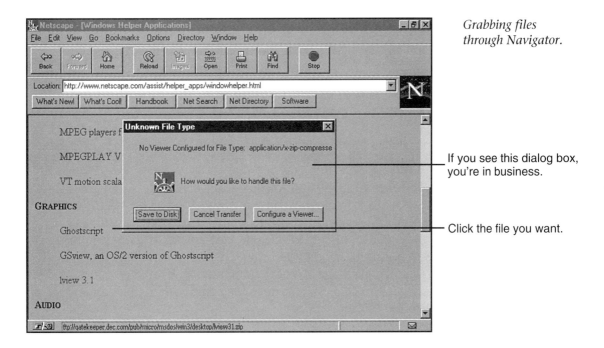

Grabbing files through Navigator.

If you see this dialog box, you're in business.

Click the file you want.

You can try later (during the Letterman show, and at the crack of dawn are good times), or you can try downloading the files from somewhere else. Try the following sites:

> http://www.ncsa.uiuc.edu/SDG/Software/WinMosaic/viewers.htm
> for links to various helper applications.
>
> http://world.std.com/~mmedia/lviewp.html
> to get LView Pro, a graphics (picture) viewer.
>
> ftp://ftp.crs4.it/mpeg
> to get the video player, MPEG Player.
>
> http://www.cs.wisc.edu/~ghost/index.html
> to get Ghostview (as if you'll need this one).

Decompressing and Installing the Software

After downloading the files, move them to separate directories or folders to keep each application in its own place. Then decompress the files. See "Unzip Me," in Chapter 6. If you don't like to go out to the DOS prompt to unzip files, use Navigator to get a copy of WinZip, a program that makes unzipping files from Windows a lot easier. Here's where you can get WinZip:

121

ftp://dorm.rutgers.edu/pub/DNP_Dist/Compressed_1994_Dist/mxwinzip.exe

ftp://ftp.edvz.uni-linz.ac.at/pub/msdos/utils/windows/utility/winzip/winzip.exe

ftp://cscnt.cit.ac.nz/PUB/WIN311/WINZIP.EXE

The WinZip file you get is a self-extracting file, so you can decompress it by running it. This file also runs an installation program that installs itself. Just run the downloaded file from the Windows Explorer or File Manager.

Once you unzip the helper application files you downloaded, read the installation instructions that came with each application for any quirky installation steps. (The instructions are usually in a file called README.TXT or INSTALL.TXT, which you can open in Windows Notepad or Wordpad.) With some applications, you can simply unzip the application, create an icon for it, and start using it. Others may require that you run a separate Setup program (in File Manager or My Computer, look for a file called SETUP.EXE, and then double-click on it). When you're done, you should have an icon you can double-click to run the application.

Cheat a Little
After installing your applications, you must tell Navigator where you stored them. You may find it easier to skip ahead to the next section, find out where Navigator already thinks the applications are stored, and create folders or directories to match those locations.

Mapping Files to Their Helper Applications

I hate to break it to you, but installing the helper applications is only half the story. Now, you must tell Navigator which applications to run for each type of multimedia file you encounter on the Web. For example, if you click a movie link, Navigator must know whether it should run the audio player, the graphic viewer, or the movie player. You need to *associate* each file type you might encounter with a helper application that can load and play that file type.

You can associate program types to helper applications on the fly. If you click a link for a file that's not associated to a helper application, Navigator displays the Unknown File Type dialog box essentially saying, "What do you want me to do?" You can then click **Save to Disk** and worry about the file later, or click **Configure a Viewer** to associate this file type to a helper application. If you click **Configure a Viewer**, you're presented with a dialog box of the same name. Click the **Browse** button, and use the dialog box that appears to select the program file for the viewer (helper application) you want to use.

Chapter 12 ➤ *Going Multimedia with Helper Applications*

Where's Navigator's Audio Player?

Funny thing: Navigator may not know where its own audio player is located. In Windows 95, the Navigator installation program sticks the player in the Program Files/Netscape/Navigator/Program folder. You may have to associate AU files with this helper application.

If you don't like that idea, you can set up your helper applications ahead of time, and completely avoid the Unknown File Type dialog box. Navigator will automatically run the helper application when you try to load a file it cannot handle. To associate files, here's what you do:

1. Run Navigator (you don't have to be connected to the Web).

2. Open the **Options** menu and select **General Preferences**. The Preferences dialog box appears.

3. Click the **Helpers** tab. You now see the page of options you can select to specify how you want Navigator to handle various file types.

4. In the **File type** list, click the type of file you want to associate with a helper application. For example, you might click **video/mpeg** to associate MPEG video files with an MPEG Player. Here's a list of common file types and the helper applications that play them:

Extension	Helper Application
JPG	LView
GIF	LView
AVI	AviPro
MPG	MPEG
MP2	MPEG
AU	Naplayer (Netscape's sound player)
AIF	Naplayer
WAV	Windows Sound Recorder

5. Click inside the File Extensions text box, and type the file name extensions for any of the files you want this helper application to play. Leave out the periods, and separate the extensions with commas. For example, the names of most MPEG video files end in mpg, mpeg, or mpe. Navigator enters the most common file name extensions for you; just check to make sure.

123

Part 2 ➤ *Mastering Navigator*

6. Click the **Launch the Application** option. This tells Navigator that whenever you choose to load a file of this type, it should run the associated helper application.

7. Click the **Browse** button. The Select an appropriate viewer dialog box appears, prompting you to select the file that runs the helper application.

8. Use the dialog box that appears, to change to the drive and folder (or directory) in which you installed the helper application.

9. In the file name list, click the executable program file (the file that launches the helper application), and then click the **Open** button. You are returned to the Preferences dialog box. In the **File Type** list, under **Action**, the name of the specified helper application is inserted.

10. Repeat steps 4 to 9 to associate additional file types with their helper applications.

11. Click **OK** when you're done.

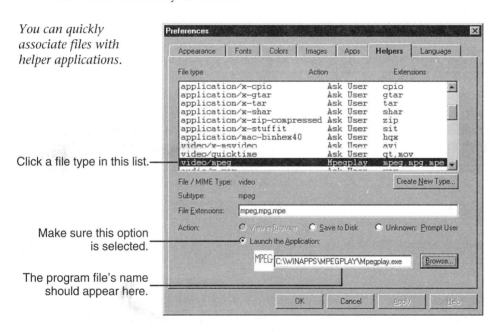

You can quickly associate files with helper applications.

Click a file type in this list.

Make sure this option is selected.

The program file's name should appear here.

Note the **View in Browser** option in the dialog box. This option tells Navigator to play the file itself. Navigator can play graphic files in the GIF or JPG format, but they won't look as clear as graphics displayed in a dedicated graphics program, such as LView. This option is available only for certain file types. Navigator can't play video clips…yet.

Although the file type list includes most of the file types you'll commonly encounter on the Web, and then some, you may come across a file type that's not on the list and that requires a special helper application. In such a case, you can click the **Create New Type**

124

button and create your own association. You'll get a dialog box asking for a Mime and Sub Mime type, which has nothing to do with Marcel Marceau.

Type the appropriate Mime and Sub Mime type in the text boxes. What's appropriate? The Mime type is the general type of file (audio, video, image). The Sub Mime type is a more specific abbreviation of the file type (for example, quicktime or jpeg). These entries don't matter much; they're more FYI (for your information). If Navigator can't recognize the Mime type of an incoming file, Navigator uses the file name extensions you enter to determine which helper application to run.

> **MIME**
> Short for *Multi-purpose Internet Mail Extensions*, MIME is a protocol that controls most file transfers on the Web. Navigator uses MIME to recognize different file types.

Click **OK** when you're done. You now have a new entry in the File Types list, and you can follow the previous steps to associate a helper application with the file type.

Playing Multimedia Links

Playing a multimedia link is as easy as clicking on the link. Navigator downloads the file and then runs the helper application, which loads and plays the file. All you have to do is sit back and watch.

Keep in mind that multimedia files can take loads of time to transfer, even if you have a direct (network) connection. The total time it takes depends on the speed of your connection, the size of the file, the amount of traffic on the server, the distance of the server from your computer, and the speed of your computer. Photos, graphics, video clips, and sound clips can be hefty. These files take a long time to transfer and consume a great deal of memory and disk space.

> **Saving Multimedia Files**
> Wait! Before you close that helper application, you might want to use the application's **File/Save** command to save the file to your disk. If you don't, when you close the application, you nuke the file. In Chapter 13, you'll learn how to save these files using Navigator.

Do It! Cinema, Sounds, and Photos

In your wanderings, you're sure to stumble across some Web sites that offer video and sound clips, photos, and on-screen art. Although I hate to spoil the thrill of discovery, I feel compelled to mention a few sites I stumbled across in my wanderings:

Internet Underground Music Archive: Stores sound clips of little-known bands. You can download short clips or entire songs.
http://www.iuma.com/

Kids Internet Delight (KID): Includes links to an MTV site and a movie database.
http://www.clark.net/pub/journalism/kid.html

MPEG Movie Archive: Contains animation clips, music videos, NASA images, auto racing pictures, and even clips of your favorite models.
http://www.eeb.ele.tue.nl/mpeg/index.html

Perry-Castaneda Library Map Collection: Offers maps of Africa, the United States, the Middle East, Europe, and maps of several major cities around the world.
http://rowan.lib.utexas.edu/Libs/PCL/Map_collection/Map_collection.html

Yahoo (a guide to the World Wide Web): Yahoo provides an index of cool Web sites, so you'll have to click a couple of links to get what you want. Click the **Entertainment** link, and then click **Comics**, **Multimedia**, or something else that catches your eye. You're sure to find some neat clips.
http://www.yahoo.com

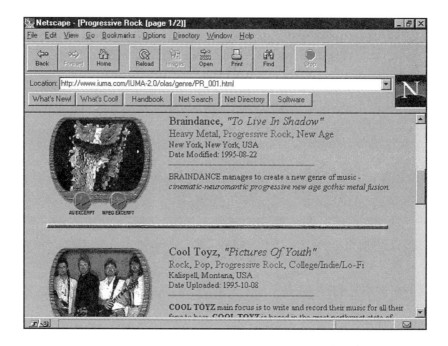

You can download music clips of lesser-known artists.

Moving Pictures with Java

The latest, greatest Web invention is Java, a programming language that allows Web developers to stick moving pictures and animations on their Web pages. And Navigator is one of the few Web browsers that you can use to view these Javimations. And, the good news is that you don't have to set up a helper application! All you do is click on an animation link, and Navigator plays the associated animation.

During the writing of this book, Netscape was in the process of incorporating Java support into Navigator. And, because the technology is relatively new, you won't find many sites with Java links. However, that will soon change.

To get a taste of Java, go to Netscape's Java support area. It contains several experimental clips. You can get to the support area by typing the following URL in the Location text box, and pressing **Enter**:

http://home.netscape.com/comprod/products/navigator/version_2.0/java_applets/index.html

If that doesn't work, open the **Help** menu, and select **Release Notes**. This takes you to Netscape Navigator's Release Notes page. Use the links on the page to find information about Java. These links will steer you to the page that has links for Java demos. Click on one of the links to play a demo.

A Word About Sound and Video Quality

Eight-bit sound cards and standard VGA monitors just can't keep up with the sounds and clips stored on the Web. If you're still stuck with the old technology, maybe the Web will provide the incentive for you to upgrade.

If you have a Super VGA monitor and a 16-bit or better sound card, make sure they're set up to play at the highest quality. If you have your Super VGA monitor set to display only 16 colors, your pictures and video clips will look like snow storms. Make sure you set your monitor to display at least 256 colors. Also, check your sound card setup to make sure it's in 16-bit, stereo mode.

The Least You Need to Know

Now that you can watch movies and listen to sound clips, you probably already know everything you want to know. However, if you get bored with all that sensory stimulation, read the following review items:

- ➤ A helper application is a small, streamlined program that can play files which Navigator is incapable of playing.
- ➤ To use a helper application, you have to get it, install it, and associate it with a specific file type.
- ➤ You can FTP from Navigator, but it's a big secret; we won't talk about anymore until Chapter 16.
- ➤ Assuming your helper applications are set up correctly, you can play a multimedia link simply by clicking on it.
- ➤ Sometimes, you're better off saving a file and then playing it later...especially if you get a juicy clip off one of the movie galleries.

Chapter 13

Saving and Printing Your Finds

By the End of This Chapter, You'll Be Able To...

➤ Save multimedia files to disk for your future enjoyment.

➤ Save a hyperdocument and open it later.

➤ Print a hyperdocument and make some minor page adjustments.

➤ Take a behind-the-scenes look at a hyperdocument.

The Web is like some big computerized flea market. You snake through the aisles picking up interesting facts, stories, bits of poetry and fiction, movie clips, sound clips, and even the occasional picture of your favorite actor or actress. You pull this stuff up in Navigator or in a helper application, give it a quick look, and then like some overstimulated kid at Christmas, you drop the item to hurry to another site.

But then it happens. You find it. A movie clip that sucks the breath right out of you. A document that answers your most profound questions. You gotta have it. What do you do? In this chapter, you'll learn various ways to preserve the treasures you discover on the Web. You'll learn how to save all your discoveries, print your favorite documents, and even see the skeletons hanging behind the HTML documents.

Saving and Playing Clips and Pics

The method of choice on the Web is to grab the loot, disconnect, and then play with the newly acquired toys later. If you have an Internet service provider who charges by the hour, you don't want to waste precious time viewing clips while you're still connected. Besides, it's considered bad manners to loiter at Web sites; other users are trying to connect.

There are a couple ways to *download* files (copy files to your hard disk) on the Web. My personal favorite is to right-click the link for the item I want, and then click the **Save this Link as** or **Save this Image as** option. This opens the Save As dialog box, which prompts you to select the drive and folder (or directory) in which you want to save the file. You can also give the file a new name. Make the appropriate selections, and then click **OK**. The reason I like this method is that it gives me the greatest flexibility: I click to view, or right-click to download. I don't have to worry about setting any options.

Right-click a link to display the shortcut menu.

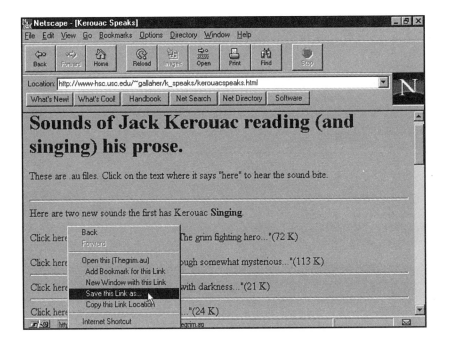

My second favorite method for saving clips and pictures is to use the helper application. Click the link to open the file in the helper application, and then use the helper application's **File/Save** command to save the file. With this method, you don't have to make any long-term commitments. You get to preview the clip before you save it to disk. Some helper applications, such as Navigator's audio player, save the file automatically in your TEMP folder or directory, and offer no **File/Save** option. Other applications will play the file, disappear, and dump the file.

If you become a serious download junkie, there's one more approach to downloading files that might appeal to you. Remember in the previous chapter where you associated particular file types to helper applications? Well there's an option in the Preferences dialog box (on the Helpers tab) called **Save to Disk**. Instead of associating a file type to an application, simply click the file type, and then click **Save to Disk**. Whenever you click a link for this file type, Navigator will display the Save As dialog box, prompting you to specify where you want the file saved.

Reassociating File Types

If you turn on the **Save to Disk** option for a particular file type, you entirely foul up the association with the helper application. If you decide later that you want to associate a file type with its helper application, skip back to Chapter 12.

Once you save a file to disk, you can open the file and play it in one of your helper applications. Run the helper application, and use its **File/Open** command as you would in any application. Then, if you have a sound or movie, use the application's controls (they'll vary, of course) to play the file.

What About Hyperdocuments?

Ever wonder what's behind one of those hyperdocuments? I'll show you. Load your favorite page. Now open the **View** menu and select **Document Source**. You should see something like the hyperdocument pictured here. Not much to look at, eh? This is the original HTML document that's stored on the server. All those bracketed codes tell Navigator how to display the document without turning you to stone.

Behind the scenes with a hyperdocument.

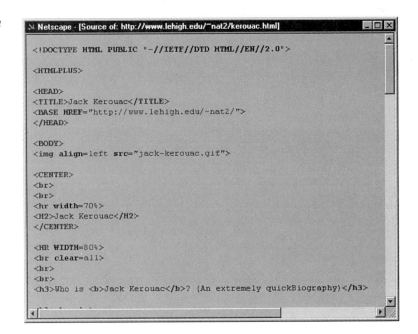

Why would anyone ever want to view one of these documents? Two reasons. First, sometimes, there's a rebel URL in the background (one with a typo in it). You click the link (which you can see), but the URL (which you can't see) isn't pointing to the page you want to go to. In such a case, you can enter the **View/Document Source** command to take a peek at the URL. You can even highlight the URL (by dragging over it), and then copy it (by pressing **Ctrl+C**). Then, close the View Source window, click inside the **Location** text box, and paste (**Ctrl+V**) the URL. You can then edit the URL to correct it (assuming it has an obvious typo).

The other reason you might want to view a source document is to learn how to code a hyperdocument (which can come in handy when you design your own home page in Chapter 23).

You can also save hyperdocuments as hyperdocuments or as text files, but don't expect too much. In Navigator, you might see a Web page with a bunch of fancy graphics, but when you save the file, all you're getting are the text and/or codes that appear on the page. Now that you've been warned, you can take the following steps to save a Web page:

1. Display the Web document you want to save.
2. Open the **File** menu, and select **Save as** (or press **Ctrl+S**). The Save As dialog box appears, prompting you to specify a drive and folder or directory.
3. Select the drive and folder in which you want the file saved.

4. To change the name of the file (you don't have to), drag over the entry in the **File name** text box, and type the desired file name.

5. Open the **Save file as type** drop-down list, and click the desired format in which you want the file saved:

    Source (*.htm,*.html) retains all the Web page codes that were inserted in the file. You can then open the file in Navigator, and it will look something like a Web page (minus the cool graphics).

    Plain Text (*.txt) strips out all the Web page codes and saves just the text. This is good if you find some text that you want to paste into a document you're creating (for example, to lift a quote).

6. Click **Save**. The file is saved in the specified format and is stored in the drive and folder you selected.

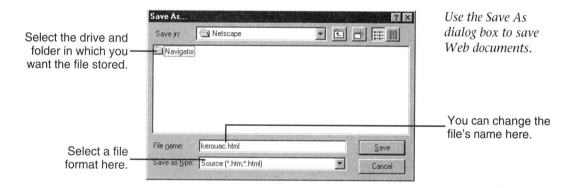

Use the Save As dialog box to save Web documents.

Taking a Peek at the Locals

Your computer has files too, you know, and Navigator can open them for you...assuming they are HTML (Web) or text documents, or that you set up a file association for that file type. (This makes it convenient to view files that you downloaded earlier.) To open a file that's on your hard disk, open the **File** menu and select **Open File** (or press **Ctrl+O**). Specify the location and name of the file you want to open (you can list all files in the folder by selecting **All Files (*.*)** from the **Files of type** drop-down list). Click **Open**.

If you selected a file that's associated to another (helper) application, Navigator runs that application, which then loads and plays the selected file. If you selected an HTML or text document, Navigator opens it just as if it were stored on a Web server. If the HTML document contains links, you can click those links to open them (assuming you are connected to the Internet with your TCP/IP software).

Part 2 ➤ *Mastering Navigator*

Making Paper—Printing

The World Wide Web is as close to paperless electronic publishing as you can get. However, you might encounter a document you want to print: maybe a Navigator help screen or an interesting quote or story. There's no trick to printing a document from Navigator. Simply display the Web document you want to print, open the **File** menu, select **Print**, and answer the dialog box that appears.

If you want to get fancy about printing, however, you can do more. You can select some page setup options to specify how you want the document to be positioned on the page and to indicate the type of information you want printed (the page's URL, for example). You might also want to preview the page before you print it. The following sections explain all this in detail.

More Control If you want any more control over the printing, go into your Windows printer setup (in the Windows Control Panel), and enter the desired settings.

Entering Your Page Preferences

If you print a Web document now, you get a basic 8.5-by-11-inch page with a header and footer, and half inch margins all around. However, you can change the page settings to reposition the text on the page or select the type of information you want printed in the header and footer.

To change the page settings, open the **File** menu and select **Page Setup**. The Page Setup dialog box appears. The settings are fairly self-explanatory, so I'm not going to bore you with the details. Just enter the desired settings, and then click **OK**.

Previewing Pages Before You Print

You can never be sure how a Web page will appear in print. Will the sparkling graphics you see on your screen transfer to paper? How will the lines and bulleted lists look? In Navigator, you can quickly see how a page will appear in print by opening the **File** menu and selecting **Print Preview**. This opens the Print Preview screen, which displays the first page of the current Web document. You can then click the following buttons to control the page display:

Print Opens the Print dialog box, which allows you to send the document to your printer. Enter your print settings, and then click **OK**.

Chapter 13 ➤ *Saving and Printing Your Finds*

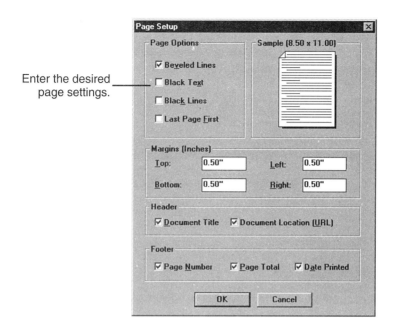

You can control how Navigator prints the page.

Enter the desired page settings.

Next Page   Displays the next page of the document (assuming the Web document consists of more than one page).

Prev Page   Opens the previous page of the document, if you clicked on the **Next Page** button.

Two Page   Displays two pages of the document side-by-side.

Zoom In   Makes the page bigger, showing more detail. You can also zoom in by moving the mouse pointer over the area you want to see in more detail and then clicking the mouse button.

Zoom Out   Returns the page to its smaller view, giving you a bird's eye view of the page.

Close   Closes this window and returns you to the Navigator window. Be sure to use this button rather than the Close button in the title bar; otherwise, you'll close Navigator altogether.

Part 2 ➤ *Mastering Navigator*

You can preview a document before printing it.

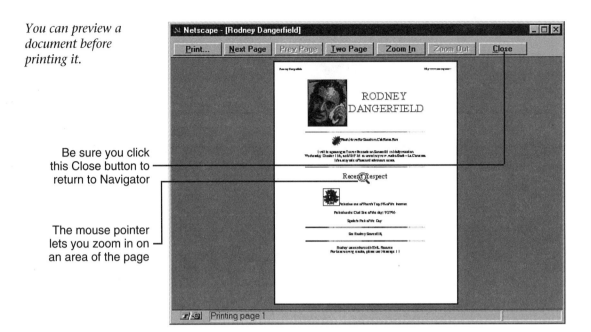

Be sure you click this Close button to return to Navigator

The mouse pointer lets you zoom in on an area of the page

The Least You Need to Know

As you ready yourself for a download binge, try to remember the following:

➤ To quickly download a file, right-click its link, and then click the **Save** option.

➤ If you plan on downloading several files, open the General Preferences dialog box, click on the **Helpers** tab, and turn on **Save to Disk** for the file type you want to download (instead of view).

➤ To view a coded hyperdocument, open the **View** menu and select **Document Source**.

➤ To open files stored on your hard disk, open the **File** menu and select **Open File**.

➤ To print a hyperdocument, open the **File** menu and select **Print**.

Chapter 14

Corresponding with Electronic Mail

By the End of This Chapter, You'll Be Able To...

- ➤ Send a letter without licking a postage stamp.
- ➤ Put your e-mail address on your business card.
- ➤ Grab mail from your mailbox.
- ➤ Write to a Webmaster to offer suggestions.

The U.S. Postal Service has made all sorts of improvements in an attempt to make their service more attractive. You want me to name one? Okay, they released the Marilyn Monroe stamp. Oh yeah, and they came out with those self-adhesive stamps, so you can still taste your coffee after applying the stamp.

But the mail is still slow. A letter you send today usually takes several days to reach its destination. Fortunately, the Internet has provided an alternative: *electronic mail* (*e-mail* for short). This postage-free alternative sends e-mail across the states, or to the other side of the world, in a matter of minutes or hours instead of days. In this chapter, you'll learn how to send and receive e-mail directly from Navigator.

You Have to Set It Up First

As with anything on the Internet, e-mail requires some setup before you can use it. You have to enter your return address, specify an e-mail server, and enter your name. Although this takes a little longer than it takes to lick a postage stamp, it's almost as easy (and you only have to do it once).

To enter the necessary e-mail information, open the **Options** menu and click **Mail and News Preferences**. The Preferences dialog box pops up on your screen. Click the **Appearance** tab, and change any of the settings to control the way messages appear. The only tricky option here is the Fixed Width Font or Variable Width Font. A fixed width font gives each character the same amount of space: an anorexic "i" gets the same space as a corpulent "m." A variable width font gives each character the room it needs.

Next, click the **Composition** tab, and change any of the following options to specify how you want mail and newsgroup messages handled:

Send and Post allows you to specify the type of file transfer protocol to use for mail messages. **8-bit** handles most type of mail servers. If you have trouble transferring a particular mail message, try changing this to **Mime Compliant**.

Deliver Mail lets you choose whether you want your e-mail messages delivered **Automatically** when you create them, or held in a queue (**Queue for Manual Delivery**) until you are ready to send them all at once.

Mail Messages lets you specify an e-mail address of someone to whom you want to send a copy of all your e-mail correspondence. You can leave this blank for now.

News Messages lets you specify an e-mail address of someone to whom you want to send a copy of all the messages you post to newsgroups. Again, you can safely leave this blank.

Mail File and **News File** allow you to specify a file in which to save the mail you send and the messages you post to a newsgroup. This file does not need to exist. Just type a path to the folder in which you want the file saved followed by the file's name (no extension is needed).

Now, for the important options. Click the **Servers** tab, and enter the following information:

Outgoing Mail (SMTP) Server The name of your e-mail post office, which is on your service provider's computer. You should have received this name from your service provider, and it should look something like **iway.com** or **mail.iway.com**. If you are unsure of this, call your service provider.

Chapter 14 ➤ *Corresponding with Electronic Mail*

Incoming Mail (POP) Server   The name of your service provider's POP (Post Office Protocol) server. This name usually starts with pop, as in **pop.iway.com**.

POP User Name   This is the part of your e-mail address to the left of the @ sign. Don't enter the @ sign or any information to the right of it.

Mail Directory   The path to the folder on your hard drive in which you want incoming mail messages stored. Initially, Navigator is set up to use the NETSCAPE\MAIL folder, but you can change it.

Maximum Message Size   Keep this set to **None**. If you decide later to limit the size of messages you receive, you can select the Size option, and then type the maximum size (in kilobytes) of incoming messages. Any part of the message over the limit will be kept on your mail server.

Removed from the Server and **Left on the Server**   Allow you to specify whether you want messages deleted from your server's computer after Navigator retrieves them. Keep this set to **Left on the Server** until you're sure that this e-mail thing works. Later, change this to **Remove from the Server**, so you don't clutter your service provider's computer with your junk mail.

Check for Mail   You can choose **Every ___ minutes** to have Netscape automatically check for incoming e-mail at the specified interval (type the number of minutes in the text box). If you prefer to check for mail manually, keep this set to **Never**.

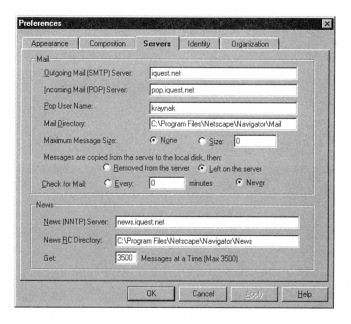

Before you can use e-mail, you need to enter some information.

139

Only two tabs left. Click the **Identity** tab to enter the following information about yourself:

Your Name is your name, duh.

Your Email is the e-mail address assigned to you by your service provider. This usually consists of your username followed by the @ sign, followed by the server name (for example, **jsmith@iway.com**).

Reply-to Address is the e-mail address that will appear when you post messages to newsgroups. Leave this blank for now.

Your Organization is an optional entry. You can type the name of your company or just leave the text box blank. If you plan on insulting someone through e-mail, don't link your company with the insult.

Signature File is another optional entry. A signature file is a small text file that is automatically attached to the end of the letters you send. It can include your name, address, and phone number, your e-mail address, and any interesting quips you want to add. You can create the file in Windows Notepad or your word processor, and save it as a text file. Then, use the **Browse** button in the Preferences dialog box to tell Navigator where the file lives.

Finally, click the **Organization** tab. This tab contains options that tell Navigator how to sort your e-mail messages. The sort options are fairly straightforward; you can sort messages by date, subject entry, or the name of the sender. You can also have mail and news messages *threaded*. If you turn on the threading options, you'll see a copy of the message you sent whenever someone sends you a response to your message. This is good if you have Alzheimer's. This tab also offers the **Remember Mail Password** option. Click on this option if you get tired of typing your password each time you check your mail. However, if you're afraid that someone will snoop, leave this option off. When you're done setting your options, click **OK**.

...you're now ready to e-mail!

Pronouncing an E-Mail Address

If you want to be cool, you have to be able to pronounce your e-mail address properly. If your address is jsmith@weidner.cyber.edu, you would say, "jsmith at weidner dot cyber dot edu." Just remember that @="at" and .="dot." E-mail addresses are usually in lowercase, so you don't have to specify case unless one or more characters is uppercase.

Writing (and Sending) an E-Mail Message

Once you enter your e-mail settings, you can start churning out e-mail messages. Open the **File** menu and click **New Mail Message** (or press **Ctrl+M**). The Message Composition dialog box appears. To complete the dialog box, you must address your message and then type it.

Click inside the **Mail To** text box, and type the e-mail address of the person to whom you're sending the message. For example, you might type **cmiller@aol.com**. Click inside the **Subject** text box, and type a brief description of the message. Now, click inside the big message area at the bottom of the dialog box, and type your message. Assuming you want to send only the message you typed, click the **Send** button to send it. If you want to attach a file or grab some text from the Web page that's displayed, read on.

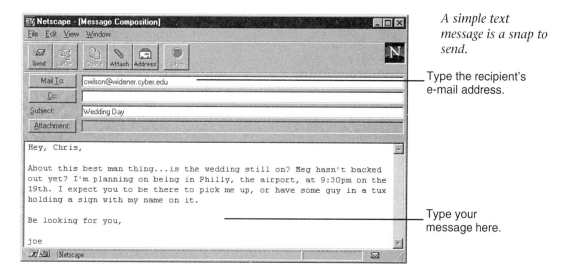

A simple text message is a snap to send.

Type the recipient's e-mail address.

Type your message here.

To send a file along with your e-mail message, click the **Attachment** button (or on the **Attach** button in the toolbar). The Attachments dialog box appears, asking you to select the file you want to send. Pick one of the following options:

> **Attach Location (URL)** Sends the Web document that's currently displayed in Navigator. Just click on the **OK** button. You can then select **As Is** to send it as an HTML document (a Web page) or select **Convert to Plain Text** to send the Web document as a text file.
>
> **Attach File** Sends a file that's on your hard disk (such as a graphic or sound file or a document you created). Use the dialog box that appears, to select the drive, folder, and name of the file you want to send, and then click on the **Open** button. (You can send more than one file by clicking on the **Attach File** button again.)

After selecting the file(s) or Web page you want to send, click the **OK** button. You're returned to the Message Composition dialog box, and the file's name(s) is inserted in the **Attachment** text box.

When you're ready to send your message (along with any attached file), click the **Send** button. Navigator sends the message. Because the message may take any of several paths on the Internet, it may not arrive for several hours (it's still faster than the Post Office). Mail typically bounces around several Internet sites before reaching its destination (especially if there's a lot of traffic).

C/O Webmaster

As you browse the Web, you'll often encounter a link that allows you to write to the person who created a particular Web page (the Webmaster). If you click the link, Navigator automatically opens the dialog box that allows you to send an e-mail message.

Finally, a Browser That Can Read Mail!

Traditionally, Navigator has always been better at sending than at receiving e-mail. Before Navigator version 2.0 came along, Navigator had no way to access incoming e-mail messages. If you wanted to check your mail, you had to use a specialized e-mail program, such as Eudora. But now Navigator comes with its own built-in e-mail reader that makes receiving e-mail as easy as sending it.

To read incoming e-mail messages, start Navigator's E-Mail program. Open the **Window** menu, and click **Netscape Mail**. A dialog box appears, prompting you to type your e-mail password (this is usually the same as your login password, supplied by your service provider). Type your password and click **OK**. Navigator checks your electronic mailbox. If you haven't received any mail, a dialog box appears, telling you that your box is empty (I hate when that happens). Click **OK**.

The Netscape Mail window appears, as shown in the next figure. Notice that the window is divided into three *panes*. The left pane shows a folder called **Inbox** for incoming messages. The first time you send a message, Navigator will create a **Sent** folder (which contains copies of all the messages you've sent). The right pane displays the contents of the active folder; initially, you have only one message, a sample message called **Mozilla**. This is a message that comes with Navigator (Mozilla is Netscape's mascot). The bottom pane displays the contents of the selected message.

Chapter 14 ➤ *Corresponding with Electronic Mail*

You can change the relative sizes and dimensions of the panes by dragging their borders. You can also change the width of columns in a pane by dragging the right column marker.

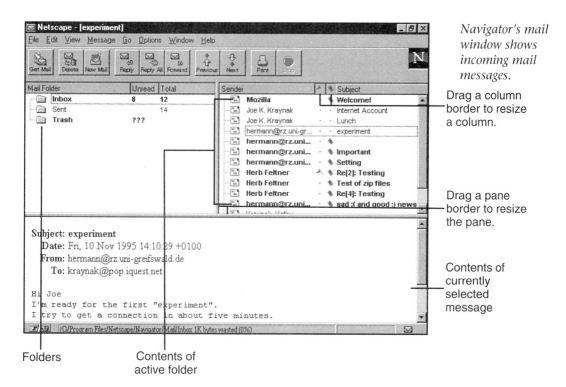

Navigator's mail window shows incoming mail messages.

Checking the Mail

When you first connect to your e-mail server using Netscape Mail, it automatically grabs any new messages and stuffs them into your inbox. If you want to check for mail yourself, you have three options: click the **Get Mail** button in the toolbar, press **Ctrl+T**, or open the **File** menu and select **Get New Mail**.

However you choose to do it, Navigator nabs any new messages, activates the Inbox folder, and displays the names of all the messages in your inbox. The names of messages you've already read appear in normal type. Names of new messages (messages you haven't read) appear bold. To read a message, click its name. The contents of the message then appears in the bottom pane.

You can continue to read messages by double-clicking on their names, but to save time, you can click the **Next** or **Previous** button in the toolbar to scroll through messages in the list. You can also use the commands on the **Go** menu to scroll through the messages: Next Message, Previous Message, First Unread, Next Unread, or Previous Unread.

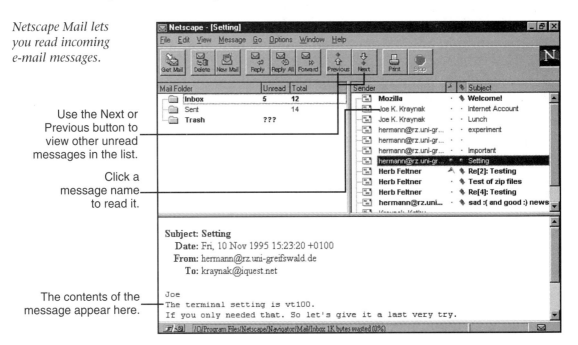

Netscape Mail lets you read incoming e-mail messages.

Use the Next or Previous button to view other unread messages in the list.

Click a message name to read it.

The contents of the message appear here.

Responding to Messages

As you read your mail, you will undoubtedly want to respond to a message, especially if you're caught up in a flame war with your ex. (For a complete description of flame wars, skip ahead to "Behave Yourself.")

To respond to an e-mail message, first click the message to which you want to respond. Then, click the **Reply** button in the toolbar (or press **Ctrl+R**, or open the **Message** menu and select **Reply**). The dialog box that appears looks a lot like the dialog box you saw earlier in this chapter (when you sent your first e-mail message). The only difference is that the Send To and Subject text boxes are already filled in for you.

Type your response in the blank message area. Netscape mail automatically inserts text from the original message into the message area as a quote. Each line of the quoted message begins with an angle bracket >, which is a standard way to show that the material is a quote. You can delete parts of the quote by using the Del or Backspace key. (You should rarely quote an entire message, because then the message becomes too long and redundant.) You can also use the **Attachment** button to send a file along with your response.

When you're ready to send the message, click the **Send** button.

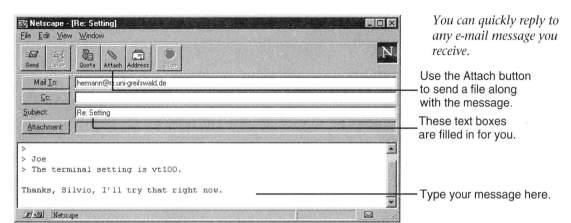

You can quickly reply to any e-mail message you receive.

Use the Attach button to send a file along with the message.

These text boxes are filled in for you.

Type your message here.

Organizing Messages with Folders

As the mail starts pouring in, you'll soon become a prolific writer, even if you never had any intentions of becoming a prolific writer. Soon, your landfill (folders) will be heaping with messages and ongoing dialogs with friends, relatives, and colleagues. You need some way to organize this opus...and clean it up.

Fortunately, Netscape Mail contains all the management tools you need to group, delete, copy, and move messages. It even comes with the equivalent of a trash compactor, which you can use to compress messages, so they take up less space.

The first step in reorganizing your messages is to create a folder. For example, you might create a folder for each person you frequently correspond with or one for business and one for personal messages. To create a folder, open the **File** menu (in the Mail window) and select **New Folder**. Type a name for the folder, and click **OK**. The new folder appears in the left pane. You can now copy and move messages to this new folder, as explained in the next section.

Selecting, Moving, Copying, and Deleting Messages

Whenever you receive a message, the message is added to the Inbox folder. When you send messages, they're added to the Sent folder. These folders quickly become overcrowded, making it nearly impossible to find a specific message later. To help, you can create folders, as explained in the previous section, and then move the messages to the folders you created.

145

Before you can move messages, you must select them. You can select a single message by clicking on its name. To select additional messages, hold down the **Ctrl** key while clicking on their names. You can select a range of neighboring messages by clicking on the top message in the range, and then holding down the **Shift** key while clicking on the bottom message in the range. The Edit menu offers some fancy commands to select messages:

Select Thread   Selects all messages that have the same title.

Select Flagged Messages   Selects all messages that you've flagged. (To flag a message, select the message, open the **Message** menu, and click on **Flag Message**.)

Select All Messages   Selects all messages in the currently open folder.

You don't select messages for the sheer joy of selecting them; you usually want to do something to the messages, such as delete them or move them. The easiest way to move messages is to select the messages you want to move, and then drag them over the folder into which you want them placed. To copy messages, hold down the Ctrl key while dragging (although I can't imagine why you would want two copies of a message cluttering up your disk).

You can also move the selected messages, by opening the **Message** menu and clicking on **Move**. This opens a submenu that contains the names of all your folders. Click the name of the folder to which you want to move the messages. You can use the **Copy** option on the **Message** menu to copy messages to another folder.

To delete messages, first select them, and then click the **Delete** button in the toolbar, or press the **Del** key. The deleted messages are sent to the TRASH folder, which Netscape Mail creates automatically when you first delete a message. If you delete a message by mistake, you can move it from the TRASH folder to one of your other folders, as explained in the previous paragraph. If you delete a message from the TRASH folder, it's gone for good.

Taking Out the Trash

You can quickly nuke all the messages in the TRASH folder. Open the **File** menu and select **Empty Trash Folder**.

Sorting Out Your Messages

Long lists of messages can become somewhat unwieldy. To help, Netscape Mail can sort the messages for you by date, subject, and even by sender. To sort your messages, click the folder whose messages you want to sort, open the **View** menu, click **Sort**, and choose one of the following options:

Again   Sorts the messages again if messages were added since the last time you sorted them.

Thread Messages   Indents responses to original messages, so you can quickly see which messages are related.

Ascending   Sorts messages in ascending order. For example, if you sort by date, earlier messages will be listed first. If you sort by subject, messages are sorted alphabetically, starting with A.

By Date   Sorts messages by date. If you turn Ascending off, recent messages appear first in the list.

By Subject   Sorts messages alphabetically by their descriptions. With Ascending off, messages that start with Z would be listed before messages that start with A.

By Sender   Sorts messages alphabetically by the sender's name.

Compacting Folders to Save Space

Text messages typically take up little space. However, if you have a bunch of messages in a particular folder, they can put a dent in your hard disk. To save disk space, consider compressing your stuffed folders. Compressing really doesn't change the messages at all—you can still read them; they just take up less of your storage space.

To compress a folder, click it, and then open the **File** menu and select **Compress This Folder** (or press **Ctrl+K**). Any messages you store in a compressed folder are automatically compressed.

Making an E-Mail Address "Book"

Internet e-mail addresses are about as easy to remember as international phone numbers. They can be a combination of long usernames, disjointed numbers, and domain names that snake across the screen, all separated with dots. Nobody expects you to remember these addresses, but if you don't enter them precisely as they appear, your mail will never reach its destination.

The solution to this problem is to create an e-mail address book. To make an address book, open the **Window** menu (in Navigator or in Netscape Mail), and click **Address Book**. The Address Book window appears.

To add an e-mail address to your book, open the **Item** menu, and click **Add User**. The Address Book dialog box appears. The Nick Name text box allows you to enter a person's username. As you establish electronic relationships, nick names become an important way of knowing people. In the **Nick Name** text box, type the person's nickname as a combination of lowercase characters and numbers (this entry is optional); you cannot use any uppercase characters. Click inside the **Name** text box, and type the person's full name (you can include uppercase characters. This name will appear in your address book).

Now for the important entry. Click inside the **E-Mail Address** text box, and type the person's Internet e-mail address, just as you would type it if you were sending the person a message. You can type additional information in the **Description** text box, such as the person's phone number and mailing address. (If you open your address book in Navigator as a Web page, the description information will appear.) To start a new line in this text box, press **Ctrl+Enter**. When you're done, click **OK**.

The Address Book shows a list of people you've added.

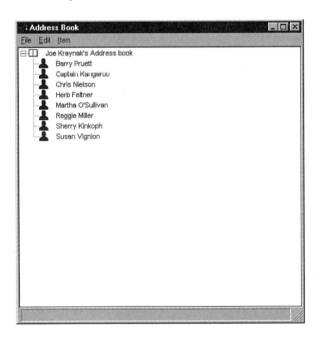

To delete a person from your address book (sorry it didn't work out), click the person's name, and press the **Del** key (or open the **Edit** menu and select **Delete**).

Chapter 14 ➤ *Corresponding with Electronic Mail*

Changing an Address Book Entry

If your friend or relative moves or picks a new e-mail address, you'll have to change it. Open the **Address Book** window, right-click the person's name, and click **Properties**. This opens the same dialog box you used to add the person to your address book.

Now that you have an address book, how do you use it? When you display the dialog box for sending an e-mail message, click inside the **Mail To** text box, and then click the **Address** button in the toolbar. This displays your list of e-mail addresses. Click the address to which you want to send this message, and then click **Mail To**. This inserts the selected e-mail address into the Mail To text box. Click on the **OK** button when you're done. Then, take any additional steps to send the message.

Displaying Your Address Book as a Web Page

Inserting addresses from your address book instead of typing them is a big time-saver, but if you really want to save some time, open your address book as a Web page. The names you entered in the address book appear as links; to e-mail someone, you simply click the link, and then type your subject and message. What could be easier?

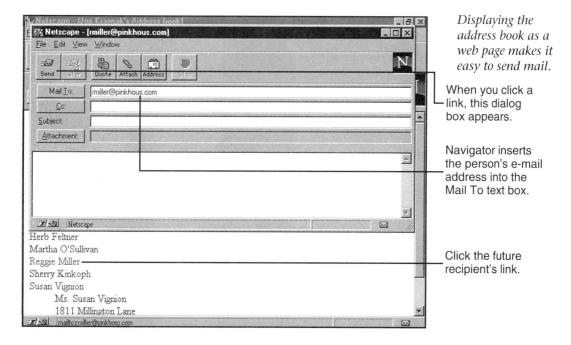

Displaying the address book as a web page makes it easy to send mail.

When you click a link, this dialog box appears.

Navigator inserts the person's e-mail address into the Mail To text box.

Click the future recipient's link.

149

To display your address book as a Web page, open Netscape Navigator's **File** menu and select **Open File** (or press **Ctrl+O**). The Open dialog box appears. Select the drive and folder where your address book is stored (in Windows 95, the address book is stored in PROGRAM FILES\NETSCAPE\NAVIGATOR), and then double-click its name (address.htm) in the file name list. This opens the address book as a Web page, showing the names you entered as links. Click a link to display the dialog box you use to send e-mail.

Behave Yourself: E-Mail Rules and Abbreviations

To avoid getting yourself into trouble by unintentionally sending an insulting e-mail message, you might want to consider the proper protocol for composing e-mail messages. The most important rule is NEVER EVER TYPE IN ALL UPPERCASE CHARACTERS. This is the equivalent of shouting, and people become very edgy when they see this text on their screen. Likewise, take it easy on the exclamation points!!!

Secondly, avoid confrontations in e-mail. When you disagree with somebody, a personal visit or a phone call is usually more tactful than a long letter that painfully describes how stupid and inconsiderate the other person is being. Of course, if you're breaking off a relationship, sometimes e-mail is the best way to do it. The person becomes so irritated, that he or she will refuse to speak, write, or otherwise communicate with you.

Flame Wars

When you strongly disagree with someone on the Internet, it's tempting to *flame* the person—to send a stinging, sarcastic message. It's even more tempting to respond to a flaming message with your own barb. The flame war that results is usually a waste of time and makes both people look bad.

:-) Emoticons: A Symbolic Internet Language

If you want to look as though you're an e-mail veteran, then pepper your messages with any of the following *emoticons* (pronounced "ee-mow-tick-cons"). You can use these symbols to show your pleasure or displeasure with a particular comment, to take the edge off a comment that you think might be misinterpreted, and to express your moods.

:) or :-)	I'm happy, or it's good to see you, or I'm smiling as I'm saying this. You can often use this to show that you're joking.
:D or :-D	I'm really happy or laughing

;) or ;-)	Winking
:(or :-(	Unhappy. You hurt me, you big brute
;(or ;-(	Crying
:| or :-|	I don't really care
:/ or :-/	Skeptical
:# or :-#	My lips are sealed. I can keep a secret
:> or :->	Devilish grin
;^)	Smirking
%-)	I've been at this too long
:p or :-p	Sticking my tongue out
<g>	Grinning. Usually takes the edge off whatever you just said
<vbg>	Very Big Grin
<l>	Laughing
<lol>	Laughing Out Loud
<i>	Ironic
<s>	Sighing
<jk>	Just kidding. (These are my initials, too.)
<>	No comment

Common Abbreviations, To Save Time

In addition to the language of emoticons, Internet chat and e-mail messages are commonly seasoned with a fair share of abbreviations. The following is a sample of some of the abbreviations you'll encounter and be expected to know:

AFAIK	As Far As I Know
BRB	Be Right Back
BTW	By The Way
CUL8R	See You Later
F2F	Face To Face (usually in reference to meeting somebody in person)

151

FAQ	Frequently Asked Questions. Many sites post a list of questions that many users ask, along with answers to those questions. They call this list a FAQ.
FOTCL	Falling Off The Chair Laughing
FTF	Another version of Face To Face
FYA	For Your Amusement
FYI	For Your Information
HHOK	Ha Ha Only Kidding
IMO	In My Opinion
IMHO	In My Humble Opinion
IOW	In Other Words
KISS	Keep It Simple, Stupid
LOL	Laughing Out Loud
MOTOS	Member Of The Opposite Sex
OIC	Oh, I See
PONA	Person Of No Account
ROTF	Rolling On The Floor (presumably in laughter)
SO	Significant Other
TIC	Tongue In Cheek
TTFN	Ta Ta For Now

The Least You Need to Know

If you really want to get into this e-mail thing, read Paul McFedries' book, *The Complete Idiot's Guide to E-Mail*. However, if you just want to send and receive e-mail messages through Netscape Mail, you have to know only two things:

1. To send an e-mail message, open Navigator's **File** menu and click **New Mail Message**. The rest of the steps are pretty obvious.

2. To check your e-mailbox, open the **Window** menu and click **Netscape Mail**.

Chapter 15

Customizing Navigator to Make It Your Own

By the End of This Chapter, You'll Be Able To...

➤ Turn screen items, including messages and toolbars, on or off.

➤ Get rid of that dingy gray document background.

➤ Wake up your documents with fancy typestyles.

Navigator has just moved in with you, toting along its old look and all its old habits and forcing you to conform. But now you're going to get your chance to mold Navigator into the Web browser of your dreams. Do you use that toolbar at the top of the screen? If not, get rid of it. You don't like the way the text looks? Change it! Consider this chapter your guide to Navigator empowerment. In the coming sections, you'll learn how to revamp Navigator to look and behave the way you want it to.

Turning Screen Things On and Off

Let's work into this customizing thing as slowly as possible, starting with some simple customization options. The easiest way to customize Navigator is to select check-mark options from the **Options** menu. This technique allows you to turn the toolbar on or off, show or hide the Location text box, and control other screen items.

The strategy here is fairly simple: You want to hide any screen objects that you don't use, giving Navigator more room to display actual Web pages. Open the **Options** menu, and select any of the following items to turn them off (if they're on) or on (if they're off):

Show Toolbar   Displays the buttons that appear directly below the menu bar. If you learn the quick-key combinations for entering these commands, you can do away with the button bar, but keep it on for now.

Show Location   Displays the Location text box. Because this text box makes it so easy to enter URLs, you might want to keep it on. However, if you develop a complete list of bookmarks for all your favorite sites, you might be able to live without this text box.

Show Directory Buttons   Displays the buttons below the Location text box that take you directly to Navigator Corporation sites. Few users really use these buttons, and all the options are on the Directory menu, anyway, so turn this puppy off.

Auto Load Images   You saw this option in Chapter 8. When this option is on, Navigator loads any graphics that are on the Web pages. When this option is off, Navigator displays icons in place of the images, which results in pages loading faster but looking worse.

Show Java Console   Displays a separate window for displaying Java Applets (animations, and other moving pictures that can be embedded in Web pages). Keep this off for now. Navigator can still display Java applets when you click on a link for an applet.

Document Encoding   Don't touch this one for now; it allows you to change the code style in the event that you connect to a Chinese, Japanese, or Korean server. If you have problems loading a page that uses this foreign encoding, go ahead and change the encoding option and try reloading the page.

Hot-Key Alternatives

If you turn off some of the screen elements, use the following key combinations:

Ctrl+L	To enter a URL
Alt+<	To display the previous Web page
Alt+>	To display the next Web page
Esc	To stop loading a page
Ctrl+R	To reload
Crtl+I	To load images

If you exit Navigator now, and then restart it, any screen objects you turned off will be turned back on. In order to start Navigator the way you configured it, open the **Options** menu, and select **Save Options**.

Giving Navigator a Makeover

Turning screen items off is pretty drastic. It's sort of like knocking out a wall in your house or demolishing an entire wing. But what if you just want to add a fresh coat of paint? You can do that in Navigator by changing the font used to display Web document text or changing the background colors. To change the appearance of Navigator, open the **Options** menu and select **General Preferences**. This displays the general Preferences dialog box.

As you can see from the picture, this dialog box has a bunch of tabs, a few of which you have already encountered. We'll skip the Helpers tab, since you spent enough time there in Chapter 12. We'll also ignore the Language tab, which has advanced options you can afford to ignore. And we'll skip the Apps tab, which you'll use for Telnetting (in Chapter 19). Now that you've whittled down the list to four tabs, let's see what's on them.

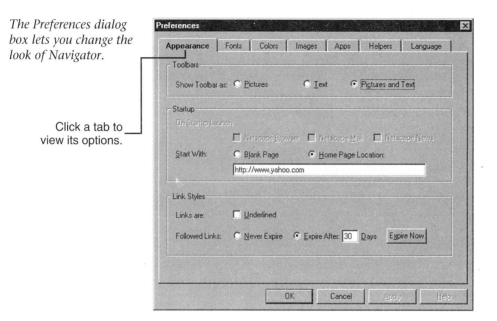

The Preferences dialog box lets you change the look of Navigator.

Click a tab to view its options.

A Peek at the Appearance Options

As soon as you open the Preferences dialog box, the Appearance tab jumps to the front, so let's deal with its options first:

Show Toolbar as Allows you to control the appearance of the buttons in the toolbar. You can choose **Pictures** (for small buttons with pictures on them), **Text** (for skinny buttons with words on them), or **Pictures and Text** (for big buttons with pictures and words).

On Startup Launch Gives you the option of starting Navigator, Netscape Mail, and Netscape News automatically when you start your computer in Windows 95.

Start With Lets you specify which page you want Navigator to load when you start it. You can select **Blank Page** if you don't want Navigator to load a page. Or select **Home Page Location**, and then type the desired page's URL in the text box. This can be the URL for a file on your hard disk, as explained in Chapter 11.

Links are This option lets you turn off underlining for links. Hey, the links are blue, anyway, so what do you need underlining for?

Followed Links As you know, Navigator keeps track of the URLs for the Web pages you've visited and displays the links for those URLs in a different color. You can use the Followed Links options to specify how far back you want Navigator to

"remember" those URLs. **Never Expire** tells Navigator to remember forever.
Expire After ___ Days specifies the number of days Navigator should remember.
The **Expire Now** button erases Navigator's memory.

Dressing Your Text in the Right Font

If you took a peek at the source document in Chapter 13, you know that Web pages consist of a bunch of text and codes. Sometimes, the codes actually outnumber the text. These codes tell Navigator (or whatever Web browser you might use) how to display a document. It specifies the colors to use, the background, and the style of text. However, codes give general orders like "make this text bigger," and "emphasize this text." The browser (Navigator for instance) interprets the codes, and there's a lot of room for interpretation.

Because of this, you can pick the fonts you want to use to style the text. With the general Preferences dialog box displayed, click the **Fonts** tab.

To refresh your memory a fixed font gives each character the same amount of room. A slender "i" gets the same space as a wide-body "w." Proportional fonts are more communistic—"to each, according to his needs, from each, according to his abilities." In other words, each character gets only the room it needs. Fixed fonts are usually used to display file names at FTP sites. Proportional fonts are used for most of the text you see on Web pages.

To change a font, click the **Choose Font** button next to the Proportional or Fixed Font option. A dialog box appears, allowing you to select the type style and size you want to use. Make your selections, and then click **OK**.

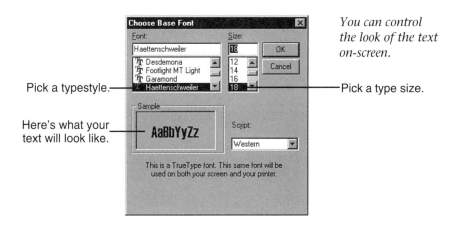

Pick a typestyle.

Here's what your text will look like.

Pick a type size.

You can control the look of the text on-screen.

Taking Your Crayolas to the Screen

Check This Out...

Carol Channing and Cal Ripken You need a bit of trivia to wake you up. Did you know that Carol Channing has missed only one day of work while performing in *Hello, Dolly!* for the past 30 years? That smashes Cal Ripken's attendance record.

You've taken it for granted, that dingy gray background that sits behind each Web page you look at is intentional, placed there by one of Navigator's many color settings. How would you like to turn that background white or display a background picture of Carol Channing starring in *Hello, Dolly!*?

Okay, maybe you don't want Carol Channing staring out at you from behind every Web document you load, but the point is that you can take control of the Navigator background and the colors that Navigator uses to display text and links. Simply click the **Colors** tab, and change any of the following options:

Links Controls the colors of the links you haven't yet tried. If you like blue links, don't change this setting. If you would prefer some other color, click **Custom**, and then click the **Change Color** button. In the dialog box that appears, click the desired color, and click **OK**.

Followed Links Sets the color for links that you've already tried. Perform the same steps to change this color setting as you performed for the Links setting.

Text Sets the color for the rest of the text (nonlink text) that makes up a Web page. Black is a good setting, but if you pick a dark background, you should pick a lighter shade of text.

Check This Out...

Power Tip Select the **Default background** option, and turn on **Always Use My Colors, Overriding Document**. This speeds up Navigator, because it won't try to download any fancy backgrounds that the Web pages try to send you.

Background Lets you pick a background color for any Web page that does not have a background color (some Web pages contain codes that display a specific color). The Default setting gives pages a white background, which makes the text easy to read. To pick a different color, click **Custom**, and then use the **Change Color** button to display a dialog box that lets you change the background color.

Optionally, you can pick a graphic image to act as your Navigator background. Click **Image File**, and then use the **Browse** button to pick the JPG or GIF image file that you want to use as the background. Be careful with this one; some images can make the text unreadable.

Always Use My Colors, Overriding Document Tells Navigator to use your colors and background setting even if the Web page you load is set to display a different color or background.

You Can Control Pictures, Too

Up to this point, you've been setting the options for boring stuff such as text and backgrounds. But what really makes a Web page come alive are its pictures. To control the way Navigator displays pictures, click the **Images** tab.

The Images tab doesn't give you a whole lot of options (two, to be exact). The Choosing Colors options specify how Navigator displays the colors that make up inline images and other graphics it displays. Leave this option set to **Automatic**; this setting will pick the best option for displaying colors in most images. Substitute Colors and Dither sometimes make the graphics look blotchy. Experiment. If you encounter a graphic that looks bad on-screen, try one of the other options.

Mr. Dithers

Dithering is used in graphics to help smooth the areas on the picture where colors and shades meet. When you turn dithering off, you force the graphics program (or the program that displays the image) to form harsh boundaries between shaded and colored areas. This gives you a sort of early '70s, Jimi Hendrix-album-cover look.

The Images option that can really make a difference in how Navigator performs is the **Display Images** option. You can choose to have images displayed while Navigator receives them or after receiving them. Personally, I don't like the way Navigator gradually displays images. I keep trying to focus in on what I'm getting before the picture actually arrives. However, if you choose **After Loading**, you won't be able to click a graphic link until Navigator is done loading *all* the graphics on the page...and this can take awhile. Pick your poison.

You might want to stick with the default settings here.

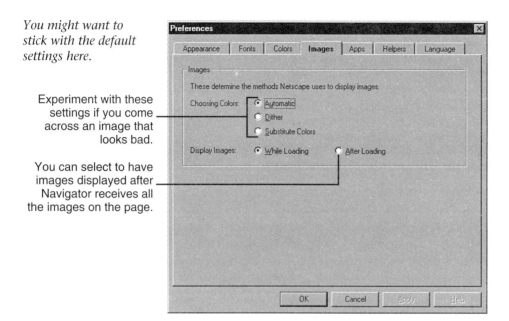

Experiment with these settings if you come across an image that looks bad.

You can select to have images displayed after Navigator receives all the images on the page.

Turning the Security Warnings On and Off

If you've filled out any search forms or order forms in your Web wanderings, you know that whenever you click the button to start the search or submit the form, a bossy dialog box appears warning you that someone might see what you just did. I don't know about you, but that always startles me and makes me glance over my shoulder. Although you can turn the warnings off, as explained later in this chapter, you should leave them on to prevent any information you enter from falling into the wrong hands.

Now that you've been warned, here's what you do if you decide to turn off the security options: Open the **Options** menu and click **Security Preferences**. This tab also contains the options for turning the security warnings on or off. Click on all the warnings you want to turn off. (You can turn off Java support by clicking on **Disable Java**, if you don't want Java applets to be running on your computer. Because Java applets are small applications, there is some risk that the applications might introduce a virus to your computer.)

Be Careful!

Regardless of whether you turn the warnings off or leave them on, you should be careful when transmitting any personal or credit card information over the Internet. For example, you should treat Internet credit card orders just as you handle a credit card order over the phone. Make sure you're dealing with a reputable company, and that the company has a secure server. You don't just call any company on the phone and give them your credit card number, so don't do it on the Internet.

This leads us to the next question: How do I know that a server is secure? First, if you leave the security warnings on, Navigator will display a dialog box, informing you of when you enter or leave a secure server or try to submit a form on an insecure server. This is by far the best way to tell.

If you turn the security warnings off, there are three main ways you can tell a secure server from an insecure one. First, before you fill out an order form, check the URL in the Location text box. If it begins with https instead of http, the document is protected by Netscape's SSL (Secure Sockets Layer) protocol. Second, look in the lower left corner of the Navigator window for a key icon. If the key is unbroken and on a blue background, the document is secure. If the key is broken and on a gray background, the document is insecure. Finally, open the **View** menu and select **Document Info**. A window appears, showing all sorts of information about the Web page. Look at **Security** to find out if the document is secure or not.

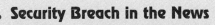

Security Breach in the News

A couple college students broke into the server at one of Netscape's client companies and managed to nab some important information. Maybe you saw the story in the newspaper. Since then, Netscape has been working hard to improve security, and has built some new protections into both Netscape Navigator and into the sites that Netscape Corporation serves.

Additional Security Options

You'll notice some other tabs in the security Preferences dialog box. Ignore these tabs for now. Currently, only the sites you are connecting to require passwords and certificates to protect their sites from security breaches. The Passwords, Site Certificates, and Personal Certificates tabs are used by the administrators of these Web servers to protect you, the Navigator user, from any unauthorized access to the information you enter. In the future, Netscape may incorporate additional security measures for users like you.

For more information about Internet security and how Netscape deals with it, open Navigator's **Help** menu, and click **On Security**. This opens Netscape's Security Web page, which contains more information about security than any three people I know really care about.

Tinkering with Some Additional Settings

You've played with the look of Navigator, but what about how it behaves? How much RAM should it use for those Web pages? How much disk space should it use? And how many connections should it manage at the same time? These settings can seriously affect Navigator's performance, so let's take a look at them. Open the **Options** menu, and click **Network Preferences**. This displays the network Preferences dialog box, which contains options you can use even if you have a lowly modem connection.

Establishing a Strong Cache Flow

The first tab, **Cache**, has the most important options. A *cache* is memory or disk space that Navigator (or any other program) uses to temporarily store data. In Navigator's case, the cache is used to store Web pages you've already loaded, so if you go back or forward to a page, Navigator doesn't have to reload the page from the Web site. The minimum numbers for the disk and memory cache are already entered for you; don't go any lower. If you have scads of disk space or memory, you can increase the numbers so Navigator will "remember" more pages.

> ### Clear That Cache!
> The buttons next to the disk and memory cache settings (**Clear Memory Cache Now** and **Clear Disk Cache Now**) are useful if you have trouble running your other Windows programs, because your system is low on memory. These buttons clear the cache, freeing that storage space for other use.

You should leave the Disk Cache Directory setting as is, unless you have some good reason to change it. When you installed Navigator, it created a CACHE folder for you, which is as good a place as any to store the cache.

The last option, **Verify Documents**, lets you specify how often you want Navigator to check a Web document you've loaded against the original. The less often Navigator has to verify documents, the faster Navigator will run. **Once per Session** is a good, safe setting. **Every Time** is excessive and will slow down an already slow process. **Never** is good if you want to speed up Navigator; you can always reload the page if it doesn't transfer right the first time.

Chapter 15 ➤ *Customizing Navigator to Make It Your Own*

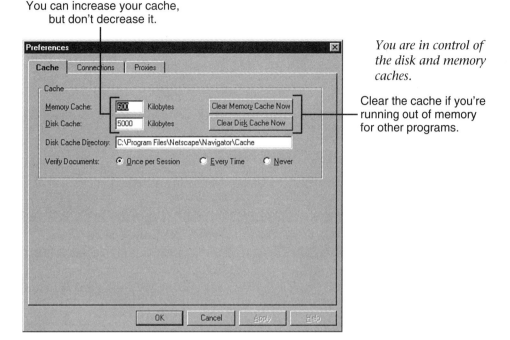

You can increase your cache, but don't decrease it.

You are in control of the disk and memory caches.

Clear the cache if you're running out of memory for other programs.

You Gotta Have the Right Connections (But How Many?)

The second tab in the network Preferences dialog box lets you control the flow of data from the remote computer to your computer. Initially, Navigator is set up to open four "channels" to the remote computer, which allows Navigator to grab several files at once. If you watch your screen and status bar as Navigator loads Web pages, you'll notice that Navigator grabs a little text, and then part of a picture, and then part of another picture, in an attempt to build the entire page at once.

If you increase the number of simultaneous connections, you'll slow down each individual connection, but you'll allow Navigator to load more parts of the page at once. It's a toss-up, but if you have a fast network connection, go ahead and crank up this setting.

If your computer is connected to the Internet through a network cable, you can also play with the **Network Buffer Size** setting. As you increase this number, Navigator allows more data to enter the connection at one time. However, if you crank this setting up too high, more data than your computer can handle may come rushing in, and it will foul up the transmission. Experiment with the setting, but increase it by only one or two kilobytes at a time.

163

Part 2 ➤ *Mastering Navigator*

Check This Out...

> **Saving Your Settings**
>
> When you turn screen items on or off, you have to enter the **Options/Save Options** command to save your settings. With dialog box options, this is unnecessary. Once you click **OK**, Navigator automatically saves the settings, and they will be in effect the next time you start Navigator.

A Word About the Proxies Tab

I know, you're curious about that Proxies tab. Go ahead and click on it. You see that the No Proxies option is selected. In case you're wondering, a proxy is a server that acts as a sort of middleman. If you're connected to the Internet through a network connection (instead of a modem), your network may have something called firewalls that protect the network from unauthorized access. The problem with these firewalls is that they may limit your access to some Internet features. Proxies act as bridges over the firewalls, allowing information to pass freely between the Internet and your network.

If you're connected to the Internet with a modem, leave No Proxies on. If you have a Network connection, ask your network administrator if you need to use proxies. If you do need proxies, the network administrator can tell you which options you need to select, and how to enter information about the proxies.

The Least You Need to Know

You don't need to know a whole lot about customizing Navigator. Just remember that the Options menu is your key to changing Navigator, that the first four options open dialog boxes, the next five options allow you to turn settings on and off, and that the last option lets you save your changes.

Now, play around some more until Navigator looks and behaves the way you want it to.

Part 3
Stretching the Web with Navigator

You've surfed the Web. You clicked links, typed URLs, set up your helper applications, downloaded files, and even sent and received some e-mail. You probably have two or three different bookmark files by now. Given the most obscure topic, you can probably find at least five Web pages with relevant information. Face it, you've mastered Navigator. You've whipped the Web. Now, you need a new quest.

In this section, you'll learn how to use Navigator and the World Wide Web to explore other areas on the Internet. You'll learn how to use Navigator to find and transfer files from FTP sites, to read messages in newsgroups, to connect to gopher servers, and much more. You'll even learn how to use Navigator along with Netscape's Chat program, to talk with other users all over the world! By the end of this part, you'll be able to use Navigator as your sole Internet tool.

Chapter 16

Grabbing Files with FTP

By the End of This Chapter, You'll Be Able To...

➤ Fake your way through a conversation about FTP.

➤ Stumble into FTP sites without even trying.

➤ Use Navigator to download files from FTP sites.

➤ Find specific files when you know their names.

➤ Identify common file types on the Internet.

Chances are you've already downloaded files from FTP sites using Navigator. The process is simple. You find a link for the file you want to download, click on the link, and specify the name of the file and where you want it stored. So why have a whole chapter on it? Because there's more you *can* know about accessing FTP sites through Navigator—information that can help you find specific FTP sites, connect to those sites, and navigate through their directory structures to download the files you want.

FTP: What's It All About?

Techno Talk

FTP Stands for *File Transfer Protocol*, a set of rules that govern the transfer of files between computers. True geeks use this acronym as a verb, for example, "I FTP'd to the to ftp-dot-netscape-dot-com to nab all my helper applications."

When the Internet started out, it wasn't much more than a gigantic file warehouse. Businesses and individuals stored files on various Internet servers, where other people could come and copy (download) those files. It was like a huge swap meet for computer geeks.

As the Internet grew and diversified, it had to assign specific jobs to different servers. World Wide Web servers were given the task of storing hyperdocuments, newsgroups were set up to act as bulletin boards, and FTP servers became the file warehouses. What does this have to do with you? You can connect to many public-access FTP servers; once there, you can copy programs, text files, graphics, and anything else that can be stored electronically.

Connecting to FTP Sites

In Chapter 7, you learned a couple of ways to connect to the Netscape FTP site to download the copy of Navigator you're now using. If you're a masochist, you probably like to connect to sites and transfer files the old-fashioned way: using the UNIX shell. You type cryptic commands at a clueless prompt and hope you get what you want.

An easier way to perform FTP file transfers is to use a special FTP program. With one of these—such as WS_FTP for Windows—you can transfer files simply by copying them from one panel to another in a dialog box. In addition to ease-of-use, an FTP program offers two important benefits: it allows you to copy the file directly to your computer, and it transfers files fairly quickly.

The third and easiest way to FTP is to use Navigator. You simply type the URL of the FTP site, and Navigator presents you with a graphical representation of the files and directories on the server. To open a directory, you click on its link. To download a file, you simply click on its name.

FTP Sites That Anyone Can Use

You'll encounter two types of FTP servers: those that let anyone transfer files (*anonymous* sites) and those that don't. To connect to an anonymous site, you usually log in as **anonymous** and then use your e-mail address as your password. As long as you have entered this information into Navigator, it will use the information to automatically log in to FTP sites for you.

Chapter 16 ➤ Grabbing Files with FTP

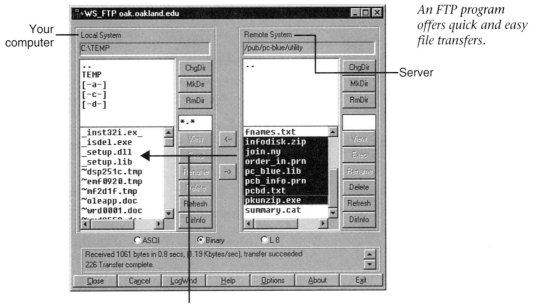

An FTP program offers quick and easy file transfers.

Nonanonymous sites require you to enter a username and a password. To connect to one of these sites, you must contact the network supervisor of the site beforehand (usually by sending the supervisor an e-mail message or by calling that person). That person will provide you with a login name and password...assuming she agrees to give you access.

If you have trouble connecting to FTP sites, make sure you've entered your e-mail address in Navigator. You probably already did this in Chapter 14, but to refresh your memory, you open the **Options** menu, click **Mail and News Preferences**, and then click the **Identity** tab. Enter your name and e-mail address. Most FTP sites won't give you access without an e-mail address.

Know the Rules

If you ruffle the administrator at an anonymous FTP site, you will quickly lose your anonymity. The administrator can use your e-mail address to lock you out. You'll try to log on as anonymous, and you'll get an **access denied** message or something similar. When you first access a site, read its rules. On most anonymous FTP servers, the only rule is, "Don't connect during business hours."

169

Using URLs to Access Specific Sites

Picture this. You work for a local underground newspaper. A friend sends you an e-mail message telling you of a great FTP site where you can get the latest dirt about members of Congress and Presidential hopefuls. You decide to do a little muckraking, but how do you get to that site?

You connect to FTP sites the same way you connect to HTTP sites: type the site's URL in the **Location** text box, and press **Enter**. You can also use the **File/Open Location** command, and then type the URL in the dialog box that appears, but that's an extra step. If the FTP site won't let you in, check to make sure you typed the URL correctly. If you still can't get in, don't be surprised. The site may not allow anonymous access, or access during high-traffic hours. Either that, or the site may be simply too busy to handle your requests.

Stumbling Around in FTP Sites

Chances are you stumbled unknowingly into a couple of FTP sites already. If you looked in the Location text box, you would see that the URL started with **ftp://** rather than **http://**. Another sign that you just stepped out of the Web is that you'll see tiny document and folder icons next to the link text. If you see any of the following icons, it's a sure sign you're in FTP country.

 A directory or folder. It may contain files and additional directories or folders.

 A text file. Navigator can probably read and display the file.

 A file that Navigator can't read and that has no helper application associated to it. The file might be a compressed file or a program file.

 A sound file. If you set up a helper application for sound files, you may be able to play this one.

 A movie file, usually a file with an MPG extension.

 A graphic, usually GIF or JPG.

The folder icons represent directories. To change to a directory, click on its link (not on the icon). You may see additional directories. Continue clicking on links until you find the desired file. You can move up the directory tree by clicking the **Up to a higher level directory** link at the top of the tree. If there is no Up to a higher directory link, click the single period (.) to move to the root directory, or the double period (..) to move up one directory.

Don't Forget About Bookmarks
When you find a great FTP site, create a bookmark for it. Open the **Bookmarks** menu and click **Add Bookmark**. You can then quickly return to a site that was too busy to give you access.

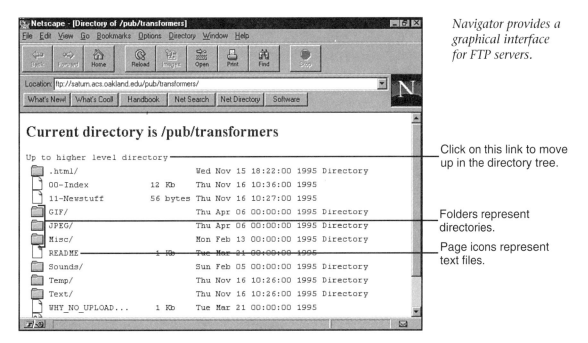

Navigator provides a graphical interface for FTP servers.

Click on this link to move up in the directory tree.

Folders represent directories.

Page icons represent text files.

Viewing and Getting Files

Once you find the file you want, you have to make a decision: do you want Navigator to "play" the file or download it? Navigator can display plain text files, and can play any other file types for which you installed helper applications. So, if you installed a GIF viewer (for example), and you come across a graphic file with the GIF extension, you can click on the link as you would click on any multimedia link in a Web document. Navigator downloads the file and then runs the associated helper application, which plays the file.

If you encounter a program file, a compressed file, or any file that Navigator is not set up to play, you must download the file to your disk. Then you can work with the file outside Navigator. Navigator displays a special icon for most files it can't play; the icon looks like a box with 010 on it, indicating that the file is binary.

To download a file, right-click on the file's link to display a shortcut menu, and then click the **Save this Link as** option. The Save As dialog box prompts you to name the file, and select the drive and folder where you want it stored on your hard drive. Enter the requested information, and then click **Save**.

ZIP, TAR, and Other Compressed Files

Many files you find at FTP sites are *compressed* in some way, so they take up less storage space and travel more quickly over Internet connections. PC files are commonly compressed into a .ZIP format, requiring you to *uncompress* the files with PKZip. Mac files are compressed into .SIT format, so you'll want to stay away from those files. Here's a list of other compressed formats you might encounter:

- **.Z**   Compressed with a UNIX compression program.
- **.z**   Compressed with a UNIX pack program.
- **.shar**   Archived with UNIX shell archive.
- **.tar**   Compressed with UNIX tar.
- **.pit**   Compressed with Macintosh Packit.
- **.zoo**   Compressed with Zoo210.
- **.arc**   Packed with PKARC for DOS.
- **.exe**   Self-extracting .ZIP file for a PC.
- **.sea**   Self-extracting .SIT file for the Mac.

When downloading files, make sure you get files that can run on your platform: DOS or Windows. In other words, you don't have a Mac, so don't bother downloading a .SIT or .SEA file. You're also not running UNIX, so you won't have much use for compressed UNIX files. Most sites also have the shareware utilities you need to decompress the files. Look for a /UTIL directory—that's where you'll usually find them.

Using Archie to Sniff Out Files

When word gets out that an anonymous FTP server has cool files, every user with a modem and a SLIP account tries to connect and grab some free stuff. The administrator

Chapter 16 ➤ *Grabbing Files with FTP*

then closes the server or restricts access, and the online locusts swarm to another server. The good news is that the files you want are probably stored on other (*mirror*) servers in addition to the swamped location. If you can't get the file at its original location, you can get it at the mirror site.

But how do you find these mirror sites? You use a program called Archie, which is sort of like a Web robot for FTP servers. Instead of sniffing out Web sites, however, Archie helps you find the FTP servers on which a file is stored.

Performing an Archie search in Navigator is easy. You display an Archie Request Form, fill out the form, and submit it. Archie acts as an automated librarian; it finds the files that match your search instructions, and displays a list of servers on which the file is stored. To display and fill out an Archie Request Form, perform the following steps:

> **Techno Talk**
>
> **Archie** Archie is a system that periodically creates an inventory of the files on many FTP servers. When you search for a file using Archie, you are actually searching through the file directory that Archie created. You're *not* searching the FTP servers themselves, although some searches can take so long that they give that impression.

1. Run Navigator.

2. Click inside the **Location** text box, and type one of the following URLs:

    http://hoohoo.ncsa.uiuc.edu/archie.html

    http://www-ns.rutgers.edu/htbin/archie

    http://www.wg.omron.co.jp/AA-eng.html

3. Press **Enter**, and wait for the Archie Request Form to appear. The form you see varies depending on the URL you entered in Step 2. (If you type a partial name, make sure you enter a setting to search for a substring instead of an exact match.)

4. Enter any other information or settings as desired. For example, most Archie search forms ask if you want the search to be case-sensitive.

5. If you're given a choice, click the **By Host** or **By Date** button to select a sorting preference. By Host tells Archie to sort the found files by host name. By Date lists newer files first.

6. If you see a **Priority** or **The impact on other users can be** drop-down list, select how pushy you want to be. **Not Nice At All** tells the Archie server to drop everything to search for your file. Select **Nicer** to be at least sort of nice. (Choosing Not Nice At All is sort of like cutting in line to see Santa. Don't do it unless you're in a big, big hurry.)

173

7. If you're given a choice of Archie servers to use, open the drop-down list, and select the Archie server you want to use for this search. A closer server may be faster in off-hours, whereas a distant server (one located in a time zone where it is evening or early morning) might work better during business hours.

8. If you see a text box that allows you to limit the number of copies of the file you want Archie to find, type a number in the text box. Archie searches can take a long time, so I usually type **30** in this text box.

9. Click the **Start Search** button (or its equivalent). Archie searches can take awhile, so don't expect a list of files to pop up immediately.

An Archie Request Form.

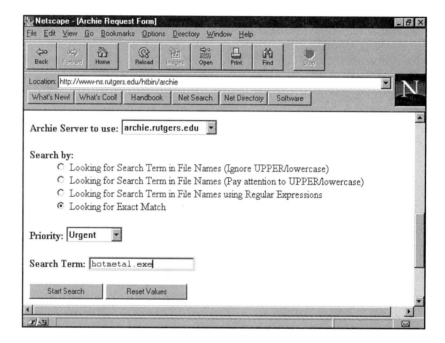

Be Specific

The first thing you'll want Archie to do is sniff out all the JPEG and MPEG video files on the Internet. Resist the temptation. Archie is designed to look for specific files. Don't clog Archie's arteries with vain searches. Archie won't help you with these overly general searches, anyway.

At this point, you can probably go get a cup of coffee...and drink it. The only thing slower than an Archie search is an Archie search through Navigator. When you come back from your break (assuming Archie is done), you can expect one of two things. If Archie found items that match your entry, you get a list of the items. You can then click on one of the listed links to connect to an FTP server and download the file. If Archie failed to find a file that matched your entry, you'll see the Archie form; you won't see any message telling you that the search failed.

The Monster FTP Site List

The Archie search technique may be a little too specific for your liking. If you prefer wandering aimlessly through FTP sites, I have the perfect place for you. It's an exhaustive directory of FTP sites listed alphabetically.

To view this list, click inside the Location text box, and type the following URL. The FTP Interface page appears, displaying links for the various alphabetical groupings of FTP sites. Click on a link to view a list of sites.

> http://www.ncsa.uiuc.edu/SDG/Software/Mosaic/Interfaces/ftp/ftp-interface.html

A Cool Trick

You can have Navigator display the directories and files on your hard disk. This gives you the opportunity to "play" files from your hard drive that you may have downloaded from the Internet. In the Location text box, type **file:///** followed by the path to the drive and directory you want to access. Your entry might look like this:

> **file:///c|/data/letters**

Make sure you use three forward slashes after **file:** and that you use a vertical line (|, the pipe symbol) after the drive letter instead of a colon.

When you press **Enter**, Navigator displays a listing of all the files and subdirectories in the directory you specified. You can then copy files to a another drive and directory: Right-click on the file, and use the dialog box that appears to specify a name and destination for the file.

You can access these files through Navigator, just as you can on an FTP site. For example, if you have a text file, you can click on it to open it in Navigator. If you have movie clips, graphics, or sound files, and you set up helper applications for those files, you can click on the file to have Navigator run the appropriate helper application and play the file. You can even set up a program such as Microsoft Word as a helper application to play .DOC files.

The Monster FTP Site List.

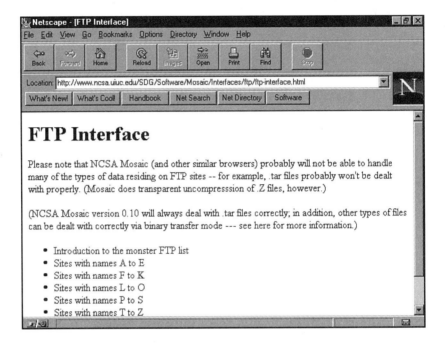

The Least You Need to Know

Before Navigator (BN), FTPing was one of the clumsiest Internet features. However, with Navigator's graphical interface, you should have no trouble connecting to anonymous FTP sites and downloading files. As you set out on your downloading venture, keep the following points in mind:

➤ Try to connect to FTP sites in the evening or on weekends.

➤ Before you FTP, make sure you've entered your e-mail address in Navigator.

➤ If you know the name or partial name of the file you want, perform an Archie search to find FTP sites where the file is stored.

➤ Here's the URL for a popular Archie Request Form:

http://hoohoo.ncsa.uiuc.edu/archie.htm

➤ To connect directly to an FTP site, type its URL in the **Location** text box, and press **Enter**. The URL for FTP sites cleverly starts with **ftp**.

Chapter 17

Chatting Online with Other Users

By the End of This Chapter, You'll Be Able To...

- ➤ Type messages back and forth with your friends.
- ➤ Swap Web pages with acquaintances and colleagues.
- ➤ Prowl cyberrooms when you can't sleep.
- ➤ Pretend you're someone you're not.

You've probably heard of it on the news. Two people wandering the Internet or some commercial online service bump into each other in a virtual talk room, realize they are soul mates, decide to get hitched, and live happily ever after.

A more likely story would have one member of the "happy couple" (not to be sexist, but usually the male) already married and pretending to be single. He woos the young computer mistress, convinces her to meet him in New York, has a one night stand, confesses that he's married, and flies back to Podunk, Illinois just in time for breakfast with the wife and kids.

But not all people try to score in chat rooms (yeah, right). Some people actually like to talk shop, discuss the weather, argue politics, or just hang out an watch other people make fools of themselves. Now, you'll get your chance.

Where to Get Netscape's Chat Program

You can't chat on the Internet with Netscape Navigator alone. You need another program, called Netscape Chat, which provides a window that displays the running dialogue.

Mirror FTP Sites If the Netscape FTP server is too busy, it shows you the courtesy of displaying a list of URLs for mirror sites (other FTP servers that have the same files). Drag over one of the URLs, and press **Ctrl+C** to copy it. Then, click inside the Location text box, press **Ctrl+V**, and press **Enter**.

To get Netscape Chat, fire up Netscape Navigator, type the URL for Netscape's FTP site (**ftp://ftp.netscape.com**) into the **Location** text box, and press **Enter**. Assuming that the FTP site lets you in (BIG assumption), you'll see a list of directories. Use the directory list to change to the pub/chat directory.

Okay, ready to download? Right-click on the file called **nc32105** (for Windows 95) or **nc16105** (for Windows 3.1). (Remember, the file name might differ, if Netscape has come out with a new version of Chat since the writing of this book.) Click **Save this Link as**, and use the dialog box that appears, to select the drive and folder in which you want the file stored (the TEMP directory on your hard drive is usually a good place).

Installing Netscape Chat

The file you just downloaded is a self-extracting ZIP file, so before you can install it, you have to unzip (the file, that is). Simply run the Windows Explorer (or File Manager, if you're using Windows 3.1), change to the folder or directory that contains the file you just downloaded, and then double-click on the file. Windows opens a DOS window, showing you the extraction process in action.

After the extraction process is complete, you can close the DOS window. You now have all the necessary Netscape Chat files on your hard drive, including the most important file of all: setup.exe. In the Windows Explorer or File Manager, double-click the **setup** icon or the **Setup.exe** file. This runs the Netscape Chat Installation program. Just follow the on-screen instructions to install the Chat program.

The Netscape Chat Installation program installs Netscape Chat for you.

Follow the on-screen instructions to complete the installation.

When you're done, you should have a Netscape Chat icon on the Windows Start menu (in Windows 95), or (if you're using Windows 3.1) in the Netscape program group. Don't run Netscape Chat just yet. If you try, you'll find yourself with no one to talk to. You first have to connect to an IRC (Internet Relay Chat) server, which you'll do next.

Finding a Chatty Cove

The hardest part about using Chat is finding a place to chat. Most Internet servers don't mind you flipping through Web pages and purloining an occasional file, but they don't like to devote their resources to a bunch of slackers. Because of this, it's tough to find a chat room, and even when you do, it might be gone the next day.

If you're very lucky, your service provider has a chat server, which you can connect to and use. Find out the chat server's URL, and ask if you need to enter a special username and password for access.

When your service provider informs you that he offers no such server, you'll have to hunt for a public chat server. The first place to search is on your service provider's Web server. If your service provider has a technical support area on the Web, you might find a list of public chat servers on one of its Web pages. Because most service providers do not have dedicated chat servers, they try to provide links to servers, so you won't feel cheated.

If you still can't find anything, try grabbing a file called **servers.950301** (or a similar name) from the following FTP site:

ftp://cs-ftp.bu.edu:/irc/support/

This file is a text file that contains a list of IRC servers throughout the world, along with each server's URL, as shown here.

You can acquire a list of chat servers.

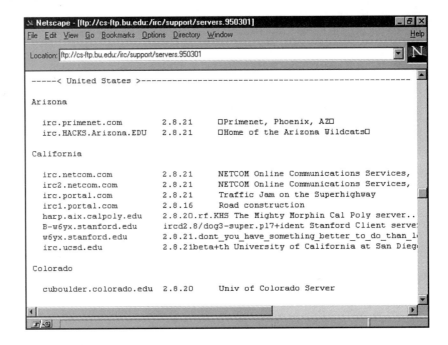

Find More Than One Chat Server Chances are that you'll have to try several chat servers before you find one that actually exists and will let you in. Make sure you have a long list to start with.

If you can't find that file, or the FTP server won't let you in, search for information in the newsgroup alt.irc. A newsgroup is like an electronic bulletin board where you can read and post messages. This particular newsgroup (alt.irc) contains messages about Internet chat. Users commonly post lists of chat servers and their URLs. For details on how to read newsgroup messages, skip ahead to Chapter 20.

Connecting to a Chat Server with Netscape Chat

With your URL list of chat servers in hand, you're ready to connect to a chat server and meet some people. If this is your first attempt at chatting, be prepared for some teasing. You'll be a *newbie*—a novice—a virgin, and seasoned Internet users will seize the opportunity to take an occasional jab at you. Don't let it rattle you; most chatters welcome a new face.

Now that you've been warned, take the following steps to connect to a chat server and start talking:

1. Run your TCP/IP program (in Windows 3.1) or Dial-Up Networking (in Windows 95), and establish your Internet connection.

2. If you're using Windows 95, click the **Start** button, rest the mouse pointer on **Programs**, point to **Netscape Chat**, and then click **Netscape Chat**. In Windows 3.1, open the Netscape program group window, and double-click the **Netscape Chat** icon. The Netscape Chat window appears, and the The Server Connection dialog box is displayed.

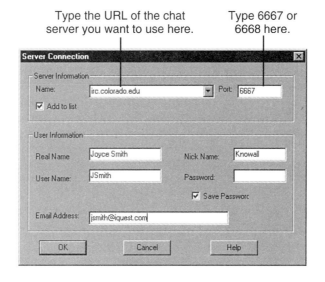

The Server Connection dialog box asks for information about the chat server.

3. Under Server Information, click inside the **Name** text box, and type the URL of the chat server you want to use (for example, irc.colorado.edu).

4. Click inside the **Port** text box, and type the server's port number (usually 6667). If 6667 doesn't connect you, try 6668 or 6669.

5. Make sure **Add to list** has a check mark next to it. This adds the server name to the Name drop-down list, so you won't have to enter all this information again next time.

6. Under User Information, type your full name (for example, Joyce Smith) inside the **Real Name** text box, and type your username (the name you use to sign on) in the **User Name** text box.

   (You don't have to use your *real name*. You can use a made-up name, or enter other information into the Real Name text box, such as, SWF32, for "single, white female, 32-years-old" or type something like "Movie buff.")

7. Click inside the **Nick Name** text box, and type the name you want to use in the chat room (up to nine characters, no spaces). This is the name that will appear on-screen whenever you send a message.

8. If you need a password to connect to a particular chat room, click inside the **Password** text box, and type the password. Make sure **Save Password** has a check mark next to it.

9. Click inside the **Email Address** text box, and type your e-mail address. (You can leave this blank if you don't want anyone to e-mail you.)

10. Click **OK**. If all goes as planned, you are connected to the chat server (**Server Connected** should appear in the status bar). If you see a message saying that the chat server has no DNS entry or won't let you in, click **OK**, and repeat steps 3 to 10 to try connecting to the same or a different chat server. (You might have to click on the **Connect** button, the one with the lightbulb on it, to display the Server Connection dialog box.)

    The Group Conversation dialog box appears, asking you to select a *channel*. Each conversation is carried on a different channel; you have to "tune in" to the channel you want to use.

11. In the list of channels (at the bottom of the dialog box), click on the conversation you'd like to join, and then click **OK**. The conversation window appears. It consists of three panels: a list of users (on the left), a running transcript of the conversation (on the right), and a text box you can use to send your own messages (at the bottom).

12. Click the **Maximize** button to expand the window. You can also drag the pane borders to change the relative sizes of the panes; for example, you might want to increase the width of the column that lists people's names.

13. Read the running transcript of the conversation to find out if it interests you. As other people type messages, they appear on the screens of all those who are involved in the conversation.

Chapter 17 ➤ *Chatting Online with Other Users*

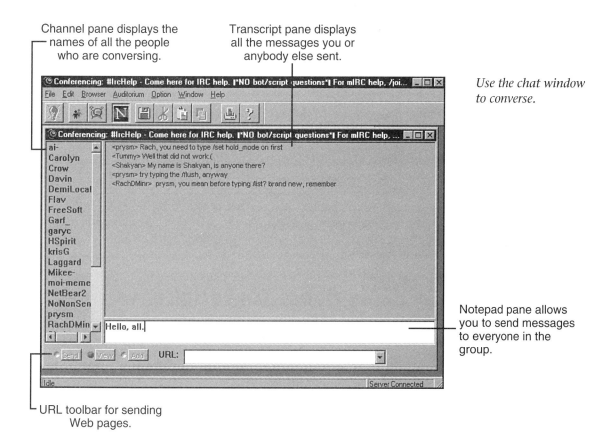

Channel pane displays the names of all the people who are conversing.

Transcript pane displays all the messages you or anybody else sent.

Use the chat window to converse.

Notepad pane allows you to send messages to everyone in the group.

URL toolbar for sending Web pages.

14. If you want to make a statement, click inside the text box directly below the transcript pane, type your statement, and then press **Enter**.

15. To find out about a particular person in the "room," double-click his or her name in the list on the left. The Personal Info dialog box appears, showing the person's real name and (sometimes) the e-mail address. Click the **Close** button when you're done.

16. To leave the conversation, say your good-byes, and then open the **File** menu and select **Exit Conversation**. You remain connected to the chat server. To join a different conversation, open the **File** menu, select **Group Conversation**, and then repeat steps 11–16.

If one discussion starts to lag, you can always leave it and join a different discussion. Or you can stay in that discussion and tune into another channel (in a separate chat window). You can enter up to ten separate discussion groups on the same channel. Simply

183

open the **File** menu, select **Group Conversation**, and then pick the conversation you want to join. You can then use the options on the Window menu to change windows or arrange them on your screen.

Check This Out...

Start Your Own Conversation

The steps here show how to enter an established chat room and start conversing. However, you can create your own chat room, and have people join *your* discussion. In steps 13 and 14, instead of picking a channel from the list, type a unique name for your channel, and click **OK**. You'll be the only one in the room for awhile, but not for long...especially if you added "sex" to your channel name.

More You Should Know About Conversations

Now that you know how to enter group conversations (and leave them), you have all the information you need to chat in groups. However, there are some additional techniques you can try in group conversations:

➤ To change the topic of conversation, open the **File** menu and select **Change Topic**. The Set new topic of conversation dialog box appears. Type a description of the topic, and click **OK**. Some servers will not allow you to change topics without permission, and even if you do change the topic, there's no guarantee that everyone in the discussion will immediately change their messages.

➤ To save a conversation transcript (the running dialog text that appears in the transcript pane), open the **File** menu and select **Save Transcript** (or press **Ctrl+S**). A dialog box appears, prompting you to name the file and select the drive and folder where you want the transcript stored. Enter your preferences, and then click the **Save** button.

➤ To print a transcript, open the **File** menu and select **Print**. (The Print option was unavailable in the beta version of Chat that this book covers.)

➤ To clear the transcript from the window (and start fresh), open the **Edit** menu and select **Clear Transcript**.

Chapter 17 ➤ *Chatting Online with Other Users*

➤ To whisper a message to another person, click his or her name in the list, and then send your message. The message appears only on the other person's screen and on your screen. To turn whispers off, click the person's name again. (You can whisper to more than one person by clicking on each person's name.)

➤ To search for a person on the current chat server, open the **File** menu, and click **Personal Info**. In the dialog box that appears, type the person's nickname in the Nick Name text box, and then click the **Get Info** button. At the bottom of the dialog box is a list of the channels on which the person is speaking.

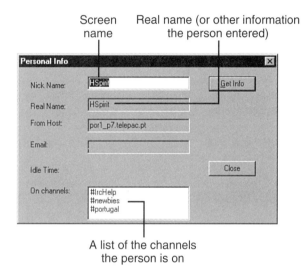

Screen name

Real name (or other information the person entered)

A list of the channels the person is on

If a person is currently logged on, you can find out which channels he or she is on.

Oh yeah, one other thing: Whenever you connect to a channel, that channel is added to a frequent channel list (which is sort of like frequent flyers without the mileage credits). To quickly connect to a channel, first connect to the chat server where you first encountered the channel. Then, open the **Edit** menu and select **Frequent Channels**. Click the desired channel in the list, and click **OK**. You can also use this dialog box to remove channels from the frequent channels list.

Person-to-Person Conversations

If you're looking for privacy, you can enter into a personal conversation with another person. The person must agree to join you, of course, but once he or she does, the two of you will be in your own cozy room, typing clever quips back and forth to one another.

185

- To enter into a private conversation, open the **File** menu, and select **Personal Conversation** (or click the **Personal** button in the toolbar). Type the name of the person with whom you would like to converse, and then click **OK**. This sends a message to the specified person, asking if he or she would like to join you. If the person agrees to join you (by clicking the **Yes** or **OK** button), the two of you are dumped into a private "room." A separate window appears, allowing you to converse. You can still be involved in group conversations as you carry on in private.

Using the Phone Book

Whenever you invite a person to have a personal conversation with you, that person's name is added to the phone book. To invite that person again later, simply connect to your chat server, open the **Edit** menu, and click **Personal Phone Book**. Click the person's nickname, and click **OK**. You can use the Personal Phone Book dialog box to remove names from the phone book, as well.

Joining an Auditorium Discussion

Group conversations are typically free and open. Anyone can join in at any time and say just about anything. However, you can join a more formal discussion group, called an *auditorium discussion*. These discussions feature a moderator and speakers, and may require permission to enter. Only the moderator and speakers talk. You can sit in and "listen" to the discussion, but if you want to talk, you must obtain permission from the moderator.

Auditorium discussions are usually scheduled ahead of time. You might hear about a particular discussion from a friend or colleague or from reading a newsgroup message. The moderator of the discussion may require that you fill out a form beforehand. The moderator will then send you (via e-mail) information about the discussion, including a list of featured speakers, the scheduled time and date, the channel on which the discussion will proceed, and the password you must enter to access the channel.

You follow the same procedure for joining an auditorium discussion as you follow for joining a group discussion. First, connect to the chat server on which the discussion is scheduled to take place. Then, open the **File** menu, and click **Group Conversation**. Use the dialog box that appears to specify the name (channel) of the auditorium discussion, click **Auditorium**, and then click **OK**.

Once you're "tuned in" to the auditorium discussion channel, you can watch the discussion, but you can't talk. If you want to speak, you can ask the moderator for the microphone. To ask permission, open the **Auditorium** menu, and select **Request Microphone**. Type a request to one of the discussion moderators, and press **Enter**. Assuming your request is granted, you can now type messages to the entire group.

If you start an auditorium discussion yourself, or are picked to be a moderator for the discussion, you have the power to grant or refuse microphone requests. Click the name of the person to whom you would like to give the mike, and then open the **Auditorium** menu, and select **Grant Speaker**. To take the microphone away, click the person's name, open the **Auditorium** menu, and select **Revoke Speaker**.

> **You're the Moderator?**
>
> To start your own auditorium discussion, enter the **File/Group Conversation** command, type a unique name for your discussion, click **Auditorium**, and click **OK**. You can then use the commands on the Auditorium menu to appoint and fire other moderators, and grant and revoke speaker requests. Hey, you're in charge.

Sending and Receiving Web Pages

Here's where Netscape Navigator comes in. You may have noticed that whenever you enter a conversation, Netscape Chat attempts to run Navigator, which allows you to send and receive Web pages while you chat.

In Windows 95, you might have a little trouble with this feature, because Chat looks for Navigator in the Netscape folder (not in the Program Files\Netscape\Navigator\Program folder). If you receive an error message indicating that Chat can't find Navigator, open the **Option** menu, and click **Preference**. Click the **Browse** button, and, using the dialog box that appears, pick the drive and folder where Navigator is stored. Click the Netscape file and click **OK**.

If you don't want Netscape Navigator to start automatically whenever you join a discussion, click **Auto Start** to turn it off. Click the **Save** button to save your changes. If you don't click Save, the next time you run Chat, you'll encounter the same problem.

You must tell Chat where Navigator is stored.

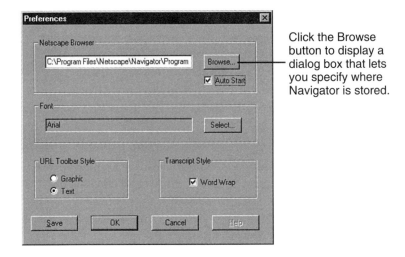

Click the Browse button to display a dialog box that lets you specify where Navigator is stored.

Sending Web Pages to Discussion Participants

Once you have Navigator set up, you can use it in tandem with Chat to send Web pages to other people in the discussion and to receive and view pages they've sent to you. To send one or more Web pages to one or more people in the discussion group, here's what you do:

Swapping GIFs and JPEGs
People love to swap pictures of themselves, so they can picture the person whom they're talking to. Consider creating your own Web page complete with a picture of yourself. You can then quickly send the Web page to anyone in the chat room who has Netscape Chat and Navigator. For details on how to create a Web page, see Chapter 23.

1. Change to Netscape Navigator, and display one of the Web pages you want to send. Whenever you display a Web page in Navigator, the page's URL is automatically inserted into the URL text box in Chat.

2. If you plan on sending more than one Web page, click the **Add to List** button. This adds the URL for the current Web page to a list of pages you want to send. You can repeat steps 1 and 2 to add URLs to the list.

3. In the panel that shows the nicknames of those involved in the discussion, click the name of each person to whom you want to send the Web page(s). To send the page to all the people in the list, make sure that *no* names are selected.

4. Click the **Send** button in the URL toolbar, or open the **Browser** menu and select **Send URL**. The specified Web pages are sent to the selected individuals, who can then view the pages in their Web browser. You can then continue to use Chat to discuss the Web page(s) you sent.

Chapter 17 ➤ *Chatting Online with Other Users*

Receiving and Viewing Web Pages Sent by Others

You can now send Web pages, but what if someone sends a Web page to you. How do you view it? The best way to view incoming Web pages is to turn on the automatic viewing feature. Open the **Browser** menu, and make sure there is a check mark next to Auto View. (The Browser menu is available only if you are currently in a discussion on one or more channels.) If the check mark is missing, click **Auto View** to turn it on.

With Auto View on, the View button in the URL toolbar has a green dot next to it. Now, whenever someone sends you a Web page, Chat opens the Web page in Netscape Navigator. The only trouble is that the Navigator window might be minimized. In Windows 95, use the Taskbar to change to Navigator, and then maximize (or restore) the Navigator window. In Windows 3.1, use **Ctrl+Esc** to display the Task List, and then use the Task List to change to Navigator.

You can continue your discussion in Netscape Chat. Using Chat and Navigator together in this way is especially useful if you're creating a Web page with someone else's help. You can discuss and change the Web page you're creating and immediately see the results of a change.

If Auto View is off, you can still view the page. Simply wait until someone sends you the URL for the page, and the URL appears in the URL text box. Then, click the **View** button. This activates Navigator, which displays the associated Web page.

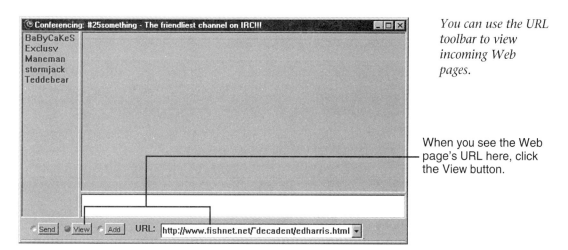

You can use the URL toolbar to view incoming Web pages.

When you see the Web page's URL here, click the View button.

Configuring Netscape Chat

You've probably configured Netscape Chat already. You had to in order to tell Chat where Netscape was located. Well, you can further customize Chat, to turn off the status bar or

189

toolbar, choose the style of text displayed in conversations, or make sure that the Chat window always stays on top of the desktop.

Since you've already dealt with the Preferences dialog box, let's start there. Open the **Option** menu, and click **Preference**. The Preferences dialog box appears. Under Font, click the **Select** button. Use the Font dialog box to select the font, style (bold or italic), and text size you want to use for the text in the transcript pane. Click **OK**. Under URL Toolbar Style, choose **Text** to have words appear on the URL toolbar buttons, or choose **Graphic** to have only pictures appear on the buttons. Click **OK** when you're done.

You can also use the Option menu to turn specific screen elements and other options on or off. Open the **Option** menu, and select any of the following settings to turn them on (if they're off) or off (if they're on):

Always on Top   Keeps the Chat Window on top of all the other windows on the Windows desktop. With this on, your Netscape Navigator window will not automatically jump to the front to display a page, so it's good to keep this off.

Show Toolbar   Turns the toolbar (below the menu bar) on or off. It does not effect the URL toolbar that appears in the conversation window. If you don't use the toolbar buttons, turn this option off, to provide more screen space for your discussion windows.

Advanced Tip #1
For all you hackers out there, here's an advanced tip: Chat still uses the old Windows INI file to configure itself. If you'd like to change something in the program, and you can't do it with the Option menu, open the **nschat.ini** file in Notepad, and enter your changes.

Show Status Bar   Turns the status bar at the bottom of the Chat window on or off. The status bar displays useful messages that tell you when you're connected to the server and when you're able to communicate, so keep this on.

Save Settings   Is not an on/off option. After setting the desired options on the Option menu, click **Save Settings** to make them permanent. (This does not save the settings entered in the Preferences dialog box; you have to use the **Save** button in the dialog box to save your settings.)

The Least You Need To Know

You don't need to know a whole lot about chatting. Once you find a chat server, and tune into a channel, you'll receive plenty of help from the other chatters. Feel free to ask questions and to try out unexplored features with other people. Also, you can find answers to most Chat questions by using Netscape Chat's Help menu. Although it's not the best Help system, it can steer you in the right direction. Happy chatting!

Chapter 18

Gophering from Navigator

By the End of This Chapter, You'll Be Able To...

> Recognize a Gopher menu outside of Navigator.
> Recognize a Gopher menu *inside* Navigator.
> Clutter your disk with even more files.
> Access a Gopher playground to get some practice.

gopher *n.* 1. Any of various short tailed, burrowing mammals of the family Geomyidae, of North America. 2. (Amer. colloq.) Native or inhabitant of Minnesota: the Gopher State. 3. (Amer. colloq.) One who runs errands, does odd jobs, fetches or delivers documents for office staff. 4. (computer tech.) Software following a simple protocol for tunneling through a TCP/IP internet.

—*Copied from the University of Minnesota Gopher site.*

You're chin-deep in the information age; swallowed up by a bottomless pit of facts, files, and data...and you don't know where to start. You need help. You need an automated online tool that can run around and find files for you, an electronic rodent that can tunnel through the Internet and sniff out interesting subject areas and useful resources, a hunter that can track down information on all the various types of Internet servers. You need Gopher.

Gopher is an indexing system that enables you to access various Internet services through menus. Whenever you connect to a Gopher site, it presents you with an opening menu. When you select a menu item, the server presents you with *another* menu containing additional options and/or files. These options may send you off to another Gopher server, an FTP server, a newsgroup, or other Internet servers. You proceed through the menus until you find the file you want…or reach a dead end.

You may already have used Gopher menus through your service provider or by using a Gopher menu program, such as the one shown here. As you can see, the Gopher menus are text-based. In this chapter, you'll learn how Navigator can provide you with a more graphical interface, one that contains links similar to those in a Web document.

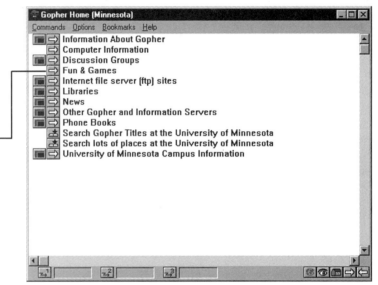

A Windows Gopher program gives the Gopher site a slick look, but it's still text-based.

Click on an option to view the next menu or a list of files. The arrows here indicate that clicking the option displays a menu.

Gopher Guts

Here's how Gopher works: Each Gopher server has a huge index of Internet resources, including the names and locations of thousands of files. You have Gopher menu software that provides a way for you to access the servers' indexes. Whenever you connect to a Gopher server, it sends index information to your menu software, which uses that information to build a menu system. All this goes on behind the scenes. The only things you see are the menu options, which you select to access various Internet resources.

Chapter 18 ➤ *Gophering from Navigator*

Gopher and FTP: What's the Difference?

Before you connect to a Gopher site, I have to warn you: the screen is going to look almost identical to the screens you encountered at FTP sites. The difference is in how the two types of servers function.

When you connect to an FTP server, you're limited to the files stored at that site. Accessing an FTP site is almost like accessing a gigantic hard disk drive. None of the links will kick you out to a different site or help you find resources on another server. You use links only to change directories and download files.

Like FTP servers, most Gopher servers contain files you can download. The similarity ends there. Gopher servers also provide links to other servers on the Internet. For example, you might click on a menu option and find yourself halfway around the world, on a Gopher server or a telnet site in another country. Gophers are designed to give you easy access to *all* Internet resources.

Connecting to a Gopher Site

You may have stumbled into a Gopher hole without realizing it, because some Web documents contain links to Gopher sites. You click on a link, and Navigator takes you to the site. So how can you tell you're at a Gopher site? First, look in the **URL** text box. If the URL starts with **gopher** rather than **http**, you're at a Gopher site. In addition, the Gopher page may have a heading such as **Gopher Menu**, which is a pretty good indication that you're in Gopherland. The third sign is that Gopher sites use menus like the one shown here.

Sure signs that you've reached a Gopher site.

"gopher" appears here.

Gopher Menu title

Gopher menu items

193

If you haven't encountered a Gopher, what are you waiting for? Check out a couple sites, just to see what you're getting yourself into. If you know the Gopher site's URL, type it in the **Location** text box and press **Enter**. For example, to go to the original Gopher, at the University of Minnesota, type the following URL, and press **Enter**:

gopher://gopher.micro.umn.edu

Romping Around in a Gopher Server

There's no trick to getting around in a Gopher server. You simply click on the desired links to follow a trail of menus. Use the Back and Forward buttons to display the previous or next screens, just as you would do with Web documents. The following icons can provide clues as to what the Gopher menu options provide. Note that most of these icons are identical to icons you encounter at FTP sites:

 A directory or folder. It may contain files and additional directories or folders.

 A searchable index. This usually displays a search screen that has a Search text box at the bottom. Type your search instruction in the text box, and press **Enter**. Refer to the following section for details.

 Telnet site. Telnetting allows you to connect to a remote computer and control it from your keyboard. See Chapter 19 for details.

 A text file. Navigator can probably read and display the file.

 A file that Navigator can't read that has no helper application associated to it. The file might be a compressed file or a program file.

 A sound file. If you set up a helper application for sound files, you may be able to play this one.

 A movie file, usually with an MPG extension.

 A graphic, usually with a GIF or JPG extension.

The top-most choice in most gopher menus is **About this Gopher.** Click on this link to find out information about the current Gopher, including general descriptions of what's stored on the Gopher and the types of services it offers. Some Gophers may also have restrictions you should read about before using them. To read this document, click on its link. Navigator loads and displays its text.

Searching Gopherspace with Veronica

Browsing the Internet with Gopher can be fun, but when you need specific information in a hurry, browsing just won't do. You need a way to search out only those Gopher sites that have the information you want. You need Veronica.

With Veronica, you type search strings that tell Veronica what to look for and how many items to find. Veronica searches its huge index of Internet resources and then assembles a menu of servers that match your search string. For example, you can enter a search string to have Veronica find all sites that contain information about IBM and Apple.

The first, and possibly most time-consuming, step in searching with Veronica is to access a Veronica server. What makes this step so difficult is that Veronica servers are in high demand; you may not be able to gain access when you need it most. The easiest way to access Veronica is to connect to a Gopher server that has a Veronica link, and then click on that link.

> **Check This Out...**
>
> **Archie, Veronica, and Jughead**
> The fact that the names **Archie** and **Veronica** stir up images of comic-book characters is no coincidence. Archie (short for "archive") started it all. Veronica, Archie's comic-book girlfriend, followed. There's even a search program called Jughead, which is a limited version of Veronica.

The sites are divided into two groups: one allows you to search all gopherspace, and one searches only for directories. For a quick search that turns up fewer finds, select one of the **Directory Only** options. For a more thorough search, select a **Gopherspace** option. Regardless of which choice you make, Veronica displays a form that allows you to enter your search string.

Click inside the text box, type the words you want to search for, and press **Enter.** For example, type **spanish literature**, and press **Enter.** Veronica looks for all entries that have "spanish" and "literature" in the title, but not necessarily in the order in which you typed the words—Veronica also turns up any occurrences of "literature" and "spanish." Make your search string as specific as possible, and read the following sections to take more control of your searches.

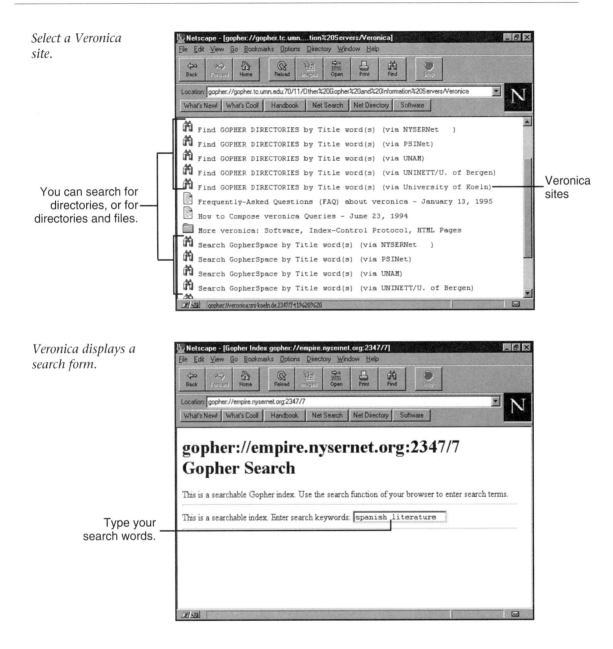

Select a Veronica site.

You can search for directories, or for directories and files.

Veronica sites

Veronica displays a search form.

Type your search words.

Searching with "And," "Or," "Not," and Wild Cards

The preferred search method (mine, anyway) is to keep it simple. Type one to three well-focused words, and press **Enter**. Veronica does, however, allow you to enter more complex search strings by using wild-card entries and link terms called *Boolean* operators.

The only wild-card entry you can use is an asterisk (*), and you can use it only at the end of a word. For example, you can type **book*** to have Veronica find "book," "books," and "bookstore." But if you type b*k, Veronica will void the search, slap your fingers, and tell everyone that you don't know how to type a proper search instruction.

You can also use Boolean operators ("and," "or," and "not") to narrow or broaden a search. The "and" operator is fairly useless. If you type three words as your search string, Veronica automatically inserts "and" between them, so don't bother typing "and." The "or" operator is also pretty useless because it broadens the search, when your primary goal is to *narrow* it. For example, if you type **spanish or literature** as your search string, the search will be too broad to do any good. The "not" operator is somewhat useful for preventing some items from being included in the search. For example, to be politically correct, you could enter **tuna not dolphins**.

To put together some fancy searches, use parentheses to group your search items. For example, if you want to find listings for only Polish and French literature, you might enter **literature (polish or french)**. This is one way to make use of the "or" operator.

Narrowing a Search with Switches

Unless you specify otherwise, Veronica limits the number of items it finds to 200, and searches for all file types. You can use the -m<*number*> and -t<*type*> switches to change these defaults. Simply type the switch before or after your search string.

The -m<*number*> switch tells Veronica the maximum number of items to list. For example, **-m5** tells Veronica to list no more than five items. (Don't type the brackets < and >.) And **-m1000** specifies 1000 items. Use the **-m** switch without a number to have Veronica list all the items it finds, no limit. When typing this switch, make sure there is no space between the **-m** and the number.

The -t<*type*> switch indicates a file type. For example, -t0 finds only text files, -ts finds sound files, and **-tg** finds GIF images. You can combine file-type symbols by typing their codes, without spaces, after the -t. For example, **-t0gs** finds text files, GIF images, *and* sound files. Here's a list of file-type codes:

0	Text File
1	Directory
2	CSO name server
4	Mac HQX file.
5	PC binary
7	Full Text Index (Gopher menu)

8	Telnet Session
9	Binary File
s	Sound
e	Event
I	Image (other than GIF)
M	MIME multipart/mixed message
T	TN3270 Session
c	Calendar (not in 2.06)
g	GIF image
h	HTML, HyperText Markup Language

In addition to these codes, you can include text after the -t switch to limit the search further. For example, type **-ti mac** to find non-GIF images that have "mac" in their titles.

Making Bookmarks for Your Gopher Sites

Once you find a great Gopher site, it's tempting to poke around and get lost in the menu system. You get lost in the play, you sign off, and an hour later you can't remember where you've been. To get back, you have to perform another search, which may not generate the same results. So, before you weave through the menu system, add a bookmark for the gopher site. Open the **Bookmarks** menu and select **Add Bookmark**.

Create a Gopher Submenu Consider creating a separate Gopher submenu on the Bookmarks menu. You can then add the URLs for your favorite Gopher sites to this submenu. Refer to Chapter 11 for details.

Searching a Single Server with Jughead

Veronica is an ambitious search tool. It searches for all Internet resources that match your entry, regardless of whether those resources are stored on the current server or on another, remote server. Jughead is a similar, though less ambitious tool, which searches only for those resources that are stored on the current server.

Most of the time, you'll use Jughead without ever knowing it. You might select a menu item, such as **Search Gopher titles at the University of Minnesota**. You get a search form that looks just like the form you would get through Veronica. The only difference is that instead of searching all Internet resources, the search is restricted to the resources at the current site. Although Jughead allows you to type a search string, your options are limited. You can type only two words, and you can't use the -t<*type*> switch.

Playing and Grabbing Files

The ultimate goal in a Gopher session is to find a file and then play it or save it. You've done the first part; you found a file that looks promising. Now for step two. You can download a file from a Gopher site the same way you download files in FTP. Right-click on the file's link. This opens a dialog box, and you know what to do.

Navigator can display text files without saving them to disk. In addition, if you set up helper applications for specific file types, you can play those files without downloading them. To open a text file or play another file type, click on the file's link, and then wait for Navigator to download and play the file.

The Least You Need to Know

To make this section a bit more interesting, I'm presenting the review material as a list of riddles and questions. The answer for each riddle or question follows it immediately, so don't peek.

- What do you get when you cross a Web document, an FTP site, and a menu?

  Answer: A Gopher.

- If Gopher and FTP had a fight, who would win...why?

  Answer: Gopher, because it contains links to other Internet services, including FTP sites.

- What does the URL for every Gopher site start with?

  Answer: gopher://

- Who rode Washington's white horse?

  Answer: If you said "White," you lose.

- If Veronica and Jughead had a fight on the Internet, who would win and why?

  Answer: Veronica, because she can search for resources stored outside the current server.

- You know about switches and Boolean operators; should you use them?

    Answer: If you're lazy, like me, probably not. You're better off spending your time thinking of two or three specific words.

- To what family of animals does the gopher belong?

    Answer: Geomyidae.

- Extra credit question: True or False—A gopher is also a type of land tortoise found in the southern United States.

    Answer: True. And this tortoise is edible. Yummy.

Chapter 19

Telnetting with Navigator (and a Little Help)

By the End of This Chapter, You'll Be Able To...

➤ Find the helper application you need to telnet from Navigator (and set it up).

➤ Poke around on another person's computer while sitting at your keyboard.

➤ Rattle off a list of ten UNIX commands (and know what they do).

➤ Connect to at least one remote computer...and act as if you know what you're doing.

Occasionally, you'll hear a story on the news about some X-Generation computer hacker who broke into a supposedly secure network to steal some credit card numbers or launch a nuclear missile. Maybe you have your own secret desires to sneak into remote networks, perhaps to steal plans for building a biological weapon or to change your Visa balance.

Well, I hate to break it to you, but this chapter won't teach you how to do any of the cool illegal stuff you hear about. However, I will teach you to log in to computer systems that provide public access, and use those systems to take advantage of resources that are unavailable at Web sites.

The Ins and Outs of Telnetting

Telnetting is short for "networking over the telephone." When you network without the "tel," you type at a *terminal*, which is connected by cable to a huge central computer, which does all the work. When you telnet, you're dialing (with your modem) into this central computer, and using your computer as a terminal.

If you've ever used a computerized card catalog at your local library, you've used a network. You use the terminal to search for books by author or title, to find out which branch library has the book, and to determine the book's status (whether it's in, or when it's due).

Some libraries allow you to dial into their networks. With your computer, a modem, and a basic communications program, you can use your computer as a terminal. Without leaving your home or office, you can dial into the network at the public library and look for books, just as if you were sitting at a terminal in the library. This is telnetting.

Whoa! You Need a Telnet Program First

The concept of telnetting from Navigator brings up all sorts of grand delusions. You might picture Navigator's smooth graphical interface replacing the prompts and texty menus you see on most terminals. Not so.

What telnetting from Navigator really means is that when you click on a link for a telnet site (or enter its URL), Navigator runs a separate program (just like a helper application). You then use *that* program (not Navigator) to do your telnetting. In other words, you still get the crude prompts and texty menus. Sorry, them's the breaks.

Getting a Telnet Program for Cheap

If you already have a telnet program, skip to the next section to learn how to set it up so Navigator can run it (if you have Windows 95, you already have a telnet program). If you don't have a telnet program, you can download a shareware program from an FTP site. Following is a list of good telnet programs you can download. I bet you'd love it if I gave you the locations of these files. Sorry, but I taught you how to fish with Archie in Chapter 13, so use Archie to find a recent copy of the file you want:

> **WinQVT Net** A telnet program for Windows. Search for **WinQVT** or **qvtws**.
>
> **NCSA Telnet** The NCSA telnet program for Windows. Search for **wintelb**. Try either of the following FTP sites:
>
> ftp.ncsa.uiuc.edu

ftp://gatekeeper.dec.com/pub/micro/msdos/win3/winsock/

Trumpet Telnet   Yet another telnet program for Windows. Search for **trmptel**, or try the following FTP site:

ftp://gatekeeper.dec.com/pub/micro/msdos/win3/winsock/

Keep in mind that most of these programs are stored in a compressed format. You'll have to unzip or expand the files after you download them. Also, these are *share*ware programs, the key term being *share*. If you choose to keep the program past the trial period, send a registration fee to the programmer. This prevents them from turning into bitter sociopaths.

Setting Telnet as a Helper Application

Once you unpack (decompress) the telnet program and perform any additional installation steps, you need to set up Navigator to run the program automatically. Open the **Options** menu and select **General Preferences**. Click the **Apps** tab. Click inside the **Telnet Application** field, and type the path and file name of your telnet program (or click the **Browse** button, and use the dialog box to select the drive, folder, and name of the telnet program). If you're using Win QVT NET, the path might look like this:

c:\network\qvt\wnqvtwsk.exe

If you have Windows 95, you have a telnet program in the Windows folder. You can type **c:\Windows\telnet.exe** in the Telnet Application text box, or click the **Browse** button and use the dialog box to select this file.

Running a Telnet Session

Have you ever tried using someone else's computer? You never know what you're going to find. Maybe a menuing system, maybe some fancy graphical interface such as Norton Desktop. Maybe you even get...horror of horrors...a DOS prompt! That's sort of what telnetting is like. You connect to another computer, never sure what you're going to encounter—a texty menu system, a UNIX prompt, or a spiteful warning explaining what will happen to you if you go any further.

In the following sections, you'll get a preview of what you'll meet at many telnet sites, and you'll learn how to manage a telnet session with a vague sense that you know what you're doing.

Part 3 ➤ *Stretching the Web with Navigator*

How Do I Connect?

One sure way you can connect to any Internet site with Navigator is to type the site's URL in the Location text box and press **Enter**. If you don't know of any telnet sites, try the library at Washington University in St. Louis:

telnet://library.wustl.edu

Navigator runs your telnet program, and connects to the specified telnet *host*, the central computer that will be serving you. (In case you're wondering how you fit in, you're the *client*.) If you connected to the server in the example, your screen should look like this.

Telnetting to a library system.

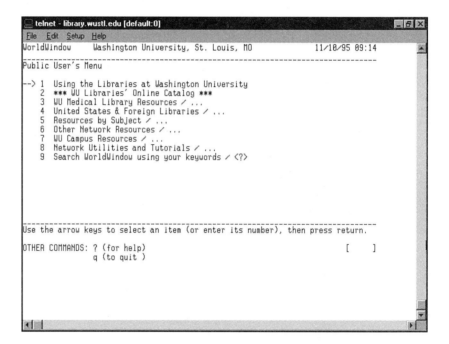

There are other ways to connect to telnet sites through Navigator. You may, for example, stumble upon a link for a telnet site. When you click on the link, Navigator automatically runs your telnet program and connects with the telnet host. You may also encounter links to telnet sites when Gophering from Navigator (see Chapter 18).

Chapter 19 ➤ *Telnetting with Navigator (and a Little Help)*

Funky Hieroglyphics

If you connect to a site, and you get a bunch of characters that look as though they've been scrawled by a possessed Egyptian, you probably picked the wrong terminal type. Change the terminal setting in your telnet program. Most telnet programs have a Terminal or Options menu that lets you change the settings.

I'm Supposed to Know My Terminal Type?

The first thing most telnet sites will ask you is what type of terminal you're emulating (not you, personally, but your computer). If you don't know, just press **Enter** to accept the default setting. Then, if that doesn't work, try to change the setting in your telnet program. Common settings are VT100, VT102, and VT220. Some telnet hosts are very accommodating, as long as you can specify which terminal emulation you're using.

Emulating Terminals

Terminal emulation is a technique used to make one computer act like another so the two computers can carry on a conversation. Some mainframe computers will interact with only a specific type of terminal. If you want to connect to that mainframe computer using your personal computer, you must make your computer act like the required terminal.

Greeting Your Telnet Host

Very few telnet hosts just fling the door open and let you in. Most ask for some sort of identification: an e-mail address, a password, maybe a fake ID. Don't get rattled. Read the entire screen to see if the server allows for anonymous telnet sessions. You may be able to log in as **guest** or **visitor**.

No two hosts will greet you the same way. Some hosts are very formal. They require that you enter your name, address, and phone number, and then type a user ID and provide a password. The next time you log in, the host prompts you to type your user ID and password. Other hosts will kick you out immediately, no questions asked, refusing the connection. And others will let you in, only to warn you that if you continue, you'll be in deep trouble. They never say what kind of trouble, or tell you who's coming to get you, but the vague threat is intended to make you disconnect.

205

What Do I Type?

When you connect with your first telnet site, you have an overall feeling of accomplishment. You start to feel like the greatest computer wizard of the century. Once the glow passes, you go into mild shock as you realize that you've never met anything quite as ugly as the screen that you're staring at right now. What do you type? How do you proceed? And most importantly, how do you get out?

The best general rule I know for proceeding from this point is to read the screens. Most telnet hosts display messages and instructions that lead you through the login process and then tell you what to do to get help or exit. If you see no instructions, try the following keystrokes:

? The question-mark key usually displays a list of telnet commands. If this key doesn't work, try pressing **Ctrl+]** and then pressing the question-mark key.

Ctrl+] Interrupts the telnet session, and usually returns you to the **telnet>** prompt. Use this command if your system locks up and prevents you from entering other telnet commands.

Ctrl+D Quits the current telnet session. This won't work on all telnet hosts.

q or **quit** If Ctrl+D doesn't quit the telnet session, press **Ctrl+]** to return to the **telnet>** prompt, and then type **q**.

close Another way to close the telnet session. Press **Ctrl+]** to return to the **telnet>** prompt, and then enter **close**.

Most public access telnet hosts offer additional command keystrokes, which are usually displayed with a caret (^). For example, the host may display **^Q to Quit**. The caret stands for Ctrl (the Control key). To enter the command, you would hold down the **Ctrl** key while typing **Q**.

If you encounter a menu system, look for instructions on how to use it. Menu systems vary widely. In one, you might type the number that appears next to the desired option. In another menu, you might press the **Tab** key to move from option to option and then press **Enter** to select an option. In other menus, you must type the first few characters of the option's name, and then press **Enter**. There's no consistency from one host to another. Just trust the experience you gained using other systems, and think creatively.

Chapter 19 ➤ *Telnetting with Navigator (and a Little Help)*

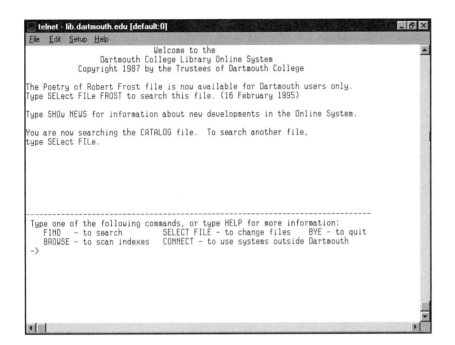

Read the screen for important instructions when you first log on.

HYTELNET, a Directory of Telnet Hosts

One way to tour various telnet hosts is to connect to HYTELNET, a directory of telnet hosts. This telnet host acts as a phone book for other telnet hosts. It contains addresses and login information for hundreds of online library catalogs, bulletin board systems (BBSs), Free-nets (free online systems), and other information resources. To telnet to this site, enter the following URL (in Navigator, not in your Telnet program):

   http://library.usask.ca

This Web page contains links to various telnet sites on the Internet. Click on the links till you find the site you want. For example, you might click on one link for libraries, another for a list of libraries arranged geographically, and another link for libraries in the Americas. Follow the links as you would on any Web site, till you find the link for the telnet site you want to use. The last screen you get should contain the site's domain name and the username you must enter to telnet anonymously.

Part 3 ➤ *Stretching the Web with Navigator*

HYTELNET provides login information for other telnet sites.

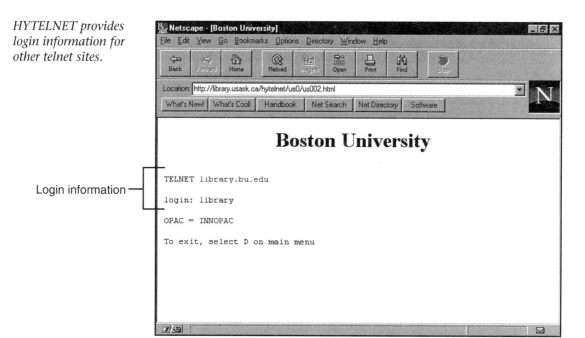

Login information

UNIX Primer

If you do much telnetting, chances are you'll wander into one or more sites that give you nothing but a UNIX prompt. If you have a Mac or use Windows exclusively, getting dumped at a UNIX prompt is like waking up surrounded by a tribe of aborigines. Although I'm not about to teach you how to speak UNIX (or "aboriginese," for that matter), I will teach you enough to survive your first encounter with UNIX.

Repeating a UNIX Command You can repeat the previous UNIX command by typing !! and pressing Enter.

Bare Bone Basics

The first lesson is that all UNIX directories are separated by forward slashes (files/files/Morefiles). Second, capitalization matters: **MYFILE.TXT** is not the same as **myfile.txt** or **MyFile.txt**. So when you're trying to get a file, make sure you type the directory and file names **eXactly** as they appear.

208

Chapter 19 ➤ *Telnetting with Navigator (and a Little Help)*

What's in This Directory, Anyway?

Now, you're at a UNIX prompt, and you want to see what's in the current directory. Type **ls** and press **Enter** to view a *list* of files and directories. Enter **ls -l** if you want more information, including file sizes and types. Enter **ls -m** to pause the file list at the end of each page; you can then view the next page by pressing the **Spacebar**.

Changing Directories

In most cases, you won't need any of the files or information stored in the root directory of the server. You'll want to change to one of the subdirectories. Type **cd** *dirname* (where *dirname* is the name of the directory you want to change to), and press **Enter**. To move back to the previous directory, type **cd ..** and press **Enter**. To find out which directory you're in, type **pwd** and press **Enter**.

Tracking Down Files

If you know the name of the file you're looking for, but you don't know which directory it's in, the UNIX **find** command can help. The **find** command searches the current directory and all its subdirectories for the specified file, so make sure you're in the correct directory, or in the root (topmost) directory, before entering this command.

Type the command as **find . -name** *filename* **-print** (where *filename* is the name of the file you're looking for). Make sure you type the command exactly as shown, and use the proper capitalization in the file name. Press **Enter**. If the file is stored in the current directory, UNIX displays its location as *./filename*. If the file is in a different directory, UNIX shows the location as *./dirname/filename*.

Taking a Peek at a Text File

If you come across a text file you want to read, type **cat** *filename* and press **Enter**. If the text scrolls off the screen, try the **more** *filename* command. With the **more** command, UNIX displays the first page of the text file. Press the **Enter** key to scroll down line by line, or press the **Spacebar** to scroll page by page.

Grabbing a File

You're at a telnet site for one or two reasons: you want to use the programs and other resources at that site, or you want to grab some files. To get a file off a UNIX server, you use the **get** command. Change to the directory that contains the file, type **get** *filename*, and press **Enter**.

209

Running a Program

Most telnet sites greet you with a menu, which pretty much limits your options. However, on the rare occasion you get dumped at a UNIX prompt, you may be able to run a program on the UNIX server. If you type **ls -l**, you see a file list. To the left of the file names are attributes, such as **-rw** or **-rwx**. The **x** stands for executable. Type the name of the program file and press **Enter**. You're on your own when it comes to navigating the program.

Telnetting to an Archie Server

In Chapter 16, you learned how to use an Archie Request form to search for files. Hands down, this is the easiest way to search for files on the Internet. However, it may not be the fastest and most flexible of search tools. If you're daring, you may want to perform your Archie searches from a telnet site. Here's what you do:

1. Click inside the Location text box, type a URL for one of the following Archie servers, and press **Enter**:

    United States:

telnet://archie.internic.net	New Jersey
telnet://archie.unl.edu	Nebraska
telnet://archie.ans.net	New York
telnet://archie.rutgers.edu	New Jersey
telnet://archie.sura.net	Maryland

    Other Countries:

telnet://archie.au	Australia
telnet://archie.cs.mcgill.ca	Canada
telnet://archie.th-darmstadt.de	Germany
telnet://archie.wide.ad.jp	Japan
telnet://archie.switch.ch	Switzerland
telnet://archie.luth.se	Sweden
telnet://archie.doc.ic.ac.uk	United Kingdom

2. Enter **archie** when prompted to type your account name.

Chapter 19 ➤ *Telnetting with Navigator (and a Little Help)*

3. Enter **set pager** to make the display easier to read.

4. Enter one of the following commands to specify the type of search:

   set search sub searches inside file names for the search text and ignores capitalization. This command tells Archie to find all file names that contain the text you enter. So, if you search for wintelb, Archie will find files such as wintelb.zip, wintelb_3.zip, and so on.

   > **Check Out the Locals** When choosing an Archie server, try the closest server listed first. That cuts down on Internet traffic, something every good Net citizen should be concerned with. Also, try accessing the servers during off hours.

   set search exact searches for only those file names that are identical to your search text. In other words, you have to know exactly what you want.

   set search subcase is like **set search sub**, but this command tells Archie to acknowledge capitalization. If you search for MYFILE.TXT, Archie won't look for myfile.txt.

5. Type **find** and follow it with a space and the name (or partial name) of the file you want to search for. Press **Enter**. If you're lucky, Archie displays your position in the search queue (line) and approximately how long the search will take. If you're less fortunate (which is more likely than not), Archie notifies you that it's too busy right now to search for your file. Try another server.

   > **Get Lots of Information** Copy the information for at least five sites. You may not be able to connect to some sites, or the file may no longer be stored at that site.

6. Wait. This could take awhile. When the search is complete, Archie displays a list of the files it found, including the location of the file and the date on which Archie last logged it in.

7. Write down the domain of the server on which each copy of the file is stored, along with any other information you need to locate the file (for example, its complete name and the directory in which it is stored). If your telnet program has a Copy command, it can come in handy here. Copy the information to a text editor or word processor.

8. If there are additional files, press the **Spacebar** to view the next screenful of finds, and then repeat step 7.

9. When you reach the bottom of the list, type **q** to go back to the Archie prompt, then type **logoff** or **quit** and press **Enter**.

After you log off, you can use Navigator to connect to one of the FTP sites you found and then download the file.

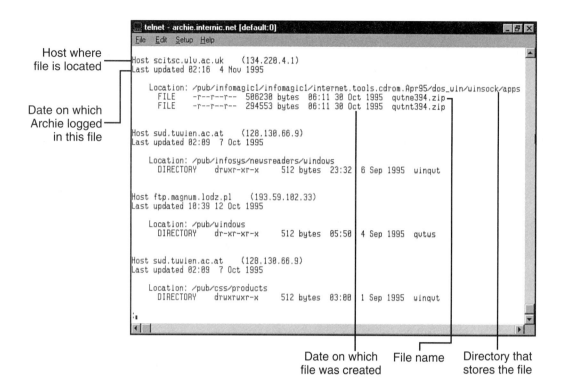

The Least You Need to Know

Okay, so you can't change the balance in your Visa account or launch nuclear warheads from your office, but you now have the power to connect to other computers all over the world. As you start your journey, keep the following in mind:

➤ To telnet from Navigator, you need to install a telnet program, which acts like a helper application.

➤ You can start a telnet session by clicking on the link of a telnet site or by entering its URL.

➤ The URL for all telnet sites starts with **telnet://**

➤ When you connect to a telnet site, specify your terminal emulation and enter a login name.

➤ Most telnet sites display instructions on how to use the system. Read the screens thoroughly.

➤ When in doubt, type **?** to get help or **q** to quit.

Chapter 20

Reading and Posting Newsgroup Messages

By the End of This Chapter, You'll Be Able To...

➤ Tell the difference between a newsgroup and a newspaper.

➤ Have a general idea of what's in a particular newsgroup just by looking at its URL.

➤ Navigate a newsgroup by clicking on links.

➤ Connect to and read messages in at least five newsgroups.

If you've never encountered newsgroups, you might have a somewhat distorted image of what they are. Maybe you think that newsgroups provide up-to-the-minute online news...news on demand. You click a link to get the latest sports scores, click another link to see a national weather map, and click still another link to view CNN Headline News.

That's not quite what Internet newsgroups are all about. A *newsgroup* is more of a discussion group, an electronic bulletin board on which users exchange messages. For example, you might post a message in a body art newsgroup asking for instructions on how to pierce your belly button. Other people will read your messages, and some of those people

USENET Most newsgroups are part of a larger organization called USENET, which is short for *user's network*. USENET sets the standards by which the various newsgroups swap information.

will post responses, telling you just what to do. They might even offer to do it for you!

There are thousands of newsgroups on the Internet, dealing with just about any topic you can think of...everything from Christianity to body art to dog training. In the past, you needed a special program called a newsgroup reader in order to read and post messages. Now, with Netscape Navigator, you can read and post messages directly from your Web browser.

Before You Can Read Newsgroups...

To read messages posted in a newsgroup, you have to tell Navigator which newsgroup server you want to use. Hopefully, your service provider already supplied you with the domain name of its newsgroup server. If you don't have this information, get on the phone to your service provider (yes, again), and find out. Because there are no public newsgroup servers, you have to use your service provider's newsgroup server.

When in Doubt, Guess

If it's 2 a.m., and you can't get ahold of your service provider, guess the domain name of your service provider's news service. You can usually just add "news." to the beginning of your service provider's domain name entry. For example, if the general domain name is iquest.com, the news server address should be news.iquest.com.

Once you have the information you need, open the **Options** menu and select **Mail and News Preferences**. Click the **Servers** tab. Now, click inside the News (NNTP) Server text box, and type the domain name of your service provider's newsgroup server. Don't change the entry in the News RC Directory, unless you have some good reason for changing it. This entry tells Navigator where to store information about the newsgroups you decide to read. Click **OK** to save your changes.

Chapter 20 ➤ Reading and Posting Newsgroup Messages

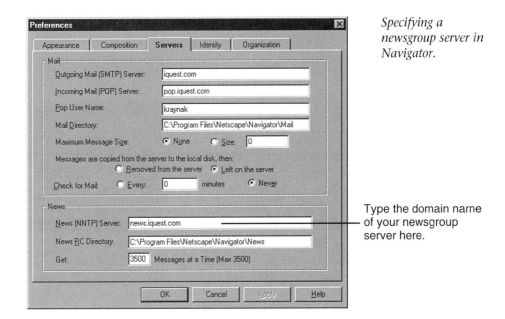

Specifying a newsgroup server in Navigator.

Type the domain name of your newsgroup server here.

Connecting to a Newsgroup

Enough preliminaries. The only way to see how a newsgroup looks in Navigator is to bring one up. You connect to a newsgroup the same way you connect to any server: you can either click a link that points to a newsgroup, or type the newsgroup's URL in the Location text box, and press **Enter**. The URL must start with **news:**. Here are some URLs to try:

> news:alt.ascii-art
>
> news:alt.comedy.british
>
> news:misc.forsale
>
> news:sci.anthropology
>
> news:sci.military

When you connect to a newsgroup, Navigator runs a special newsgroup reader. It's sort of a helper application that's built into Navigator. The newsgroup you chose to connect to is listed on the left, along with a count of new messages and messages you haven't yet read. On the right is a list of the messages that have been posted. To read a message, skip ahead to the "Reading Newsgroup Messages" section later in this chapter.

215

You may not be able to connect to all newsgroups. There are over ten thousand newsgroups, but your service provider may subscribe to only a few thousand. Check with your service provider to find out which newsgroups are available. Your service provider can probably send you a list of newsgroups along with their URLs.

Navigator lists the messages in the specified newsgroup.

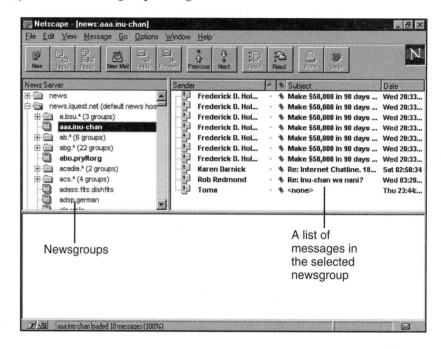

Newsgroups

A list of messages in the selected newsgroup

Dissecting Newsgroup Addresses

Where Did It Go? If you get a message saying that the newsgroup no longer exists, you may have mistyped its URL...or the newsgroup may no longer exist. Also, some less active newsgroups may have no messages. In that case, you'll get a message saying that the newsgroup is empty.

Maybe you noticed the unique format of newsgroup addresses. (Then again, maybe you didn't.) These addresses can tell you a lot about the newsgroup's focus; most are made up of two to three parts.

The first part of the address indicates the newsgroup's overall subject area: **comp** stands for computer, **news** is for general information about newsgroups, **rec** is for recreation (hobbies, sports), **sci** stands for science, **soc** is for social topics, **talk** is for controversial debates, **misc** is for general topics such as jobs and selling, and **alt** is for topics that may offend some people, and...well...you get the idea.

The second part of the address indicates, more specifically, what the newsgroup offers. For example, **comp.ai** is about computers, specifically covering artificial intelligence. If the address has a third part (most do), it focuses even further. For example, **comp.ai.philosophy** discusses how artificial intelligence can be applied to philosophical questions, which is probably a philosophical question in itself. **rec.arts.bodyart** discusses the art of tattoos and other body decorations.

Chain Letters

If you're wondering how the Internet broadcasts messages throughout the world, just think of it as a huge chain-letter system. Whenever someone posts a message in a newsgroup, the message is stored on that person's newsgroup server and is sent out to other newsgroup servers. These newsgroup servers send copies of the message to other newsgroup servers; the process continues until all the participants in the particular newsgroup have received the message. This usually takes no more than a couple of hours.

Searching for Newsgroups

You can make Navigator display a list of all the newsgroups in a specified category. Simply enter the newsgroup category followed by the asterisk. For example, to display all the newsgroups in the sci category, type **news:sci.*** in the Location text box, and press **Enter**. You can narrow the search by adding a subcategory name to your entry. For example, enter **news:sci.space.*** to display the names of all newsgroups that deal with space exploration.

Download a List of Newsgroups

You can download lists of newsgroups from various FTP servers. Try the following site:

ftp://pit-manager.mit.edu/pub/usenet-by-group/news.answers/active-newsgroups

You'll find two files called **Part1** and **Part2**. Assuming you are FTPing from Navigator, right-click one of the files, and use the dialog box that appears to save it as a text file (give it the **.txt** extension). Then repeat the step for the second file. All together, these two files make up a newsgroup address book of about 40 pages!

217

Part 3 ➤ *Stretching the Web with Navigator*

To view the names of all the newsgroups (this can take awhile), type **news:*.*** in the Location text box, and press **Enter**. Or when the newsgroup reader window appears, open the **Options** menu and click **Show All Newsgroups**. A dialog box appears, telling you that this will take some time. Click **OK** to proceed.

Reading Newsgroup Messages

Okay, now that you know all about connecting to newsgroups, you're probably dying to read some messages. Take a gander at Navigator's newsgroup window. It's divided into three panes:

➤ The left pane displays the names of the newsgroups.

➤ The right pane displays the names of messages in the selected newsgroup.

➤ The bottom pane displays the contents of the selected message. (You can change the relative sizes of the panes by dragging the bars that separate them.)

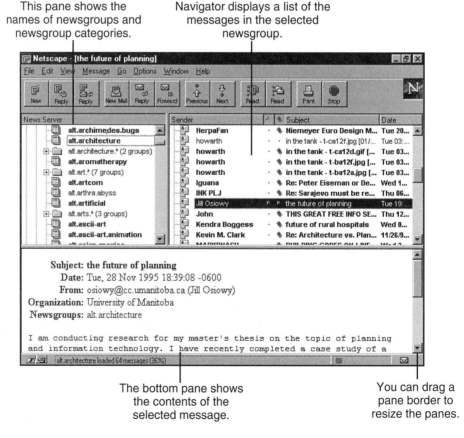

This pane shows the names of newsgroups and newsgroup categories.

Navigator displays a list of the messages in the selected newsgroup.

Navigator's newsgroup window is divided into three panes.

The bottom pane shows the contents of the selected message.

You can drag a pane border to resize the panes.

218

Chapter 20 ➤ Reading and Posting Newsgroup Messages

Let's start with the left pane. If you chose to display all the newsgroups, the contents of the left pane look something like a directory or folder tree, listing newsgroups and newsgroup categories in alphabetical order. Newsgroup categories appear as folders. To open a folder (and display the newsgroups in it), click the folder. The names of the newsgroups in the folder appear. Next to each newsgroup are two numbers, indicating the number of messages in the newsgroup and the number of messages you haven't yet read.

If a newsgroup has no numbers next to it, either your service provider does not recognize the newsgroup or the newsgroup is empty. In either case, don't waste your time with these newsgroups. When you see a newsgroup in which you are interested (and one that has some messages in it), double-click its name. Navigator retrieves the message descriptions and displays the names of the messages in the right pane.

Speaking of the right pane, it does not simply display a list of messages in chronological order. It displays messages as ongoing conversations. The first message in a topic of conversation is listed first. If another person responded to the first message, the response is indented from the topmost message, to indicate that it is related. This method of displaying messages in called *threading* and is designed to make newsgroup discussions easy to follow.

To read a message, double-click the name of the message in the right pane. This displays the message contents in the pane at the bottom of the window. The contents may be a text file or a graphic, and it may take Navigator some time to decode the message, so the information can be displayed. You can continue to read messages by double-clicking their names. Or you can use the options on the **Go** menu to move from message to message:

Next Message displays the contents of the next message. (Or click the **Next** button in the toolbar.)

Previous Message displays the contents of the previous message in the list. (Or click on the **Previous** button in the toolbar.)

First Unread displays the contents of the first message that you haven't read in the newsgroup.

Next Unread displays the contents of the next message that you haven't read in the newsgroup.

Previous Unread displays the contents of any previous message that you haven't read.

You can also search for newsgroups or messages. To search for a newsgroup, click inside the pane that displays the newsgroup names, and then open the **Edit** menu and select **Find**. Type the name of the newsgroup, and then press **Enter**. To search for a message in a newsgroup, click inside the pane that lists the message titles, and then open the **Edit** menu and select **Find**. Type one or two words that might appear inside the message description you're looking for, and press **Enter**.

> **Check This Out...**
>
> **Sorting Messages**
>
> Netscape News can sort the newsgroup messages by date, subject, or sender. Open the **View** menu, click **Sort**, and select the desired sorting option. Be sure to keep the **Thread Messages** option on, so you can easily see which messages belong to a separate discussion.

Replying to Newsgroup Messages

Before you post messages to a newsgroup, familiarize yourself with the newsgroup. Hang out, and read existing messages to obtain a clear idea of the focus and tone of the newsgroup. Reading messages without posting your own messages is known as *lurking*. Newsgroups encourage lurking, because it provides you with the knowledge you need to respond intelligently and to avoid repeating what was already said.

If you read a message and decide to respond, make sure the message is selected, and then open the **Message** menu and select one of the Reply options: **Post Reply** (to post a response in the newsgroup, where everyone can read it), **Mail Reply** (to respond to the person privately with an e-mail message), or **Post and Mail Reply** (to reply privately with e-mail and post the message in the newsgroup).

If you select **Post Reply**, Navigator displays the dialog box shown here, allowing you to type your response. Notice that the From, Newsgroups, and Subject text boxes are already filled in for you. Don't change any of this information. Simply type your response in the large text box at the bottom of the dialog box, and click the **Send** button. Your reply is then posted to the newsgroup, where everyone can open and read it.

> **Check This Out...**
>
> **Newsgroup Etiquette**
>
> To avoid getting verbally battered in a newsgroup, follow a few simple rules. Don't insult any person or attack any topic of conversation. Post messages that pertain to the newsgroup and topic of conversation (read the entire conversation before adding your own two cents). And don't advertise in a newsgroup unless the newsgroup is especially designed for advertising. Oh yeah—DON'T SHOUT by using all capital letters in your message.

Chapter 20 ➤ *Reading and Posting Newsgroup Messages*

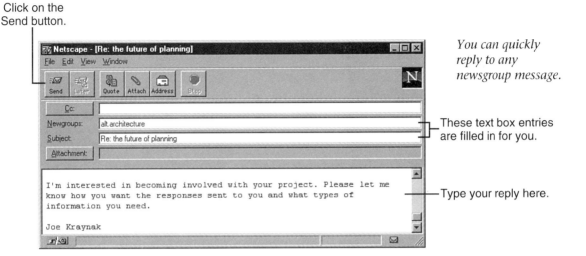

Click on the Send button.

You can quickly reply to any newsgroup message.

These text box entries are filled in for you.

Type your reply here.

Starting a New Discussion

As you gain experience in a particular newsgroup, you might decide to venture out and start your own conversation. For example, if you're into hot rods, and you need a bumper for your '64 Corvette, you might want to post a message asking if anyone knows where you can find the bumper.

To start a conversation, first activate the newsgroup in which you want to post your message. Then, open the **File** menu and select **New News Message**. The dialog box that appears is very similar to the dialog box you use to reply to messages, except in this dialog box, the Subject text box is blank. Click inside the Subject text box, and type a description for your message.

Now, click inside the big text box at the bottom of the dialog box, and type your message. When you're done typing, click the **Send** button. Your message is posted in the active newsgroup. You can now check the newsgroup on a regular basis, to see if anyone has replied to your message. And don't be surprised if you receive replies via e-mail!

Receiving and Sending Files in Newsgroups

What's cool about newsgroups is that they allow you to trade files (in addition to text messages) with other newsgroup members. The only trouble is that these files are usually encoded, so they can be transferred over the phone lines. Whenever you send a file, the file has to be encoded, and whenever you receive a file, you have to decode it before you can open or use it. Fortunately, Netscape News can handle the coding and decoding for you.

In most cases, when you come across a file that has been uploaded to a newsgroup by another user, the file is usually in numbered parts. You'll see a list of messages something like...

> **dog.gif (0/4)**
>
> **dog.gif (1/4)**
>
> **dog.gif (2/4)**
>
> **dog.gif (3/4)**

The first part of the message, dog.gif (0/4) usually contains a brief description of the file. The remaining parts of the message contain the coded version of the file that was uploaded. If you click the dog.gif (1/4) message, Netscape News grabs all parts of the file, decodes them, and displays the file (in this case, a graphic file) in the message area.

Other times, you'll see a link for the file in the message area (at the bottom of the screen). If you click on the link, and Netscape News or one of your helper applications can play the file, Netscape News automatically downloads the file and plays it. If News or one of your helper applications cannot play the file, a dialog box appears, allowing you to save the file to your hard disk.

You can also send a file along with the message you post. In the dialog box you use for posting your message or reply, click the **Attach** button. Use the dialog box that appears, to select the document or file you want to send, and then click the **Attach** button.

The Least You Need to Know

You've just read one of the shortest chapters in the book...and you want less?! Okay, here goes:

- ➤ Newsgroups are discussion groups.
- ➤ To connect to a newsgroup, type the group's URL in the Location text box, and press **Enter**.
- ➤ Navigator lists the messages in a newsgroup from newest to oldest and threads messages on a specific subject to keep them together.
- ➤ To see a list of messages in a newsgroup, double-click the newsgroup's name in the left pane of the Netscape News window.
- ➤ To read a message, double-click its name in the right pane of the Netscape News window.
- ➤ To reply to a message, first open the message you want to reply to, and then open the **Message** menu and click **Post Reply**.

Chapter 21

Other WAIS of Finding Information

By the End of This Chapter, You'll Be Able To...

➤ Pronounce the acronym WAIS (and define it).

➤ Find articles on everything from rock climbing to nuclear physics.

➤ Connect to some services that have merged WAIS and the Web.

➤ Find a couple of back doors to WAIS servers.

If you're independently wealthy, you have all sorts of time to wander the Web and happen upon intriguing sites. But most of us have work to do. We need to find specific information or research a particular topic. And we don't have time to follow a trail of links that might lead to fruitless pages. We need WAIS.

WAIS (pronounced "ways") stands for *Wide Area Information Server*. WAIS is a system that allows you to search various databases on the Internet for specific articles and other resources. For example, you might connect to a WAIS server and find a list of 500 or more databases for everything from stocks to cooking. You pick the database you want to search, and type your subject title or other unique search text. WAIS finds the articles and other resources that match your entry and lets you know where you can find them. In most cases, you can even view the articles immediately.

Cheating Your Way to WAIS

Navigator has a very convoluted way of connecting to a WAIS server and performing a search. We'll save that for later, so you'll have something to do if you get snowed in this winter. For now, we'll look at some easier methods of performing WAIS searches. You see, some companies on the Internet have established Web pages that take care of all the WAIS mumbo jumbo behind the scenes. You simply open the WAIS search form, enter the topic you want to search for, click the **Start Search** button, and wait for a list of articles to pop up on your screen.

One service that offers these WAIS search forms is the EINet Galaxy. This service provides a search tool that spans several Internet sources, including WAIS, Gopher, and Telnet. To access this service, type the following URL in the Location text box, and press **Enter**:

http://www.einet.net

Galaxy provides you with a list of subject areas. You can search by clicking the links in these subject areas, or by scrolling down to the bottom of the page and entering your search instructions. If you choose to enter search instructions, Galaxy searches its online databases to find the resources that match your instructions. You can then click a link for the desired item.

EINet Galaxy offers some powerful search tools.

...or enter search instructions here.

Click a link...

Chapter 21 ➤ *Other WAIS of Finding Information*

Another service, which provides a more standard connection to WAIS, is WAIS, Inc. To connect to the WAIS, Inc. server, enter the following URL:

http://wais.com

This opens the WAIS, Inc. home page. Scroll down the page, click inside the Find text box, and type the word or words you want to search for. Open the ___ **titles** drop-down list, and select the maximum number of articles you want the WAIS search to find. Click the **Search** button to start the search.

Assuming WAIS finds some articles that match your search instructions, it displays links for the articles. You can then click a link.

WAIS finds a list of articles that match your search instructions.

Articles that the WAIS search found

Click on a link to read the article.

Okay, here are a couple more sites you might try. Type one of the following URLs in the Location text box, and press **Enter**:

http://www.ai.mit.edu/the-net/wais.html
http://www.ecrc.gmu.edu/title.html

225

Composing Your Search Instructions

WAIS searches differ slightly from other searches you may have performed. For one, if you enter two words as your search text, WAIS finds all articles that contain both terms. For example, if you search a pet database for "dog training," WAIS finds all articles that contain "dog" and "training," although the two words do not have to be next to each other.

Secondly, the databases may mark common words as *stop words*, and refuse to search for such words. For example, most databases don't allow common words including "the" and "an." A computer database may not allow you to search for "software" or "computer." Stop words allow you to compose searches in plain English. For example, you might type a search instruction, such as "Find me the passing records for college quarterbacks in 1967." The database will ignore the stop words, such as "find," "me," and "the," and search for the words "college," "quarterbacks," and "1967."

Some databases, such as WAIS.COM, allow you to control the search by using the following operators:

> **AND** tells the search tool to search the database for all articles that have *both* of the specified terms. For example, if you're searching for articles about violent crimes in Chicago, you would type **violent AND crimes AND Chicago**. This would ensure that you didn't get articles about nonviolent crimes in Chicago or about crimes in New York. (Some search tools assume that you want a list of articles that contain either of the search terms you enter.)

> **OR** broadens the search. For example, if you're researching tropical storms in the Eastern and Western hemispheres, you might search for **hurricane OR typhoon**.

> **NOT** prevents the search tool from finding any articles that contain specific text. For example, if you're searching for articles about high-school and professional baseball, but not college baseball, you might search for **baseball NOT college**.

> **ADJ** makes sure two search words are next to each other in the article. For example, if you're searching for articles about fly fishing, you would search for **fly ADJ fishing**. This would omit any articles that talk about fishing with flies or getting bitten by flies while fishing.

> **()** allows you to group search terms and expressions. If you're looking for articles about violent crimes in Chicago and San Francisco, you might enter (violent ADJ crimes) AND (Chicago OR San ADJ Francisco).

> ***** allows you to search for partial words, to broaden a search. For example, you might search for **psych*** to find articles about psychology, psychologists, and psychoanalysts.

Now for the Complicated Stuff

STOP! Go back! Don't read any further! The remainder of this chapter provides overly complicated instructions about the overly complex process of using Navigator to access WAIS through a *proxy WAIS server* or *gateway*, a special connection that allows two incompatible networks (the Web and WAIS in this case) to communicate.

Because so many organizations have developed easier methods for performing WAIS searches, there's no reason to use this method to do your research. I'm providing these instructions only for the masochists and overly curious individuals who are reading this book.

Choosing a WAIS Proxy or Gateway

Because Navigator cannot deal directly with WAIS, you have to set up Navigator to use a WAIS gateway or proxy. NCSA and CERN (two organizations that have been central in building the World Wide Web) offer such gateways, though neither provides reliable access, because so many people want to use them. In addition, your service provider may have a private WAIS server that you can use (call to find out). If you don't have access to a private WAIS gateway, here are the URLs of some public gateways you can try:

> www.w3.org at port **8001**
>
> info.cern.ch at port **8001**
>
> www.ncsa.uiuc.edu at port **8001**
>
> nxoc01.cern.ch at port **8001**

To set up a gateway for Navigator, open Navigator's **Options** menu, and click **Network Preferences**. Click the **Proxies** tab, and then click the **View** button next to Manual Proxy Configuration. Click inside the WAIS text box. Type the gateway's URL, press **Tab**, and type the gateway's port number (8001) in the Port text box. Click **OK** to save your change and return to the Preferences dialog box; then click **OK** in the Preferences dialog box.

> **Check This Out...**
>
> **Gateway Is Busy** Don't count on gaining access to the first gateway you try. Gateways are usually busy, and they won't let you in when there's a lot of Internet traffic.

Performing a WAIS Search

Once you set up Navigator to use the WAIS gateway, you can start searching WAIS databases. Because this is so complicated, let me tell you beforehand what you're about to do. First, you'll connect with Navigator (through the WAIS gateway) to a WAIS server, where you'll be asked to specify what you're looking for. When you specify your search topic, the WAIS server will display a list of databases that might have what you need. You then enter the URL of one of the databases, and enter your search topic (yes, again). This gives you a list of articles that (hopefully) has the answers you're looking for.

All this is very tough to visualize when you haven't tried doing it. I just want you to know that the process is pretty weird; it's not as simple as clicking links and typing search topics. Okay, now that you've been warned, take the following steps to perform an actual search:

1. Type one of the following URLs in the URL text box, and press **Enter**:

   wais://quake.think.com/directory-of-servers
   wais://ftp.wais.com/directory-of-servers
   wais://sunsite.unc.edu/directory-of-servers

   This brings up a form that allows you to search for databases that might have articles that contain the information you're looking for.

2. Click inside the Search Index text box, and type the words you want to look for; for example, you might type **classical music**.

3. Press **Enter**. Navigator displays a list of databases that contain your search text. The links point to files that end in .SRC (which stands for "source"), and which Navigator can't open, but click the link anyway to display the Unknown File Type dialog box.

4. Click the **Configurer Viewer** button, and in the dialog box that appears, set up WordPad or Write as the viewer for this file type. (Write is in your WINDOWS directory. WordPad is in the Program Files/Accessories folder.)

   (This is weird, isn't it? The trouble is that the links you see point to files, not to URLs for the databases you might want to search. In this step, and the next step, you'll open the file, to find the URL of the database you want to search.)

5. Click **OK**. Windows runs Write or WordPad (in Windows 95) and opens the selected source file. This file contains the IP name of the WAIS server you want to search, along with the name of the specific database.

6. Write down the IP name of the WAIS server, its port number (if any), and the name of the database *exactly* as it appears.

Chapter 21 ➤ *Other WAIS of Finding Information*

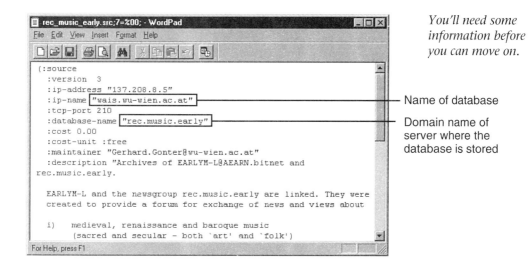

You'll need some information before you can move on.

Name of database

Domain name of server where the database is stored

7. Switch back to Navigator, click inside the Location text box, and type **wais://** followed by the IP name of the WAIS server, followed by the name of the database. For example, if you used the information from the previous figure, you would type the following:

   wais://wais.wu-wien.ac.at/rec.music.early

8. Press **Enter**. A form appears, allowing you to search the specified database.

9. Click inside the search text box, type the words you want to search for, and press **Enter**. Assuming all goes according to plan, a list of articles that match your search instructions should appear.

Tip: Instead of writing down the IP and database names and then typing them, consider cutting and pasting them from the source file into the Location text box. Just remember to type **wais://** at the beginning, and to separate the IP name and the database name with a forward slash.

Did You Score?

Most WAIS lists contain a **score** and a number of **hits**. The number of hits indicates how many times the search word occurs in the article. The scores listed are relative. The topmost file has a score of 1,000, indicating that it contained the most hits. Subsequent scores indicate the relative number of hits compared to the topmost document. So a score of 500 would mean that the article had half as many hits as the topmost article.

229

Part 3 ➤ *Stretching the Web with Navigator*

WAIS finds articles that match your search instructions.

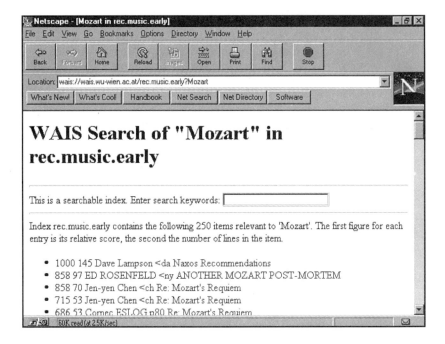

The Least You Need to Know

By now, your head should be spinning with all the options presented in this chapter. To get over the spins, grab onto a sturdy piece of furniture, and read the following list:

➤ Pick one of the WAIS methods described in this chapter and stick with it.

➤ The easiest way to WAIS is to use a server that has bridged the WAIS/Web chasm:

http://www.einet.net

or

http://wais.com

➤ To WAIS from Navigator, open the **Options** menu, select **Network**, click the **Proxies** tab. Enter the URL and port number for the WAIS gateway you want to use.

Chapter 21 ➤ *Other WAIS of Finding Information*

➤ To search for a list of databases, try the following URL:

   wais://quake.think.com/directory-of-servers?

➤ To WAIS through Gopher, connect to one of the following Gopher sites:

   gopher://gopher-gw.micro.umn.edu

   or

   gopher://launchpad.unc.edu

Chapter 22

Finding People on the Internet

By the End of this Chapter, You'll Be Able To...

- ➤ List three ways to search for people on the Internet.
- ➤ Understand why it is so difficult to find someone on the Internet.
- ➤ View a list of users at a given site.
- ➤ Find a person's e-mail address by searching for his name.

If you've ever used CompuServe, Prodigy, or America Online, you know how easy it is to find a member. You enter the command to look for a member, and then you enter the member's real name or screen name. Seconds after you give your okay, a list pops up, showing you the names of all the people who fit your description. With such power, it's easy to find friends and long lost relatives...assuming they're using the same online service.

Because the Internet consists of a loose collection of other computers, there's no master list of the millions of users who sign on. At best, each network within the Internet has a list of users at that site. In other words, you have to know where a person hangs out if you're going to have any chance of finding that person.

And that's not the only problem. Some sites don't allow you to view their lists of users. They consider such information confidential. Other sites allow their users to decide whether or not they want to make their e-mail addresses and other information publicly accessible. And even when this information is available, it may only provide a list of login names and e-mail addresses, names that may not exactly match the names as you would normally search for them. In short, as you work through this chapter, don't get your hopes up.

Fingering Your Friends

The best way to find people on the Internet is to search for them by e-mail address, using a program called *Finger*. Finger pokes around through the directory of users, and finds information about the person you're looking for. This info includes the person's e-mail address, and whether or not that person has read her mail recently (or even logged in).

If you've been paying attention, you're probably wondering, "What's the point? If you have to have a person's e-mail address to find the person, why not just send the person an e-mail message?" Admittedly, Finger isn't the best tool for tracking down lost contacts.

The most useful aspect of Finger is that it allows you to check on mail you may have sent to that person. If you finger the person and find out that they've never logged on or checked their mail, it's a good sign that you may need to call the person instead. In addition, Finger may dredge up the person's address or phone number, so you can contact the person if your e-mail isn't getting through.

To finger from Navigator, simply enter the URL of the finger gateway you want to use. (Remember from Chapter 21 that a gateway is a bridge between two noncompatible computer networks.) Type one of the following URLs in the Location text box, and press **Enter**:

http://www.nova.edu/Inter-Links/cgi-bin/finger.pl

http://www.cs.indiana.edu/finger/gateway

In moments, Navigator displays a page with a text box on it. Click inside the text box and type the e-mail address of the person you're looking for (for example, type jsmith@iquest.net). Press **Enter**. Assuming that Finger can find any information about the e-mail address you entered, Finger displays the information.

Chapter 22 ➤ *Finding People on the Internet*

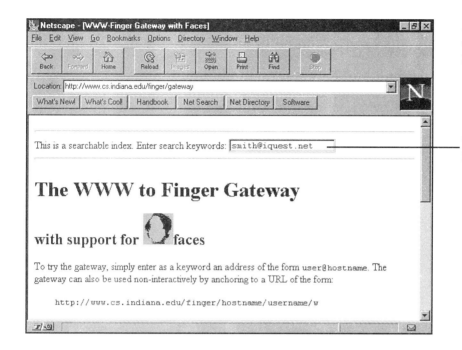

Indiana University can help you finger friends and relatives.

Type your search instruction here.

Other Things You Can Finger

Although Finger isn't the ideal tool for tracking down people, it does offer some interesting peripheral uses. For example, some users include something called a *plan* that appears when you finger that person. A plan is actually a hidden UNIX text file that can include additional information, including the person's address and phone number, job qualifications, interests, or anything else the user wants to include. When you finger someone, look at the bottom of the information screen. If the person has no plan, you'll see No Plan. If the person has a plan, you'll see Plan: followed by the plan text.

> **Check This Out...**
>
> **Draw Up Your Own .Plan** For instructions on how to create and attach your own .plan files, buy *The Complete Idiot's Next Step with the Internet.*

In addition, people commonly use Finger files (no relation to finger food) to distribute information on the Internet. These files may contain the latest earthquake information for various regions, area weather forecasts, football scores, NASA news, and anything else that'll fit in a text file. To see for yourself, connect to the Finger Gateway, as explained in the previous section, and search for the following:

    quake@fm.gi.alaska.edu   nfl@spam.wicat.com

    weather@indiana.edu   drink@csh.rit.edu

Whois This Person?

If you can't finger the person you want, you might be able to find the person using Whois. *Whois* is just another UNIX search command that is customarily used locally. Whois is particularly useful for finding a person's phone number and e-mail address if you know the person's last name. For example, if you know an employee at Bell Laboratories, you may be able to get that person's phone number by using Whois.

To use Whois from Navigator, you have to work through a Whois gateway. Click inside the Location text box, and enter the following URL:

gopher://sipb.mit.edu:70

This connects you to the Gopher server at MIT. Now, click on **Internet Whois Servers**. This displays a list of publicly accessible sites that allow Whois searches. Click the desired site to display a search form. Then click inside the Search Index text box.

Type the name or partial name of the person you're looking for. Use only one name; if you're looking for Bill Clinton, type **Bill** or **Clinton**, but not **Bill Clinton**. If you're searching for a name, and you can't remember how it's spelled, type a portion of the name followed by a period. For example, if you can't remember how to spell Olieskieviezc, type **Olie.** and press **Enter**. You should get a list of all the names that matched your entry.

You're not done yet. In some cases, a Whois search displays the person's *handle*, the user's computerized nickname. You can usually get more details about a person by searching again, this time using the person's handle.

Repeat the search using the person's handle.

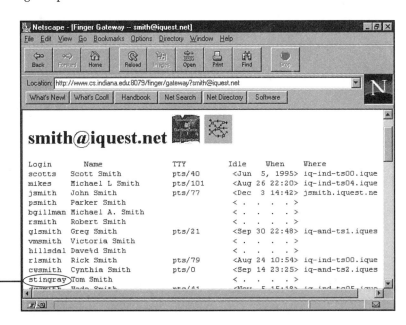

Person's handle

Other Tools and Services for Finding Lost Souls

Finger and Whois are the standard Internet tools you use to search for people, but new tools are constantly being developed. To try some of the more experimental tools, connect to the following site, and click a link for one of these tools:

http://www.nova.edu/Inter-Links/phone.html

This site also contains links to Finger and Whois, and telephone directories of several organizations.

If your husband just cleaned out your savings account and flew off to some exotic land with mistress in tow, Finger and Whois probably won't help you track him down. For that, you need a professional service…and the Internet has links for those services, as well:

http://www.cache.net/finders/

http://rmc.net/finders-seekers

When All Else Fails, Write the Postmaster

You've tried Finger. You've done Whois. No luck. Your only option at this point is to try the postmaster at the Internet site where you think you're friend hangs out. Fire up your e-mail program, and send a message to *postmaster@hostname*, inquiring as to the whereabouts of your friend or colleague. (In place of *hostname*, type the domain name of the server that the person uses—for example, compuserve.com). Be sure to tell the postmaster why you are looking for this person. You might also include your e-mail address and phone number. The postmaster may have a policy of not releasing information about members, but will gladly pass along any information about how to contact you.

The Least You Need to Know

Now that you know how to search for people, you can look up all your old college buddies, at least the ones who decided to stick around for their graduate degrees. Here are some things to keep in mind as you search:

- ➤ To use Finger or Whois, you have to go through a gateway.
- ➤ The URL for one of the Finger gateways is

    http://www.cs.indiana.edu/finger/gateway

- The URL for a Whois gateway is

  gopher://sipb.mit.edu:70

- To do a Finger search, enter your search text in the form

  person@hostname

- To do a Whois search, enter the person's first name or last name, or enter a partial name followed by a period.

- If you can't find someone with Whois or Finger, try writing the postmaster at **postmaster@hostname.**

- If you still can't find someone, hang the person's photo in the post office.

Chapter 23

Forging Your Own Hyperdocuments

By the End of This Chapter, You'll Be Able To...
- ➤ Create your very own hyperdocuments.
- ➤ Give your home page a professional look.
- ➤ Nab someone else's home page and use it as your own.
- ➤ Add graphics and sounds to your home page.

Now that you're a bona fide Web spider, you can snare just about any page that might fly into your web. You can track down any information you need, and pull it up on your screen in a matter of seconds. But now you want more. You want to start giving back a little of what you've been taking…or you at least want to make your creative presence know on the Web. How do you create your own Web page? And how do you use it to your benefit?

In this chapter, you'll learn how to use the codes that transform a simple text document into a Web page. And, you'll learn how to use your Web page to save loads of time on the Web.

Crafting a Simple Home Page

To make hyperdocuments, you use a coding system called *HTML* (HyperText Markup Language). Don't worry, I'm not going to slap a bunch of codes at you in a vain attempt to impress you with the complexity of HTML. Instead, I'll teach you how to make a simple document using just five HTML codes. If I use any more, you can call me for a complete refund. My number is (555) NOT-HERE.

Cheat a Little
If you have bookmarks for all your favorite places, start with your Bookmark.htm file. Open Bookmark.htm in Notepad, and use the **File/Save As** command to clone the file under another name. Then, edit the file to change the title of the page, and enter any other changes.

First, run your favorite text editor or word processing program. You need a program that lets you save *plain* (ASCII) *text* files. Windows Notepad will do (turn on Word Wrap by opening the **Edit** menu and selecting **Word Wrap**). You don't want any fancy formatting codes that can confuse Navigator. Open an empty window for a text file. You'll type a series of lines in this text file to create your document.

The first line in your home page should be the document's title. Now, you'd think a title would appear at the top of your document. It doesn't. It appears only in the Navigator title bar when you open the document. Although this doesn't do you much good, you still need a title line, so model yours on the following sample:

<title>Peeble's Home Page</title>

Note that the title is sandwiched between two codes. The first code turns the title on, and the second one turns it off. Most (but not all) HTML codes are paired like this. Also, the codes can be uppercase or lowercase; it doesn't matter.

Tagged Ya!
HTML codes are often referred to as *tags*. Tags can control the look of text (as in titles and headings), insert anchors that link this document to other documents, and control character formatting (by making it bold or italic).

Since the title won't appear at the top of your page, you need something that *will* appear: a top-level heading. You can use the same text you used for the title, or you can use something more unique. Wedge this text between two heading codes: <h1> and </h1>. Here's a sample:

<h1>Peeble's Points of Interest</h1>

In case you're wondering, HTML lets you use up to six heading levels: h1 to h6. Think of h1 as a chapter title, h2 as major heading levels, and h3 as minor heading levels. If you get down to h6, your page is too long, you're too ambitious, and you probably need some counseling.

Now, divide the page into two or three sections with level 2 headings. For example, say you have a bunch of URLs you want to include on your home page. You can use level-2 headings to divide your links into logical groups. The following headings divide the page into four groups:

```
<h2>Hairy Tunes</h2>
<h2>Fun Stuff</h2>
<h2>News Centers</h2>
<h2>Philosophical Rags</h2>
```

Finally, add links for all your favorite URLs. This is the hard part. You use what are called *anchor codes* to insert two items in the document: a URL and link text. The URL remains invisible; it simply tells Navigator which document to load when you click the link. The *link text* is the actual word or phrase that appears in your document (link text is usually blue and underlined). Here's a sample anchor code to get you started:

```
<a href="http://www.yahoo.com">Yahoo's Starting Points</a>
```

In this example, **<a href=>** is the code that tells the link where the Web page is located. The URL is **http://www.yahoo.com** (it must be surrounded by quotation marks and be embedded inside the <a href=> code). The link text (which will appear in the document) is **Yahoo's Starting Points**. And the **</a>** represents the end of this command line. Add each link on a line of its own, and add a **<p>** (*paragraph*) code at the end of each line. The **<p>** code tells Navigator to insert a line break. You can type the codes in uppercase or lowercase, but when you type URLs, make sure the captilization matches that of the URL.

Check This Out...

URL Extravaganza

Where you get the URLs for these links is your business. However, if you hate to type, consider copying and pasting these URLs. You can copy a URL wherever you see one: in a hotlist, in the URL text box, in a menu item edit box. Highlight the URL and then press **Ctrl+C**. You can then switch to your text editor and paste the URL where desired.

Save the document (be sure to give it the extension **.htm**), close your text editor, and you're done. You've created your first hyperdocument. In the next section, you'll get to take it for a test drive.

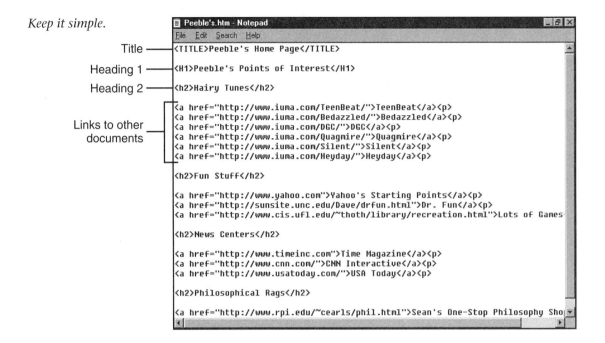

Does It Work?

You can slap together HTML documents in any number of ways. The only thing that matters is whether or not the document works when you're done. To test your document, establish your Internet connection, and then start Navigator. Open the **File** menu and select **Open File**. A dialog box appears, prompting you to specify the location and name of the file you want to open.

Select the drive and directory, or folder, that contains the HTML document you created. Select the name of the file, and then click **OK** or the **Open** button. Navigator loads the document from your hard disk and displays it on-screen. To have your home page load automatically, look back at Chapter 10 in the "Starting from Your Home (Page)" section.

Chapter 23 ➤ *Forging Your Own Hyperdocuments*

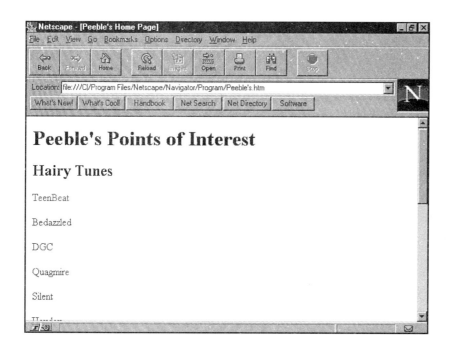

Your home page in Navigator.

More Stuff You Can Stick in a Home Page

If you show your five-code home page to an experienced Web-walker, they'll laugh you off the server. To give your home page a professional flair, you need to add some lines, include a couple of paragraphs and lists, add an inline image or two, and maybe use some bold and italic text.

Because the paragraph is the bread and butter of any document, let's start there. The rule is pretty simple. Wherever you want to end a paragraph, type a **<p>** code. Although pressing the Enter key in your text editor inserts a line break in your document, Navigator doesn't recognize that line break. Navigator breaks a line only when it sees a <p> code.

Another simple, commonly used code is <hr>, which stands for *horizontal rule*. Use this code at the end of a section, to separate it from the next section. To add space before the horizontal line, precede the **<hr>** code with a **<p>** code. To insert space after the line, add a **<p>** code after the **<hr>** code.

You want to emphasize a word or phrase by making it bold or italic—what do you do? To italicize text, bracket it with <i></i> codes. To make text bold, use <b></b> codes. Underlining? You guessed it; use <u></u>. For example, <i>increased spending</i> results in *increased spending*. You can also make text bold *and* italic, but if you plan on sharing your home page with people who use a browser other than Netscape Navigator, the text may not appear bold and italic on their screen. To add two text enhancements, simply embed one pair of codes in the other: <i><b>increased spending</i></b>.

Inserting Inline Images and Sounds

Now, for the more advanced codes. Say you have a graphic or sound file on disk, and you want to insert it into your document. You must create a link that tells the document where to look for the file. To add an inline image, insert a code like the following:

<IMG SRC="file:///C|/DIR/SUBDIR/FILE.GIF" ALIGN=middle>

Translation: IMG stands for *image*, which tells Navigator to insert the specified image. **SRC** stands for *source*, which indicates where the image is stored. Make sure you start with **file:///**, because your inline image is stored locally (that is, on your hard disk). Also be sure to use three forward slashes (NOT two), follow the drive letter with | (not a colon), and use forward slashes to separate directory names. **ALIGN** is an optional code that tells Navigator how to position the image in relation to the text that follows it: top, middle, or bottom.

Check This Out...

Relative References When you look at professional hyperdocuments, you may not see a lot of long directory paths. An anchor may specify only a file name. You can do this too by storing all your linked files in the same directory or folder in which you store your hyperdocument. The anchor then "knows" to search in the current directory for the file.

Creating links for sound files is a little different; it's more like inserting a link for a URL. You use the anchor codes <a> and </a> to insert the link. Here's a sample:

<a href="file:///C|/WINDOWS/CHIMES.WAV">Click here for sound</a>

In the example, **Click here for sound** appears highlighted in the document. When you click on that text, Navigator opens the associated application you use for playing WAV files. You can then click the **Play** button to play the sound.

You might want to use a speaker icon to represent the sound link you inserted in your document. To use an icon in your document, store a small GIF file on your hard disk, and then replace *Click here for sound* with an image link that points to the .GIF. Your code might look like the following:

    <A HREF="file:///C|/WINDOWS/CHIMES.WAV"><IMG SRC="file:///C|/DIR/SOUND.GIF"></A>

The <IMG SRC=> code tells Navigator to insert the specified GIF image in the document. You can then click on this image to play the sound.

Listing Things

People love lists. I love lists. You can scan a list and skip right to the item that catches your eye. You may have already figured out that you can create rudimentary lists by writing short sentences and ending each one with a couple of **<p>** commands. Hey, if it works, why not? You'll find, however, that HTML offers some additional codes for creating fancy lists with bullets and numbers.

The most popular list is the *unordered list* (or bulleted list). You bracket the entire list with **<ul></ul>** codes, and then start each list item with an **<li>** code. Here's a sample of a 3-item list:

    <ul>
    <li>4 pork chops
    <li>1 egg
    <li>1 can Italian bread crumbs
    </ul>

If you're giving step-by-step instructions, the *ordered list* (or numbered list) is better. With ordered lists, you bracket the entire list with **<ol></ol>** codes, and start each list item with an **<li>** code (just as you did with the unordered list). When a Web browser displays the list, it inserts the numbers where required. Here's a sample of a three-step list:

    <ol>
    <li>Preheat the oven to 350 degrees.
    <li>Bread the pork chops.
    <li>Bake the pork chops for 45 minutes.
    </ol>

One final list. If you want to create your own online glossary of terms, you can create a *definition list*. Bracket the entire list with **<dl></dl>** codes. Precede each term you want to define with a **<dt>** code; follow it with the definition, preceded by a **<dd>** code. Here's a sample list for two terms:

```
<dl>
<dt>Clipper Chip
<dd>A hardware encryption device promoted by the government that's designed to keep data communications private from anyone . . . except the government.
<dt>Download
<dd>To snatch a file from another computer or online service and drag it to your computer. You usually download using a modem.
</dl>
```

Check This Out...

Embedding Codes Keep in mind that you can insert additional codes in a list. For example, you can insert links to your favorite URLs. You can also use the <b> and <i> codes to format text within a list.

The Philosophy of Logical Codes

Earlier, I'm not sure when, you learned how to use the codes <b> <i> and <u> to make text bold, italic, and underlined. In HTML lingo, these codes are called *physical* codes, as opposed to *logical* codes. Personally, I try not to separate the physical from the logical. Whenever I do, I end up walking into a wall or driving through red lights.

Nevertheless, there *is* a difference. Physical codes are absolute. A <b> code tells Web browsers to make text bold, no questions asked. Logical codes, such as **<em>** (for *emphasis*), tell the browsers to emphasize the word; the method is up to the browser. One browser might underline the marked text, another might make it bold, and another might add italics. You can save time by using logical codes, because they're usually easier to remember. Here are a list of some of the more popular logical codes:

<em></em>	Adds emphasis.
<strong></strong>	Adds stronger emphasis.
<cite></cite>	Use this for a citation to another work or authority.

Proper Form (for the Culturally Elite)

If you're doing home pages for yourself and friends, you don't have to worry too much about following the proper HTML format. As long as the page works, you're in business. However, if you're doing this for money, or you get serious about it and start putting your pages on the Web (making them accessible to other users), you should follow some HTML conventions.

First, start each document with an **<html>** code and end with an **</html>** code. These codes tell whatever Web browser is being used that this document is, in fact, an HTML document. Currently, these <html> codes don't do much of anything, because HTML is the only game in town. However, sometime in the future, other hyperdocument languages may come into use, and when they do, the <html> codes will help Web browsers distinguish between document types.

Another currently useless code pair is the **<head></head>** pair. Not to be confused with the <h1></h1> head*ing* pair, the <head> codes indicate a head. In most current HTML documents, the <head> codes bracket the <title> codes, and do nothing. In some documents, the <head> codes bracket some advanced codes that are way beyond the scope of this book. For example, if your home page describes a database that you can search, you can insert the **<isindex>** code. This code inserts a Search Index text box at the bottom of the Navigator window into which a user can enter search instructions. But as I said, that's too complicated for this book.

Now that you have a head, you need a body, so after the </head> code, you need a <body> code that indicates the beginning of the rest of the document. At the very end of the document, but before the </html> code, you must insert a **</body>** code that indicates the end of the body.

Cheating Your Way to HTML

The best way to learn proper HTML coding—and to get ideas for how to create your own home pages—is to nab a few home pages and look at their codes. Find a willing victim, download it, and then open it up in your text editor take a peek. Think of it as a biology lesson without the stench of formaldehyde. Here's the URL of a great place to pick up some home pages…and share your own:

    http://web.city.ac.uk/citylive/pages.html

The CityLive! Complete Home Page Directory.

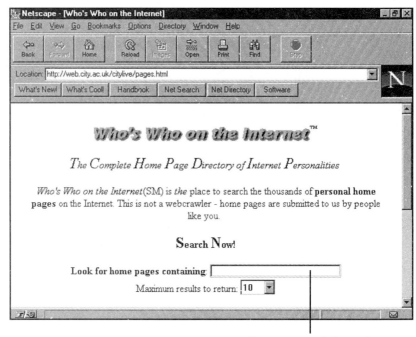

You can search for and download home pages.

Using HTML Authoring Tools

You've done the manual coding. You created your first HTML document in a text editor. Now I'll tell you: There are a couple of HTML language programs that can help you create home pages and other hyperdocuments. The most popular HTML editor for Windows is HotDog, which you can download from the following Web site:

http://www.sausage.com/

HotDog makes it a lot easier to create HTML documents. Instead of typing codes, you select them from menus or lists. If you select a *paired code* (one that has on and off codes), the editor inserts both codes for you. In addition, the editor can check your document for errors and help you correct them.

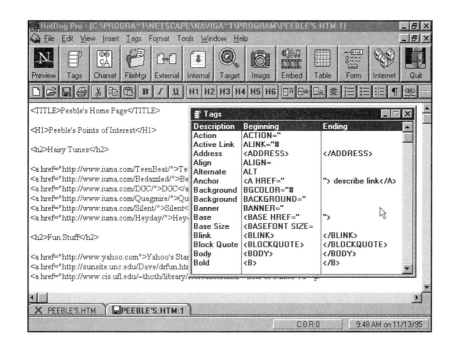

HotDog can simplify the creation of hyperdocuments.

Learning More About HTML

If you find HTML exciting and you want to make a career of it, you can get additional information, codes, and instructions from a number of sources. The best source is a book by Paul McFedries, called *The Complete Idiot's Guide to Creating an HTML Web Page*. (Okay, it's a cheap plug, but McFedries is an HTML guru, who writes in a very entertaining and informative style, so I don't feel too guilty.)

You can also find HTML information on the Web. Here are a couple of sites to check out. The first two sites provide some simple instructions on how to start with HTML. The third site provides a quick overview of many of the HTML commands:

> http://www.ncsa.uiuc.edu/demoweb/html-primer.html
>
> http://www.ncsa.uiuc.edu/General/Internet/WWW/HTMLPrimer.html
>
> http://kuhttp.cc.ukans.edu/lynx_help/HTML_quick.html

The Least You Need to Know

You can spend days wandering the Web to learn the intricacies of HTML. The following list will teach you the basics in less than 30 seconds:

- Create hyperdocuments in a text editor or in a word processing application that lets you save plain text files.
- Every home page needs a title line bracketed with **<title>** and **</title>** codes.
- Use **<h1></h1>** codes to mark the text that you want to appear as the title at the top of your home page.
- Use **<h2></h2>** codes to mark any headings under the <h1> heading.
- Use anchor codes to insert links to your favorite URL.
- The proper form for an anchor code is:

   <a href="URL">Link Text</a>

Chapter 24

More Internet Sites Than You'll Ever Have Time to Visit

Quick Guide to Web Sites

The Arts, Fine and Otherwise   p. 252

Books, Magazines, and Other Rags   p. 255

Business, Not Pleasure   p. 259

Computers, Hard and Soft   p. 261

Education for Students and Teachers   p. 264

Fun, Games, and Entertainment   p. 266

Health and Fitness   p. 269

Hobbies and Recreation   p. 271

Internet News and Information   p. 273

Investing Your Money   p. 274

Job Hunting   p. 275

Laws and Other Legal Stuff   p. 277

Musical Notes   p. 278

Movies and Videos   p. 279

News, Real News   p. 280

Philosophy and Religion   p. 282

Politics and Government   p. 284

Shopping Networks   p. 285

Sports Scores and Schedules   p. 286

Travel   p. 288

Weather Reports and Maps   p. 289

The Uncategorical Category   p. 290

Fasten your seat belt, and squeeze your mouse tight. You're about to take a joy ride on the Web. This chapter provides you with a list of the best Web sites organized by category (in alphabetical order, of course). You get the name of each site, its URL, and a brief description of the best site in each category (in my humble opinion). Enjoy!

Mark It!
As you drive along, don't forget to make bookmarks for your favorite sites. Some of these URLs are pretty long.

CMA Legal Disclaimer: Because of the dynamic nature of the Web, some of the URLs in this chapter may not work for you. People are constantly moving their home pages and making life miserable for us computer book authors. However, usually when a page moves, the mover (or shaker) inserts a link at the old location that kicks you out to the new location, so you won't even notice the move. Another problem is that the pages shown in this chapter might not look the same as the pages you see when you connect. Okay, now that you're aware of all this nonsense, get on with your life.

The Arts, Fine and Otherwise

World Wide Arts Resources

http://www.concourse.com/wwar/default.html

Although this page doesn't have any artworks of its own, it contains links to over 250 art museums, 560 galleries and exhibitions, 50 publications, 40 art institutes, and much much more. Use this site as your starting point, and fly to any of the museums listed, without even boarding a plane. This page can also help you contact art dealers and other people who may share your aesthetic tastes.

If you're interested in art, there's no better starting point than this.

The Web Museum

http://sunsite.unc.edu/louvre/

Art on the Net

http://www.art.net

Norton Museum of Art

http://www.gate.net/~iii/norton/main.html

Fine Art Print Emporium

http://www.airmail.net/~tself/

Arts Gopher

gopher://marvel.loc.gov/11/global/arts

Arts and Images

gopher://gopher.cs.ttu.edu/

Michael C. Carlos Museum

http://www.cc.emory.edu/CARLOS/carlos.html

FineArt Forum Online

http://www.msstate.edu/Fineart_Online/index.html

Krannert Art Museum

http://www.ncsa.uiuc.edu/General/UIUC/KrannertArtMuseum/KrannertArtHome.html

New York Art Online

gopher://gopher.panix.com/11/nyart

dEPARTURE fROM nORMAL Art Magazine

http://www.teleport.com/~xwinds/dfn.html

Techno-Impressionist Gallery

http://www.tlc-systems.com/techno/index.html

FotoFolio

http://www.digitalrag.com/mirror/fotofolio/FotoFolio.HTML

Specific Artists

Salvador Dali Museum in St. Petersburg

http://www.webcoast.com/Dali/

Francisco Goya, "Father of Modern Art"

http://www.primenet.com/~image1/goya/goya.html

Frida Kahlo's Electronic Gallery

http://www.hypergraphia.com/frida/

Kandinsky Image Archive

http://libra.caup.umich.edu/ArchiGopher/Kandinsky/Kandinsky.html

M. C. Escher Patterns

http://cs1.sfc.keio.ac.jp/~t93827ya/escher/escher.html

The Georges Seurat Homepage

http://k12.ucs.umass.edu/user/dbirnbau/seurat.html

Leonardo da Vinci Museum

http://www.leonardo.net/museum/main.html

Chapter 24 ➤ *More Internet Sites Than You'll Ever Have Time to Visit*

Books, Magazines, and Other Rags

The Gutenberg Project

http://jg.cso.uiuc.edu/PG/welcome.html

The Gutenberg Project is an attempt to transform the great (and not so great) works of literature into electronic form (text files). When you connect to this site, you'll get a glimpse of how extensive this project is. You can find everything from the complete works of William Shakespeare to Ed Krol's *Hitchhiker's Guide to the Internet.* If you like to read books on a computer screen, or if you like to count the number of times the word "see" appears in *King Lear,* you'll love this list.

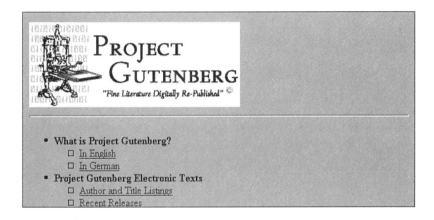

For electronic books, visit the Gutenberg list.

OnLine Books

http://www.cs.cmu.edu/Web/books.html

Internet Book Information Center

http://sunsite.unc.edu/ibic/IBIC-homepage.html

The Web's Best Bookstore

http://intertain.com/store/ibic.html

The English Server at Carnegie-Mellon University

http://english-server.hss.cmu.edu/

Electronic Text Center

http://www.lib.virginia.edu/etext/ETC.html

Macmillan Computer Publishing

http://www.mcp.com

The Electronic Newsstand

gopher://gopher.enews.com:70/11

Future Fantasy Bookstore

http://futfan.com/home.html

The Speculative Fiction Clearing House

http://agent2.lycos.com:8001/sf-clearing-house/

The Freethought Web

http://freethought.tamu.edu/freethought/

The E-Zine List

http://www.meer.net/~johnl/e-zine-list/index.html

Your Favorite Magazines

HotWired: Wired Magazine Online

http://www.hotwired.com/

Mother Jones

http://www.mojones.com/

The New Republic

http://www.enews.com/magazines/tnr/

Prison Life Magazine

http://www.NeoSoft.com/plmag/

Playboy

http://www.playboy.com

(Sorry, ladies, *Playgirl* hasn't made the Net yet.)

PC Computing

http://www.zdnet.com/~pccomp/

Esquire

http://www.esquireb2b.com/

A Woman's Perspective

http://www.uvol.com/woman/

Sports Illustrated

http://pathfinder.com

Go to pathfinder.com, then click on the link for the magazine you want.

More Cool Magazine Sites...

MIT's Oldest Newspaper: The Tech

http://the-tech.mit.edu/The-Tech

Some Weird Stuff

http://www.cs.washington.edu/homes/pauld/fishnet/

Famous Authors

Shakespeare's Complete Works

http://the-tech.mit.edu/Shakespeare/works.html

gopher://joeboy.micro.umn.edu/11/Ebooks/By%20Title/shake

Beat Generation Authors

http://www.charm.net/~brooklyn/LitKicks.html

Edward Abbey

http://www.abalon.se/beach/aw/abbey.html

Jane Austen

http://uts.cc.utexas.edu/~churchh/janeinfo.html

Orson Scott Card

http://www.libby.org/~cjolson/orson.html

Lewis Carroll

http://www.wonderland.org/Works/Lewis-Carroll/

Tom Clancy (Newsgroup)

news:alt.books.tom-clancy

Mark Twain

http://www.wonderland.org/Works/Mark-Twain/

William Faulkner

http://www.mcsr.olemiss.edu/~egjbp/faulkner/faulkner.html

Winston Groom (Forrest Gump)

http://gump.sgi.com/

Herman Melville

http://www.melville.org/

Ayn Rand

http://www.rpi.edu/~pier1/phil/works-AR/list.html

Salman Rushdie

http://www.nyu.edu/pages/wsn/subir/rushdie.html

J.R.R. Tolkien

http://www.math.uni-hamburg.de/.relippert/tolkien/rootpage.html

Walt Whitman

http://www.yahoo.com/Arts/Literature/Poetry/Poets/Whitman__Walt___1819_1892_/

Business, Not Pleasure

Dunn & Bradstreet Information Services

http://www.dbisna.com/

If you go to no other business site, at least visit Dunn & Bradstreet. At this site, you can learn how draft a successful business plan, get money from reluctant customers, market your products and services, and manage vendors. This service, like most, is still under construction, so it will probably offer a lot more by the time you sign on. And by that time, you'll probably have to pay for it.

Part 3 ➤ *Stretching the Web with Navigator*

At Dunn & Bradstreet, you can learn how to start and manage a business.

Wall Street Journal

http://www.wsj.com

SoHo Central (Home Office Center)

http://www.hoaa.com/

Internal Revenue Service

http://www.ustreas.gov

Tax Tips and Facts

http://www.rak-1.com/users/kahan/

Business Opportunities Handbook

http://www.w2.com/businop.html

Entrepreneurial Edge Online

http://www.edgeonline.com/

Entrepreneurs on the Web

http://sashimi.wwa.com/~notime/eotw/EOTW.html

Chapter 24 ▸ More Internet Sites Than You'll Ever Have Time to Visit

Internet Business Center

http://www.tig.com/cgi-bin/genobject/ibcindex

Interesting Internet Business Sites

http://www.rpi.edu/~okeefe/business.html

Commerce Business Daily

gopher://usic.savvy.com/

Curious About GATT and NAFTA?

http://ananse.irv.uit.no/trade_law/gatt/nav/toc.html

http://the-tech.mit.edu/Bulletins/nafta.html

Asian Pacific Chamber of Commerce

http://oneworld.wa.com/apcc/apcc1.html

Computers, Hard and Soft

Microsoft Corporation

http://www.microsoft.com/

If you're having trouble with Windows 95, you own Microsoft stock, or you're just curious about Microsoft's new products, connect to Microsoft's Web site for answers. Like most Microsoft projects, this site is carefully constructed, and easy to navigate. Although it may be a bit busy at times, when you do gain access, you'll find lots of cool computer information here.

Part 3 ➤ *Stretching the Web with Navigator*

Of course Microsoft has a Web site!

IBM

http://www.ibm.com/

Compaq Computer Corporation

http://www.compaq.com/

Dell Computer

http://www.dell.com/

Gateway 2000

http://www.gw2k.com/

Midwest Micro

http://www.mwmicro.com/

Packard Bell

http://www.packardbell.com/

Windows Magazine

http://techweb.cmp.com/win/current/

Windows Sources Magazine

http://www.zdnet.com

Ed Tiley's Windows 95 Home Page

http://www.supernet.net/~edtiley/win95/win95unl.html

Micro Media CD Kiosk

http://micromedia.com/

Novell's Tech Support Site

http://www.novell.com

The Boston Computer Society

http://www.bcs.org/bcs/

Ziff-Davis Publications

http://www.ziff.com/

Hewlett-Packard

http://www.hp.com/

Sun Microsystems

http://www.sun.com/

Kestrel Institute

http://kestrel.edu/

More Computer Companies

http://www.hal.com/pages/hops.html

Education for Students and Teachers

Cyberspace Middle School

http://www.scri.fsu.edu/~dennisl/CMS.html

The Cyberspace Middle School is directed toward students from sixth to ninth grades who are interested in using the Web to further their education. The site also has a link for teacher resources. If you have kids, and you'd like to introduce them to the Internet, you can't find a better Web page than this. (Well, maybe *you* can, but I sure couldn't.)

Cyberspace Middle School focuses on using the Web to educate.

Kids On Campus Internet Tour

http://www.tc.cornell.edu/Kids.on.Campus/

The Teacher Education Internet Server

http://curry.edschool.Virginia.EDU/teis/

SchoolNet

gopher://gopher.nstn.ca/11/info_kiosks/SchoolNet

Franklin Institute Virtual Science Museum

http://sln.fi.edu/

Dewey Web

http://ics.soe.umich.edu

NASA's K-12 Internet Initiative

http://quest.arc.nasa.gov/

http://quest.arc.nasa.gov/trc/toc.html

Map Reading 101

http://info.er.usgs.gov/education/teacher/what-do-maps-show/index.html

U. S. Geological Survey

http://info.er.usgs.gov/

The Vatican Exhibit

http://sunsite.unc.edu/expo/vatican.exhibit/Vatican.exhibit.html

The Dead Sea Scrolls

http://sunsite.unc.edu/expo/deadsea.scrolls.exhibit/intro.html

Dinosaurs in Hawaii!

http://www.hcc.hawaii.edu/dinos/dinos.1.html

Homespun Web of Home Educational Resources

http://www.ICtheWeb.com/hs-web/

Web Spanish Lessons

http://www.willamette.edu/~tjones/Spanish/Spanish-main.html

Introductory Accounting Course

http://www.people.memphis.edu/~fdeng/acct/2010.html

Financial Aid Information

http://www.cs.cmu.edu/afs/cs/user/mkant/Public/FinAid/finaid.html

Grantseeker's Resource Center

http://oeonline.com/~ricknot2/grant_seekers.html

Educational Online Sources

http://netspace.students.brown.edu/eos/main_image.html

KIDLINK

http://www.kidlink.org/

National Teachers Enhancement Network

http://www.montana.edu/~wwwxs/

On-Line English Grammar

http://www.edunet.com/english/grammar/index.html

Teaching and Learning on the Web

http://www.mcli.dist.maricopa.edu/cgi-bin/index_tl

TeeNet

http://www.dnai.com/~aaronv/teenet/

The Village Learning Center

http://www.snowcrest.net/villcen/vlchp.html

Fun, Games, and Entertainment

Yahoo's Entertainment Page

http://www.yahoo.com/Entertainment/

Chapter 24 ➤ *More Internet Sites Than You'll Ever Have Time to Visit*

Yahoo provides links to thousands of other Internet sites, including sites for business, education, and law. Their fun and games links are so incredible, however, that I had to place Yahoo in the games section. Here, you'll find links to comics, food recipes, drink recipes, pranks, hobbies, toys, virtual reality, and anything else you might find entertaining.

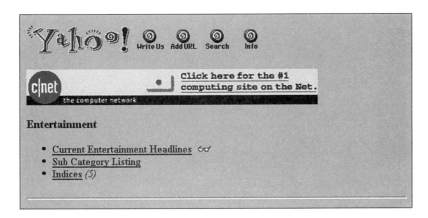

Check out the best in entertainment at Yahoo.

MUDs and MOOs

gopher://spinaltap.micro.umn.edu/11/fun/Games/MUDs/Links

MUDs, MOOs, and MUSHes

These hip games all started with MUDs, Multi-User Dimensions (or Dungeons or Dialogues). The term was derived from the game Dungeons and Dragons. MOO stands for MUD Object-Oriented, which makes use of a more dynamic programming language. There are several other types of games available, as well, including MUSHes, MUSEs, and LPMUDs.

Doctor Fun and Other Comic Strips

http://sunsite.unc.edu/Dave/drfun.html

Comic Books in Print and Not

http://www.eden.com/comics/comics.html

Barney's Home Page

http://www.galcit.caltech.edu/~ta/barney/barney.html

267

The Captain James T. Kirk Sing-a-long Page

http://www.ama.caltech.edu/users/mrm/kirk.html

Fortune Cookie (Without the Cookie)

http://www.twentymule.com/Fortune.acgi

Dr. Love's Office

http://www.prairienet.org/~connor/love.html

Punchy Advice

http://www.pacificrim.net/~lbrodie/punch/advice.html

Calvin and Hobbes Gallery

http://eos.kub.nl:2080/calvin_hobbes/

Dilbert (A Daily Cartoon Strip)

http://www.unitedmedia.com/comics/dilbert/todays_dilbert.gif

The Far Side

http://www.cad.uni-sb.de/elzer/farside.html

The BOG (Internet Graffiti)

http://www.technet.sg/BOG/

Cool Site of the Day

http://cool.infi.net/

tap online

http://www.taponline.com/

Alien On Line

http://www.crs4.it/~mameli/Alien.html

Web-Tender: Online Bartender

http://www.pvv.unit.no/~pallo/webtender/

Cook's Corner

http://wchat.on.ca/merlene/cook.htm

Sin City (Penn & Teller Home Page)

http://www.sincity.com/

Letterman's Top Ten List

http://www.cbs.com/lateshow/ttlist.html

Mr. Smarty Pants Knows (Trivia Page)

http://www.auschron.com/mrpants/

Write a Letter to Santa Claus

http://north.pole.org/santa/talk_to_santa.html

Health and Fitness

The Weightlifting Page

http://www.cs.unc.edu/~wilsonk/weights.html

The Weightlifting Page is for hard core weightlifters. Here, you'll find links to hundreds of sites that deal with weightlifting techniques, stretching, diets, gyms, videos, training equipment, newsgroups, and anything else that's even remotely helpful to weightlifters. In addition, the page contains pictures of pumped up bodies, so be prepared to feel grossly inadequate.

Part 3 ➤ *Stretching the Web with Navigator*

This page will pump you up.

Global Health Network

http://www.pitt.edu/HOME/GHNet/GHNet.html

Aerobics and Fitness Association of America

http://www.cybercise.com/affa.html

MetroSports (Magazine)

http://virtumall.com/newsstand/metrosports/

The Exercise Gopher

gopher://gopher.uiuc.edu/11/UI/CSF/health/heainfo/Fitness

HealthNet

http://debra.dgbt.doc.ca/~mike/healthnet/

USF Health Sciences News

http://www.med.usf.edu/PUBAFF/news1.html

Welch Medical Library

gopher://welchlink.welch.jhu.edu/

Chapter 24 ➤ *More Internet Sites Than You'll Ever Have Time to Visit*

Cancer Research with OncoLink

gopher://cancer.med.upenn.edu:70/11/

gopher://gan.ncc.go.jp/

AIDS/HIV Information and Resources

http://www.hivnet.fr/ircam/index-e.html

Online Allergy Center

http://www.sig.net/~allergy/welcome.html

Lyme Disease Resource

http://www.sky.net/~dporter/lyme1.html

Arthritis Foundation

http://www.arthritis.org/

Center for Food Safety and Nutrition

http://vm.cfsan.fda.gov/list.html

Yahoo's Health Page

http://www.yahoo.com/Health/

Naturopathic Physicians

http://infinity.dorsai.org/Naturopathic.Physician/

Hobbies and Recreation

Antiques and Other Collectibles

http://www.ic.mankato.mn.us/antiques/Antiques.html

If you're interested in becoming an antique collector, this should be your first stop. The mission of the Antiques & Collectibles site is to bring beginners up to speed so they won't get ripped off at antique shows. In addition to texty explanations of what to look for, this site offers graphics that can help you tell an original from a fake and help you judge the value of a particular item.

Learn about antiques and collectibles here.

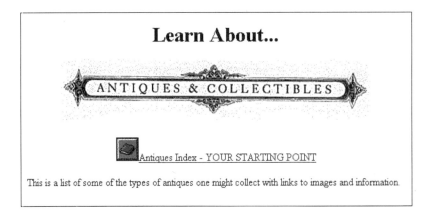

Spencer's Beer Page

http://www-personal.umich.edu/~spencer/beer/

Caffeine Injection

http://www.quadralay.com/www/Caffeine/Caffeine.html

Callahan's Cookbook

http://www.ruhr-uni-bochum.de/callahans/cookbook.html

The Garden Gate (Gardening)

http://www.prairienet.org/ag/garden/homepage.htm

Juggling

http://www.hal.com/services/juggle/

Woodworking Ideas and Techniques

http://access.digex.com/~mds/woodwork.html

Chapter 24 ➤ *More Internet Sites Than You'll Ever Have Time to Visit*

Dogs and Cats

http://snapple.cs.washington.edu:600/canine/canine.html

http://www.ai.mit.edu/fanciers/fanciers.html

The Potter's Page (Pottery)

http://www.aztec.co.za/users/theo/

Firework's Page

http://bronze.ucs.indiana.edu/~wwarf/firework.html

Hobby World

http://www.hobbyworld.com/

Internet News and Information

Lycos Internet Catalog

http://www.lycos.com/

Lycos is the "catalogue of the Internet." Each day, Lycos searches the Internet for new and interesting sites, and then catalogues these sites. You can then use the Lycos search form to look for sites that pertain to a specific topic.

Lycos can help you navigate the Internet.

273

The Internet Society

http://info.isoc.org/home.html

Internet Services Directory

http://www.directory.net/

Internet Search Form

http://www.cmpcmm.com/cc/

Zen and the Art of the Internet

http://sundance.cso.uiuc.edu/Publications/Other/Zen/zen-1.0_toc.html

Easy Internet

http://www.futurenet.co.uk/netmag/Issue1/Easy/index.html

Investing Your Money

100% No Load Mutual Fund Council

http://networth.galt.com/www/home/mutual/100/100guide.htm

Don't invest in mutual funds until you've visited this site. It offers an online book about investing in mutual funds. You'll learn how to choose funds, put together a portfolio that's right for you, and invest once you've made your decision.

Before you invest in mutual funds, stop here.

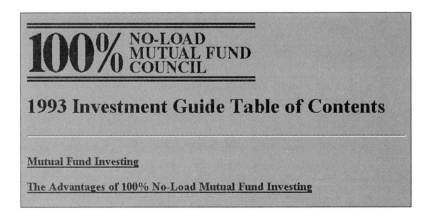

Chapter 24 ➤ *More Internet Sites Than You'll Ever Have Time to Visit*

The Morningstar Spotlight

http://networth.galt.com/www/home/mutual/morning/mspot.htm

Streetlink Corporate Financial Reports

http://www.streetlink.com/SL/STLKFIN.HTM

QuoteCom Investment Service

http://www.quote.com/

Stock Broker Information

http://www.cs.cmu.edu/afs/cs.cmu.edu/user/jdg/www/invest_brokers.html

DTN Wall Street

http://www.secapl.com/dtn/info/top.html

The New York University EDGAR Project

http://edgar.stern.nyu.edu

The Chicago Mercantile Exchange

http://www.cme.com/

NASDAQ Financial Executive Journal

http://www.law.cornell.edu/nasdaq/nasdtoc.html

Business News and Information (Lots of Links)

http://umbc7.umbc.edu:81/news/business.html

Job Hunting

E-Span Interactive Employment

http://www.espan.com

Part 3 ➤ *Stretching the Web with Navigator*

Start your career planning and job searches here. The E-Span service provides advice on writing resumés, networking, and interviewing. Have you ever mulled over the thought of salary requirements? At E-Span, you can view lists of national averages for various positions in different parts of the country. The online job database lets you perform a WAIS search of job openings by state, city, job title, or anything else you want to search for. You can even post your own resumé. For additional job search advice, check out the Dunn & Bradstreet site described earlier:

http://www.dbisna.com/

Your first stop for job-hunting hints.

JobHunt

http://rescomp.stanford.edu/jobs.html

The Monster Board

http://www.monster.com/home.html

Growth Careers

http://www20.mindlink.net/interweb/growthcareers.html

Career Magazine

http://www.careermag.com/careermag

Resumé Bank

http://www.careermag.com/careermag/resumes/index.html

Chapter 24 ➤ More Internet Sites Than You'll Ever Have Time to Visit

Laws and Other Legal Stuff

The Seamless WEBsite

http://www.ingress.com/tsw/index.html

If you're a lawyer or student of law, you'll find all the resources (and links to other resources) you'll need. From this Web page, you can advertise, find legal documents, acquire lists of expert witnesses, chat with other lawyers, and even look for a job.

The Seamless WEBsite is a hangout for lawyers.

Nolo Press Self-Help Law Center

http://gnn.com/gnn/bus/nolo/

LawTalk—Business Law and Personal Finance

http://www.law.indiana.edu/law/bizlaw.html

Supreme Court Decisions

http://www.law.cornell.edu/supct/

Labor Law

http://www.webcom.com/~garnet/labor/labor.html

Case Western Reserve Law Library

http://lawwww.cwru.edu/cwrulaw/library/libinfo.html

277

Lawyer Jokes

http://deputy.law.utexas.edu/jokes1.htm

Musical Notes

Adam Curry's The Vibe

http://metaverse.com/vibe/index.html

Adam Curry, former MTV video jock, has his own Internet site. Here you can read Curry's newsletter (the *Cyber-Sleaze Report*) for musical reviews, musician interviews, and even Adam Curry's quote of the day. You can listen to sound clips, view music videos, get concert information, and check out the charts.

Adam Curry's Vibe.

Eden Matrix Music Online

http://www.eden.com/music/music.html

American Recordings

http://american.recordings.com/

The Internet Underground Music Archive

http://www.iuma.com/

CDnow! The Internet Music Store

http://cdworld.com/

Tom Waits Page

http://www.nwu.edu/waits/

Links to Other Artists

http://www.yahoo.com/Entertainment/Music/Artists/

WZLX Classic Rock Trivia

http://www.wzlx.com/scripts/fishtriv.cgi?prezoom=31,0&postzoom=0,0

Global Music Outlet

http://www.iuma.com/GMO/

Jerry Garcia's Haight Street Shrine

http://www.sirius.com/~jmelloy/jerry.html

And Still More Music Areas

http://www.yahoo.com/Business_and_Economy/Companies/Music/Labels/

Movies and Videos

The Internet Movie Database

http://www.msstate.edu/Movies/

To search for movies by title, actor, or director, visit The Internet Movie Database (formerly known as Cardiff's Movie Database). This place also offers a ballot that allows you to cast a vote for your favorite movie, and a movie quiz to test your expertise.

MPEG Movie Archive

http://www.eeb.ele.tue.nl/mpeg/index.html

Movies Directory

http://www.cs.cmu.edu/afs/cs.cmu.edu/user/mleone/web/movies.html

The Internet Movie Database is a great place for film buffs.

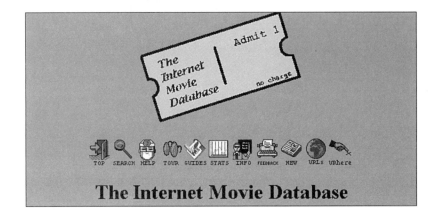

Buena Vista Movieplex

http://www.disney.com/

The Envelope, Please (Academy Awards)

http://guide.oscars.org/

Hollywood Online

http://www.hollywood.com/

The Stanley Kubrick Page

http://www.lehigh.edu/~pjl2/kubrick.html

The Rocky Horror Picture Show

http://www.cs.wvu.edu/~paulr/rhps/rhps.html

How-To Videos

http://branch.com/infovid/infovid.html

News, Real News

Time Magazine

http://www.timeinc.com

Chapter 24 ➤ *More Internet Sites Than You'll Ever Have Time to Visit*

This online version of the *Time Magazine* offers articles from the latest issue, and you don't even have to run out to the newsstand! Of course, the articles are teasers, but if all you want is the cover story and a few other tidbits, this will satisfy your thirst for weekly news. You can also use this site to send letters to the editor.

When you enter this URL, you'll automatically be kicked out to another page at **http://pathfinder.com**. This page seems to have a monopoly on digitized versions of magazines. Here, you'll find links to *People, Money, Fortune, Sports Illustrated*, and a host of other rags.

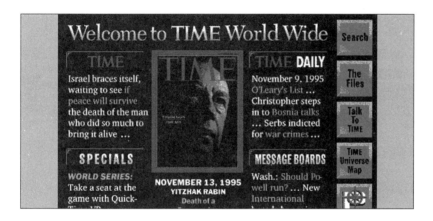

Time Magazine in its digitized form.

CNN Interactive

http://www.cnn.com/

New York Times Electronic Edition

http://nytimesfax.com/

USA Today

http://www.usatoday.com/

Chicago Tribune

http://www.chicago.tribune.com/

Indianapolis Star and News

http://www.starnews.com/

281

Philadelphia Online

http://www.phillynews.com/

Washington Weekly

http://dolphin.gulf.net/

The Detroit Free Press

http://gopher.det-freepress.com:9002/

San Francisco Chronicle and Examiner

http://www.sfgate.com/

The Seattle Times

http://www.seatimes.com/

Today.com

http://today.com/

Vocal Point (A Student Newspaper for K-12)

http://bvsd.k12.co.us/cent/Newspaper/Newspaper.html

International News

http://www.yahoo.com/News/International/

Philosophy and Religion

Sean's One-Stop Philosophy Shop

http://www.rpi.edu/~cearls/phil.html

Why do you exist? Why should you care? And who is this Kierkegaard fellow? On this Web page, you'll find answers to all your existential and metaphysical questions...or at least, you'll have a place to start looking. This page, rated in the top 5% of all Web sites, is

Chapter 24 ➤ *More Internet Sites Than You'll Ever Have Time to Visit*

more of a starting point in your future intellectual, Internet travels. In addition, you'll find links to humorous philosophical sites, and links to all your favorite philosophers—from Aristotle to Zeno.

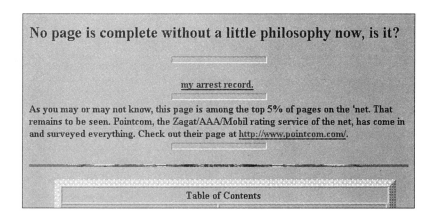

Sean's One-Stop Philosophy Shop combines humor and thought.

Philosophy Around the Web

http://info.ox.ac.uk:80/~shil0124/

American Philosophical Association

gopher://apa.oxy.edu/

The Kierkegaard Gopher

gopher://info.utas.edu.au/11/Publications/Kierkegaard

Jewish Web World Online

http://www.nauticom.net/users/rafie/judaica-world.html

Unofficial Pope John Paul II Page

http://www.zpub.com/un/pope/

Guide to Christian Literature

http://www.calvin.edu/Christian/pw.html

283

1-800-JUDAISM Online

gopher://israel.nysernet.org/11/800judaism

Politics and Government

The White House

http://www.whitehouse.gov/

Visit the White House without leaving your home! Here you can find out about the First Family, take an online tour of the White House (with a personal greeting from Mr. Clinton), sign the guest book, hear Al Gore welcome you, and select from a list of government publications. You can even visit the New and Improved Hillary Rodham Clinton Home Page (I'm not sure whether "New and Improved" modifies "Hillary" or "Home Page.")

Take an online tour of the White House.

United States Information Center

http://www.usia.gov/usis.html

Congressional E-Mail Addresses

http://www.webcom.com/~leavitt/cong.html

The Deficit Page

http://www.texas.net/users/andyn/deficit.html

Chapter 24 ➤ More Internet Sites Than You'll Ever Have Time to Visit

The CIA Page

http://www.odci.gov/cia/

FBI's Ten "Most Wanted Fugitives"

http://www.fbi.gov/toplist.htm

All Things Political

http://dolphin.gulf.net/Political.html

The Black Panther Coloring Book

http://www.cybergate.com:80/~jonco/thebpcb.html

Countdown '96

http://www.comeback.com/countdown/

Shopping Networks

The Branch Mall

http://branch.com/

The Branch Mall is the Mall of America of mail order. In the Branch Mall, you can shop for everything from bonsai trees to exercise equipment, from flowers and candy to computers and vacuum cleaners. You can even find a divorce lawyer! Of course, you don't get the same feel as a real mall. You won't see people with blank looks on their faces talking into cellular phones, but the storefronts might look familiar.

Gigaplex (Entertainment Complex)

http://www.gigaplex.com/wow/homepage.htm

Above and Beyond Mall

http://www.abmall.com/

The Branch Mall dwarfs the Mall of America.

- **Clothing**
  - Netsurfer - Internet T-Shirts
  - Computer T-Shirts from Elswear
  - Cyberspace Navigator Apparel
  - America's T-Shirt Catalog - 40 Scholarly T-Shirts NEW
  - Netgear
  - Sputnik T-Shirts - Unique T-Shirt Designs
  - The Warehouse - Elegant Tuxedos
  - The Commuter CoverUp (tm) - Protection Against Spills While Driving

- **Jewelry and Accessories**
  - Milne Jewelry Company - A Southwest Tradition Since 1951
  - KCS Imports - Photoengraved 18 Karat Gold Pendants

Brookstone

http://www.netplaza.com/plaza/strfrnts/1015/storepg1.html

FTD Online

http://www0.internet.net/cgi-bin/getNode?node=1&source=DYHO&session=2208644

The World Wide Marketplace

http://www.cygnus.nb.ca/mall/mall.html

Sports Scores and Schedules

Nando X Sports Server

http://www.nando.net/SportServer/

This sports service is for serious sports nuts who want the latest scores and stats. When you first sign on, you'll have to fill out a form and subscribe to the service. This sports service is so slick, I suspect it will soon become a pay service.

The NFL Football Server

http://www.netgen.com/sis/NFL/NFL.html

Chapter 24 ➤ *More Internet Sites Than You'll Ever Have Time to Visit*

The Nando X Sports Server is for mondo sports nuts.

Dirt Rag (Mountain Biking Magazine)

http://cyclery.com/dirt_rag/text-index.html

CyberSki (Snow Skiing)

http://www.iaccess.com.au/cyberski/

1996 Summer Olympics

http://www.intadv.com/olympic.html

College Basketball Page

http://www.cs.cmu.edu/afs/cs.cmu.edu/user/wsr/Web/bball/bball.html

ESPN Sports Page

http://espnet.sportszone.com/

Golf Data Web

http://www.gdol.com/

RaceNet (Auto Racing)

http://www.primenet.com/~bobwest/index.html

WWW Women's Sports Page

http://fiat.gslis.utexas.edu/~lewisa/womsprt.html

Travel

Conde Nast Traveler

http://www.cntraveler.com/

If you're planning a vacation (a real getaway), and you're not sure where you want to go, then start here. The Conde Nast Traveler is the online version of the printed version of this jet set vacation guide. However, this online version is much more than just an electronic magazine. It includes digitized photos, online games, and interactive maps that will keep you clicking for hours.

Visit the Conde Nast Traveler for exotic getaways.

Foreign Languages for Travelers

http://insti.physics.sunysb.edu/~mmartin/languages/languages.html

The Grand (Canyon) Tour

http://insti.physics.sunysb.edu/~mmartin/languages/languages.html

Internet Guide to Bed & Breakfast Inns

http://paradiso.com:80/inns/

Chapter 24 ➤ *More Internet Sites Than You'll Ever Have Time to Visit*

PC Travel (Airline Ticketing)

http://www.pctravel.com/

rec.travel Library

ftp://ftp.cc.umanitoba.ca/rec-travel/

Weather Reports and Maps

University of Illinois Weather World

http://www.atmos.uiuc.edu/wxworld/html/top.html

Weather World, no relation to Wayne's World, is a site where you can view the latest satellite images from around the world. Simply click a link, and you're flying above the earth, watching the clouds spin.

At Weather World, you get a seat above the clouds.

Weather Information Service

http://www.nstn.ca/kiosks/weather.html

WebWeather

http://www.princeton.edu/Webweather/ww.html

Weather Information (Links to Other Sites)

http://atmos.es.mq.edu.au/weather/

289

The Uncategorical Category

Top 5% Web Sites

http://www.pointcom.com/

As you bounce around to the various Web pages that my URLs point to, you'll notice that some have a tiny badge that says "Top 5% of All Web Sites." Well, these special sites were awarded their badges from this site. You'll find links to the top 5% of all Web pages here...at least the top 5% in some people's eyes.

The best of the Web.

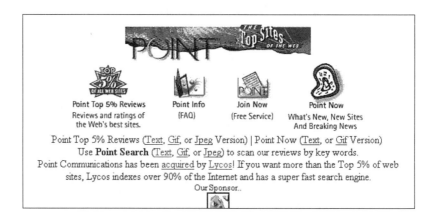

News of the Weird

http://www.cs.su.oz.au/giovanni/humour/wierd.html

Peeping Tom Home Page (It's Not What You Think)

http://www.ts.umu.se/~spaceman/camera.html

Virtual Voyager—In Search of Elvis

http://www1.chron.com/voyager/elvis/

Speak Like a Geek: The Complete Archive

absolute reference   In a Web document, a link that refers to a specific document regardless of the current document's address. Think of it like this: If you give a person an absolute reference, it's sort of like telling them to go to a specific address. A relative reference would be like saying, "It's two blocks west of the Village Pantry."

anchor   The part of a link that causes the mouse pointer to turn into a pointing finger. See also *links*.

anonymous login   The process of connecting to a system incognito. Many FTP sites (places where you can get files) allow users to connect anonymously and access public areas. Anonymous login privileges usually do not allow you to place files on the server or change anything.

Archie   An Internet search tool that helps you find files. In most cases, you need to know the exact name of the file or a partial file name. See also *Jughead* and *Veronica*.

associate   To establish a connection between a given file type and the helper application needed to view or play that file type. In Navigator, you must create file associations so Navigator will "know" which application to run when you choose to view, watch, or listen to a file. For example, you might associate movie files that end in .mpg with an MPEG movie player.

BBS   Short for *bulletin board system*, a BBS is a computer that's set up to automatically answer the phone and allow callers to exchange messages, files, and information. Special interest groups, professional organizations, and software companies commonly set up BBSs.

bookmark   A Navigator tool that lets you mark your favorite Web pages so you can quickly return to them later.

Boolean operators   Conjunctions, including "and" and "or," used to separate search terms. For example, if you search for "Clinton and Whitewater," you get a list of all resources that relate to both "Clinton" and "Whitewater." If you use "or" the search is much broader, finding anything that relates to either "Clinton" or "Whitewater."

bps Short for *bits per second*, this is a unit used to measure the speed of data transfer between two computers. As far as the Web is concerned, anything slower than 14,400 bps is a snail's pace.

browser See *Web browser*.

cache A temporary storage area the Navigator creates both in RAM and on your hard disk. Navigator stores Web pages in the cache, so it can quickly load these pages if you decide to return to them. In other words, Navigator doesn't have to yank the pages back through the phone lines.

channel The equivalent of a conference room. When you chat on the Internet, you first connect to a chat server, and then you tune in to a channel. Each channel is supposed to deal with a different topic, but people mostly talk about the weather and where they're from, or they simply flirt with one another. See also *chat*.

chat To "talk" to another person by typing at your computer. What you type appears on the other person's screen, and what the other person types appears on your screen. You can't chat with Navigator; you need another program such as Netscape Chat if you want to get chatty.

client Of two computers, the computer that's being served. Whenever you connect to a Web site, the computer at that site is the *server*, and you are the *client*. Think of yourself as the *customer*.

compressed file A file that's been squished so it takes up less disk space and travels faster through network and modem connections. Before you can use the file, you must *decompress* (or expand) it using a special program. Popular decompression programs include PKZip (for DOS) and WinZip (for Windows).

cyberspace The universe created by the connection of thousands of computers. Computer users can use modems to enter cyberspace and converse with other users. This term was first used by William Gibson in his novel *Neuromancer*. In the novel, people plugged their brains into cyberspace. If you've ever seen the glazed look people get when they're wired to the Web, you know that Gibson's notion is not too far from the truth.

decompress To unsquish a squished file and make it usable.

Dial-Up Networking A program that comes with Windows 95 that establishes the Internet connection you need in order to run Navigator and access the World Wide Web.

document On the Web, this could be anything: an index of topics, several screenfuls of text, a page full of pictures, or even a picture of Pamela Anderson in various stages of undress.

document source The coded document that controls the way Web pages appear. This is like the proverbial ugly twin.

domain name A unique identification for an Internet site. Each computer on the Internet has a domain name that distinguishes it from other computers on the Internet. Domain names usually provide some vague indication of the establishment that runs the server. For example, here's the domain name of the Whitehouse server: www.whitehouse.gov.

domain name server (DNS)   A computer that matches a site's name to a number that identifies that site. All servers on the Internet have a domain name, for example, ncsa.uiuc.edu. Each server also has a unique IP (Internet Protocol) number, such as 128.252.135.4. Your Internet service provider has an electronic database, called a *DNS (Domain Name Server)* that matches the domain to the IP number to find the server that has the requested data. As you innocently click links, the DNS is matching domain names and IP numbers to make sure you get where you're supposed to be.

download   To copy a file from another computer (usually an FTP server) to your computer.

e-mail   Mail that requires no postage and usually gets there on time. E-mail is a system in which people can send and receive messages through their computers, on a network or using modems. Each person has a designated mail box that stores messages sent by other users. He can then retrieve and read messages from the mail box.

e-zine   Pronounced "eee-zeen," this is an electronic rendition of a *zine*, a noncommercial magazine that leans toward the bizarre, twisted, or edgy side. One person or a small group of people typically put together zines, which rarely contain advertisements.

FAQ   Pronounced "fack," short for *frequently asked questions*, this is a list of answers to the most-often-asked questions at a particular Internet site. Good Internet etiquette demands that you read the FAQ at a site before you post any questions. That way, you won't risk getting flamed. See *flame*.

finger   A special UNIX command that pokes around through the directory of users and finds information about that person, including the person's e-mail address, and whether or not that person has read her mail recently or even logged in.

flame   To verbally abuse another user during an online discussion, via e-mail, or in a newsgroup. Common flaming techniques include name-calling, abusive innuendos about one's parents, and other puerile gems of wit.

form   A fill-in-the-blank Web document. Sites commonly use forms to take credit card orders, ask for your password, or let you enter search instructions.

frame   A new Navigator feature that allows two parts of the same Web document to appear in the same window. One frame might contain an outline of the document. When you click on a heading in the outline, the other frame shows the contents of that heading.

FTP   Short for *File Transfer Protocol*, a set of rules that govern the transfer of files between computers. True geeks use this acronym as a verb. For example, "I FTP'd to ftp-dot-netscape-dot-com to nab the latest Navigator beta."

geek 1. An overly obsessive computer user who will sacrifice food, sleep, sex, and other pleasantries of life to spend more time at the keyboard. 2. A carnival performer whose act usually includes biting off the head of a live snake or chicken.

GIF file Pronounced "giff file" or "jiff file," a picture file, commonly a photograph or painting. GIF is short for *Graphic Interchange Format*, a format developed by CompuServe for transferring graphic files. The format stores lots of graphic information in little space.

Gopher An indexing system that allows you to access various Internet services by selecting menu options. Whenever you connect to a Gopher site, it presents you with an opening menu. When you select a menu item, the server presents you with another submenu containing additional options and/or files. These options may kick you out to another Gopher server, an FTP server, a newsgroup, or other Internet servers. You proceed through the menus until you find the information you want...or reach a dead end.

handle A user's computerized nickname or ID number. When you look for a person using Whois, you might find the person's handle. You can often find out more about a person by performing the search again using the person's handle.

helper application A program that performs a specialized job that Navigator is unfit to manage. Whenever you click a link that Navigator can't play, Navigator loads the file to disk and then summons (spawns) the helper application associated with that file. The helper application loads the file and plays it.

history list A directory of all the Web sites you visited since you connected. You can view the history list in Navigator by opening the **Window** menu and clicking **History**.

hits In a WAIS search, the number of times a search word was found in an article. The higher the number, the more likely it is that the article contains the information you're looking for. See also *score*.

home page The page that greets you when you first start Navigator or first connect to a Web site. No relation to "home boy."

host 1. In biology, the being that is leeched on by a parasite. 2. On the Internet, it pretty much means the same thing. The host is the computer that has the information. Your computer is the client, sucking the lifeblood out of the host.

HTML Short for *HyperText Markup Language*, the code used to create Web documents. These codes tell the Navigator how to display the text (titles, headings, lists, and so on), insert anchors that link this document to other documents, and control character formatting (by making it bold or italic).

HTTP Short for *HyperText Transfer Protocol*, a set of rules that govern the exchange of data between a Web host and a client (your computer). The address for every Web server starts with **http**. If you see an address that starts with different letters (for example **ftp** or **gopher**) the address is for a different type of server: Gopher (**gopher**), FTP (**ftp**), WAIS (**wais**), USENET (**news**), or Telnet (**telnet**).

hyperdocument   A Web page that contains links connecting it to other pages. On the Web, a hyperdocument might contain links to other text, graphics, sounds, or movies.

hyperlinks   Icons, pictures, or highlighted chunks of text that connect two documents. For example, a document about pork might contain a link for sausage. If you click the link, Navigator displays a document about how to make sausage. Sausage is the link, although it's not actually a sausage link.

hypermedia   A dynamic computerized soup that contains movie clips, graphics, sound files, text, and anything else that can be stored in a digitized form. That's the "media" part, anyway. The "hyper" part deals with the fact that these ingredients are interlinked, so you can jump quickly from one to another.

HYTELNET   A phone book for other telnet hosts. It contains addresses and login information for hundreds of online library catalogs, bulletin board systems (BBSs), Free-nets (free on-line systems), and other information resources. See also *Telnet*.

inline image   A graphic that appears inside a Web document. You can tell Navigator not to display these images...if you can't stand waiting for them to load.

interactive   A user-controlled program, document, or game. Interactive programs commonly display on-screen *prompts* asking the user for input so he can decide how to carry out a particular task. These programs are popular in education, allowing children to follow their natural curiosity to solve problems and gather information.

Internet   The world's largest system of interconnected networks. The Internet was originally named ARPAnet after the Advanced Research Projects Agency in the Defense department. The agency developed the ARPAnet in the mid-1970s as an experimental project to allow various university and military sources to continue to communicate in a state of national emergency. Nowadays, the Internet is used mostly by private citizens for connecting to databases, exchanging electronic mail, and wasting loads of productive time.

IP address   A unique number assigned to each computer on the Internet. Most of the time, you work with domain names, such as nasa.uiuc.edu. Behind the scenes, whenever you enter a domain name, your service provider matches that name to the site's IP number (for example 128.252.135.4), and then calls that site. The idea here is that it's easier for you to remember names and easier for computers to remember numbers. The domain name/IP number link makes everyone happy.

IRC   Short for Internet Relay Chat, this is a technology that allows users to type messages back and forth using their keyboards. It's sort of like talking on the phone but less expensive and much slower.

Java 1. Coffee. 2. Also, a relatively new technology that allows you (or at least someone who knows how to use Java) to create animations and other moving video clips and embed them in Web pages. All you need to know about Java is that if you click a link for a Java applet (application), Navigator will play it.

JPG Short for *Joint Photograph Group*, a file-compression format used for storing graphic files. If you come across a file that ends in .JPG, you can view it in Netscape Navigator, or you can have one of your helper applications display it.

Jughead An Internet search tool used to find resources at a specific site. Archie, Veronica, and Jughead (all Internet search tools) are related. Archie searches for FTP servers that contain the files you want to download. Veronica searches all Gopher sites to find the ones that store various resources. Jughead searches only the current Gopher site to find the specified resources.

links Aka *hyperlinks*, these are icons, pictures, or highlighted chunks of text that connect the current page to other pages, Internet sites, graphics, movies, or sounds.

logical codes In a Web document, codes that provide general directions on how to display text. For example, <em> stands for emphasis, which might mean bold or italic. Physical codes give more precise instructions. For example, <b> means bold.

login To connect to another computer on a network or on the Internet so you can use that computer's resources. The login procedure usually requires you to enter your username (or user ID) and a password.

logout To disconnect from another computer on a network or on the Internet.

lurk To read newsgroup messages posted by other people but not respond to them or post any messages of your own. This is sort of like being a peeping Tom, but you rarely see anything to get excited about.

map A graphical navigational tool used on many Web pages. Think of it as one of those mall maps with the **YOU ARE HERE** arrow on it, but with a Web map, you can actually go places by clicking on different areas of the map.

MIME Short for *Multi-purpose Internet Mail Extensions*, a protocol that controls all file transfers on the Web. Navigator uses MIME to recognize different file types. If an HTML document arrives, Navigator "knows" to play that file itself. If an .MPG file arrives, Navigator calls the associated helper application. MIME was originally developed to attach different types of files (usually multimedia files) to e-mail messages.

mirror site A server that contains the same files as the original site. Why the redundancy? Because some sites are so busy that users might have trouble connecting during peak hours. The mirror sites offer an alternate location that helps users avoid Internet traffic jams.

MOO Acronym for *MUD Object-Oriented*, another type of hip interactive computer game that involves several players. MOOs are written in a more dynamic programming language than the one used for MUDs.

MPEG Short for *Moving Pictures Expert Group*, a video-compression and movie presentation standard used for most video clips stored on the Web. The only thing that matters is that if you encounter a file that ends in .MPG, you need an MPG or MPEG player to watch it.

MUD Short for *Multi-User Dimensions* (or *Dungeons* or *Dialogues*), hip interactive computer games that usually involve several players. The term was derived from the game Dungeons and Dragons.

Navigator A navigational program for the World Wide Web. Navigator transforms Web documents (which consist of boring codes) into exciting multimedia documents, complete with sounds, pictures, and movies.

newbie Derogatory term for a new user on the Internet. Newbies are often the target of obnoxious Internet junkies who are bitter because their little secret is not so little nor so secret as it once was.

newsgroup An Internet bulletin board for users who share common interests. There are thousands of newsgroups ranging from body arts to pets (to body art with pets). Newsgroups let you post messages and read messages from other users.

pane A portion of a window. Netscape Mail uses panes to divide its window into logical areas.

physical codes In a Web document, codes that provide specific directions on how to display text. For example, <b> stands for bold. *Logical codes* give less precise instructions. For example, <em> means emphasis, which might mean bold or italic.

Pink Slip 1. The little piece of paper you get after your boss catches you downloading a GIF of Pamela Anderson. 2. The packet-switching protocol used by The Pipeline.

plan A file that a user might attach to her finger file that includes more information. A plan might include the person's address, phone number, job interests, and anything else that person wants to make publicly accessible.

port 1. A sweet, robust wine that has a rich taste and aroma. 2. Also, the hardware connection through which a computer sends and/or receives data. (And one more thing; a port can be an application that's set up on a server. When you specify the server's port, you're actually telling it to run one of its applications.)

post To tack up a message in a bulletin board or newsgroup for all to see.

postmaster The person at a given site who is in charge of assigning users their e-mail addresses. You can usually send a message to the postmaster by addressing it to **postmaster@sitename**.

PPP Short for Point-to-Point Protocol, which probably means as little to me as it does to you. What's important is that when you choose an Internet service provider, you get the right connection: SLIP or PPP; otherwise, you won't be able to use Navigator.

protocol A set of rules that govern the transfer of data between two computers.

proxy A special connection that allows two incompatible networks to communicate. For example, say you're on the Web with Navigator and you decide to use WAIS to search for a list of articles. You can't use WAIS directly from Navigator, so you have to work through a Web/WAIS proxy. The proxy acts as a middleman, ensuring that the data transfer goes smoothly.

relative reference In a Web document, a link that refers to the location of another page or file in relation to the address of the current page. For example, if the page is in the /PUB directory, and a linked page is in /PUB/HOME, a relative reference might specify /HOME. An absolute reference would have to give the complete path: /PUB/HOME.

score In WAIS searches, a number that indicates the relative likelihood that an article will contain the information you need. The topmost article gets a score of 1,000. Subsequent scores are relative to 1,000, so 500 would mean that the article had half as many occurrences of the search term than the top article.

server In the politically incorrect world of the Internet, the computer that serves up all the data. The other computer, the client, acts as a customer, demanding specific information.

service provider The company that you pay in order to connect to their computer and get on the Internet.

shareware Computer programs you can use for free and then pay for if you decide to continue using them. Many programmers use the Internet to distribute their programs, relying on the honesty and goodwill of Internet users for their income. That's why most of these programmers have day jobs.

SLIP Short for *Serial Line Internet Protocol*, a type of Internet connection that allows you to connect directly to the Internet without having to run programs off your Internet service provider's computer.

spam To talk passionately about a variety of topics about which the speaker is ill-informed. People commonly spam to hide their ignorance behind a facade of conviction and verbosity.

SSL Short for *Secure Sockets Layer*, this is Netscape's new security technology. Web pages protected with SSL prevent misanthropic hackers from nabbing personal information that you might enter on the page (including your credit card number).

status bar The area at the bottom of the Navigator window that shows you what's going on as you work. The little key in the status bar indicates whether a document is or is not secure; if the key looks broken, the document is not secure.

stop word   In a search, any word that is excluded from the search. For example, if you are searching a computer database, the database may refuse to look for common words, such as "and" and "computer."

tags   HTML codes that work behind the scenes to tell Navigator how to display a document and how to open other linked documents. Tags can control the look of text (as in titles and headings), insert anchors that link this document to other documents, and control character formatting (by making it bold or italic).

TCP/IP   Acronym for *Transmission Control Protocol/Internet Protocol*, the preferred method of data transfer over the Internet. With TCP/IP, the sending computer stuffs data into packets and sends it. The receiving computer unstuffs the packets and assembles them into some meaningful and useful form. The most famous TCP/IP program is Winsock.

telnet   The process of connecting to a server and using it to run programs, just as if you were sitting at its keyboard (or sitting at the keyboard of a terminal that's connected to the server). Think of it as using the computerized card catalog at the local library.

terminal connection   The type of connection you don't want to have if you're using Navigator. A terminal connection makes your computer act like one of your service provider's workstations. You run programs on the service provider's computer, and connect to the Internet indirectly through that computer. With a SLIP or PPP connection, you connect through the service provider's computer, but you use software on your computer to do all your work.

terminal emulation   A technique used to make one computer act like another so the two computers can carry on a conversation. Some mainframe computers will interact with only a specific type of terminal. If you want to connect to that mainframe computer using your personal computer, you must make your computer act like the required terminal.

thread   In newsgroups and e-mail, a way of grouping messages, so that you can quickly tell that they belong to the same topic of conversation.

UNIX shell   The equivalent of a DOS prompt for computers that are running the UNIX operating system. You type commands at the prompt, just as if you were using a PC.

upload   To copy a file from your computer to another computer. You usually upload files to share them with other users.

URL   Short for *Uniform Resource Locator* (or *Unreliable Resource Location*, depending on the URL), an address for an Internet site. The Web uses URLs to specify the addresses of the various servers on the Internet and the documents on each server. For example, the URL for the Whitehouse server is **http://www.whitehouse.gov**. The **http** stands for HyperText Transfer Protocol, which means this is a Web document. **www** stands for World Wide Web. **whitehouse** stands for Whitehouse. And **gov** stands for Government.

USENET Short for *user's network*, USENET sets the standards by which the various newsgroups swap information. See also *newsgroup*.

Veronica One of many Internet search tools, this one finds Gopher sites that have what you're looking for. For a comparison of popular search tools, see *Archie* and *Jughead*.

viewer A program that Navigator uses to play movie clips, sound clips, PostScript files, graphics, and any other file Navigator itself cannot handle. See also *helper application*.

virtual memory Disk storage that is treated as RAM. Why am I including it in this glossary? Because Navigator uses so much memory that you'll need some virtual memory just to use it.

W3 Another name for the World Wide Web.

WAIS Pronounced "ways," short for Wide Area Information Server, a system that allows you to search various databases on the Internet for specific articles and other resources.

Web browser Any of several programs you can use to navigate the World Wide Web. The Web browser controls the look of the Web documents and provides additional tools for jumping from one Web document to another. Navigator is a Web browser.

Web robot A search tool that regularly searches the Internet for Web sites and indexes the Web documents it finds. The robot then allows you to search its indexes for Web sites that contain the resources you need.

Webmaster The person who created and maintains a Web document. If you find an error in a Web document, you should notify the Webmaster (in a nice way).

Web server A specialized computer on the Internet devoted to storing and serving up Web documents.

Whois Just another UNIX command that you can use to find out a person's e-mail address, mailing address, phone number, or other information, if you know the person's last name and the location of the server that person logs in to.

World Wide Web A collection of interconnected documents stored on computers all over the world. These documents can contain text, pictures, movie clips, sounds, and links to other documents. You move from one document to another by clicking links.

zine A noncommercial magazine that leans toward the bizarre, twisted, or edgy side. Zines started on paper but soon moved to the Internet in the form of e-zines. See also *e-zine*.

zip The process of compressing a file so that it takes up less space and transfers more quickly. If you have a zipped file, you must unzip it before you can use it.

Index

Symbols

<cite> citation code, 246
<dl> definition list code, 246
<em> emphasis code, 246-250
<h1> heading code, 240
<hr> horizontal rule code, 243
<i> italic code, 244
<li> list code, 245
<ol> ordered list code, 245
<p> paragraph code, 243
<strong> code, 246
<ul> unordered list code, 245
16-bit sound cards, 6
100% No Load Mutual Fund Council Web site, 274
403 Forbidden error message, 89

A

abbreviations, e-mail, 151-152
absolute references, 98, 291
acronyms, e-mail messages, 151-152
Adam Curry's The Vibe Web site, 278
Add Bookmark command (Bookmarks menu), 107
Address Book command (Window menu), 147
address books, e-mail, 147-149
addresses, newsgroups, 216-217
alt (alternative) newsgroups, 216
anchors, 80, 241, 291
anonymous FTP servers, 168-169
anonymous logins, 291
Antiques and Other Collectibles Web site, 271
Appearance options, 156-159
Archie, 291
    FTP searches, 172-175
    Jughead, 18
    telnetting, 210-211
    Veronica, 18
art Web sites, 252-254
articles (newsgroups)
    files, attaching, 221-222
    posting, 220, 297
    posting new, 221
    reading, 218-220
    replying, 220
    sorting, 220
    threads, 219
associates, 291
attaching files, newsgroup articles, 221-222
audio player, 123
auditorium discussions, chat rooms, 186-187

B

Back button, 80, 95
background, changing, 158-159
BBS (bulletin board system), 291, 297
Binary Transfers command (Settings menu), 50
bits per second, see *bps*
Bookmark Properties dialog box, 109
bookmarks, 107-108, 291
    deleting, 109-110
    Gopher, creating, 198
    lists, creating additional, 114
    managing, 108-114
    manually adding, 114
    organizing, 110
    renaming, 109-110
    separators, 111-113
    submenus, 111-113
    trading, 115-116
    URLs, changing, 114
Bookmarks menu commands
    Add Bookmark, 107
    Go to Bookmarks, 113
    More Bookmarks, 108
Boolean operators, 196, 291
bps (bits per second), 292
Branch Mall Web site, 285
browsers, 300
    FTP services, 71-72
    see also Navigator

bugs, 86
bulletin board system, see *BBS*
business oriented Web sites, 259-261

C

caches, memory, 81, 162, 292
channels, 292
chat rooms
  auditorium discussions, 186-187
  connecting to, 181-184
  finding, 179-180
  private conversations, 185-186
  transcripts, printing, 184
  Web pages, sending, 187-189
chatting, 19, 292
classifieds Web sites, 275-276
clickable image maps, see *maps*
clients, 204, 292
  see also browsers
Close command (File menu), 113
codes (HTML)
  <cite> citation code, 246
  <dl> definition list code, 246
  <em> emphasis code, 246-250
  <h1> heading code, 240
  <hr> horizontal rule code, 243
  <i> italic code, 244
  <li> list code, 245
  <ol> ordered list code, 245
  <p> paragraph code, 243
  <strong> code, 246
  <ul> unordered list code, 245
  anchors, 241
  logical codes, 246
  paired codes, 248
  physical codes, 246
  viewing, 247

colors, background, changing, 158-159
commands
  Bookmarks menu
    Add Bookmark, 107
    Go to Bookmarks, 113
    More Bookmarks, 108
  Directory menu, Netscape's Home, 120
  Edit menu
    Delete, 110
    Find, 103
    Word Wrap, 240
  File menu
    Close, 113
    Compress This Folder, 147
    Empty Trash Folder, 146
    Exit, 8
    Import, 115
    New, 53
    New Folder, 145
    New Web Browser, 100
    Open Location, 98
    Page Setup, 134
    Print, 134
    Print Preview, 134
    Quit, 83
    Save as, 132
  Finger (Unix), 293
  Go menu, Stop Loading, 96
  Help menu
    Frequently Asked Questions, 90
    Handbook, 90
    On Security, 161
    Release Notes, 90
  Item menu, Set to New Bookmarks Menu Folder, 113
  Message menu
    Flag Message, 146
    Post Reply, 220
    Reply, 144
  Options menu
    General Preferences, 94
    Mail and News Preferences, 138

separators, 111-114
Settings menu, Binary Transfers, 50
Start menu, Setting, 37
UNIX
  Finger, 234, 293
  Whois, 236, 300
View menu
  Document Info, 161
  Document Source, 131
  Reload, 96
  Whois (Unix), 302
Window menu
  Address Book, 147
  History, 106, 294
commercial online services, 23
communications programs, 28
comp (computer) newsgroups, 216
Complete Idiot's Guide to Creating an HTML Web Page, 249
Complete Idiot's Guide to E-Mail, 152
Complete Idiot's Guide to Modems & Online Services, 33
Complete Idiot's Guide to the Internet, 33
composing e-mail messages, 141-142
Compress This Folder command (File menu), 147
compression, 292
  e-mail folders, 147
  file types, FTP, 172
  JPG (Joint Photograph Group), 296
  zip, 300
computer oriented Web sites, 261-263
Conde Nast Traveler Web site, 288
configuring
  connections, 27-33, 54-57
  e-mail, 138-140
  Netscape Chat, 189-190

Index

PPP connections, 38-40
SLIP connections, 36, 41-43
connect-time charges, service providers, 24
Connection Refused by Host error message, 90
connections, 23-27
　associates, 291
　configuring, 27-33, 54-57
　dedicated connections, 23
　dial-in terminal accounts, 25
　dial-in-direct connections, 24
　direct Internet connections, 6, 22
　logging out, 33
　logons, 27-28, 296
　PPP (Point-to-Point Protocol) connections, 23, 36
　service providers, 23-24, 298
　settings, 163-164
　SLIP (Serial Line Internet Protocol) connections, 23, 36, 41-43
　terminal connections, 24, 299
　troubleshooting, 32-33, 45
copying e-mail messages, 145-146
CPUs (central processing units), 6
credit card orders, security, 160-161
cyberspace, 292
Cyberspace Middle School Web site, 264

D

decompression, 292
　helper applications, 121-122
　programs, 7

dedicated connections, 23
definition lists, documents, creating, 246
Delete command (Edit menu), 110
deleting
　bookmarks, 109-110
　e-mail messages, 145-146
dial icons, creating, Dial-Up Networking, 40-41, 292
dial-in terminal accounts, 25
dial-in-direct connections, 24
Dial-Up Networking, 36
　connections, troubleshooting, 45
　dial icons, creating, 40-41
　installing, 36-37
　PPP connections, configuring, 36, 38-40
　SLIP connections, configuring, 41-43
　TCP/IP, binding, 37-38
　terminal window, 41
direct Internet connections, 6, 22
directories, UNIX, 208
Directory menu commands, Netscape's Home, 120
dithering graphics, 159
DNS (domain name server), 87, 293
Document Contains No Data error message, 89
Document Info command (View menu), 161
document location errors, 88-89
Document Source command (View menu), 131
document sources, 292
documents, 292
　attaching, e-mail messages, 141
　bookmarks, leaving, 107-108
　caches, 81

codes, viewing, 247
conventions, 247
creating, 240-241
enhancing, 243-244
graphics, inserting, 244-245
hyperdocuments, 77, 131-133, 295
hyperlinks, 13
link text, 241
lists, creating, 245-246
logical codes, 296
maps, 99-100
　multiple, viewing, 100-101
　opening, 98-99
paragraphs, 243
physical codes, 297
printing, 134-135
relative references, 298
searches, 103
sending, chat rooms, 187-189
shortcut icons, creating, 107
sound, adding, 244-245
text editors, 248
domain name servers, see DNS
domain names, 40, 292
downloading, 293
　FTP files, 171-172
　Gopher files, 199
　helper applications, 119-121
　multimedia files, 130-131
Dunn & Bradstreet Information Services Web site, 259

E

e-mail, 16, 137, 293
　address books, 147-149
　addresses, phonetics, 140
　configuring, 138-140
　e-mail only accounts, 25
　folders, 145-147
　Inbox, 142

303

messages
  abbreviations, 151-152
  attaching files, 141
  checking, 143-144
  composing, 141-142
  copying, 145-146
  deleting, 145-146
  emoticons, 150-151
  flames, 150
  reading, 142-147
  replying, 144-145
  selecting, 145-146
  sending, 141-142
  shouting, 150
  sorting, 140, 146-147
  threads, 140, 301
nettiquette, 150-152
postmasters, 297
threads, 299
Whois command (UNIX), 300
E-Span Interactive Employment Web site, 275
e-zine, 295
Edit menu commands
  Delete, 110
  Find, 103
  Word Wrap, 240
educational Web sites, 264-266
emoticons, 150-151
Empty Trash Folder command (File menu), 146
encyclopedias (CD-ROM), hypermedia documents, 4
entertainment Web sites, 266-269
error messages, 85
  403 Forbidden, 89
  Connection Refused by Host, 90
  Document Contains No Data, 89
  NNTP Server Error, 90
  server location errors, 86-88
  TCP Error, 90
  Too Many Users, 90

troubleshooting, 90
Unable to Locate Document, 88-89
evening only access, service providers, 25
Exit command (File menu), 8

F

FAQs (Frequently Asked Questions), 90, 293
File menu commands
  Close, 113
  Compress This Folder, 147
  Empty Trash Folder, 146
  Exit, 8
  Import, 115
  New, 53
  New Folder, 145
  New Web Browser, 100
  Open Location, 98
  Page Setup, 134
  Print, 134
  Print Preview, 134
  Quit, 83
  Save as, 132
files
  attaching, e-mail messages, 141
  compression, 292
  decompression, 7, 292
  dispalying, FTP, 175-176
  downloading, 293
    FTP, 171-172
    Gopher, 199
  GIF (Graphic Interchange Format), 294
  local files, opening, 133
  MPEG (Moving Pictures Expert Group) files, 294
  multimedia
    downloading, 130-131
    helper applications, 123
  plans, 297
  self-extracting files, 52

sending, newsgroups, 221-222
transfers, protocols, 50-52
UNIX, 209
unzipping, 52-53
uploading, 299
financial information Web sites, 274-275
Find command (Edit menu), 103
Find Next button, 103
Finger command (UNIX), 20, 234, 293
fitness and health Web sites, 269-271
Flag Message command (Message menu), 146
flames, 150, 293
folders, e-mail, 145-147
fonts, changing, 157
forms, 101, 293
Forward button, 80, 95
frames, 79, 293
freezes, status bar, 82
Frequently Asked Questions, see FAQs
Frequently Asked Questions command (Help menu), 90
FTP (File Transfer Protocol), 17, 167-176, 293
  accessing URLs, 170
  anonymous FTP servers, 168-169
  Archie, file searches, 172-175
  browsers, 71-72
  compression, file types, 172
  files, downloading, 171-172
  Gopher, compared, 193
  Monster FTP Site list, 175
  navigating, 170-171
  Navigator, attaining copy of, 67-69
  nonanonymous FTP servers, 168-169
  origin, 168
  sites, connecting to, 168
  terminal accounts, 70-71

304

Index

G

game Web sites, 266-269
Games Domain Web site, 14
gateways, 40, 227
geeks, 294
General Preferences command (Options menu), 94
Gibson, William, *Neuromancer*, 292
GIF (Graphic Interchange Format) files, 294
Go menu commands, Stop Loading, 96
Go to Bookmarks command (Bookmarks menu), 113
Go to button, 106
Gopher, 16-17, 191-200, 294
   bookmarks, creating, 198
   connecting to, 193-194
   files, downloading, 199
   FTP, compared, 193
   Jughead searches, 198-199
   navigating, 194-195
   Veronica searches, 195-198
   WAIS servers, accessing, 230-231
governmental Web sites, 284-285
graphics
   display settings, 159
   displaying, helper applications, 82-83
   dithering, 159
   documents, inserting, 244-245
   inline images, 77, 295
Gutenberg Project Web site, 255

H

Handbook command (Help menu), 90
handles (user nicknames), 236, 294
hardware
   modems, 6, 22
   ports, 297
   processors, 6
   sound cards, 6, 22
   Super VGA (SVGA) monitors, 6, 22
health and fitness Web sites, 269-271
Help menu commands
   Frequently Asked Questions, 90
   Handbook, 90
   On Security, 161
   Release Notes, 90
helper applications, 8, 82-83, 117-119, 294
   decompressing, 121-122
   downloading, 119-121
   installing, 121-122
   mapping files to, 122-125
   movies, playing, 130-131
   multimedia files, playing, 123
   multimedia links, playing, 125
   reassociating files, 131
   telnetting, 203
   viewers, 300
History command (Window menu), 106, 294
history lists, 95, 106-107, 294
hits, WAIS searches, 296
hobby and recreational Web sites, 271-273
Home button, 81, 95
home pages, 11, 240-241, 294
   see also, documents; hyperdocuments
hosts, 204-205, 294

HTML (HyperText Markup Language), 97, 294
   codes
      <cite> citation code, 246
      <dl> definition list code, 246
      <em> emphasis code, 246-250
      <h1> heading code, 240
      <hr> horizontal rule codes, 243
      <i> italic code, 244
      <li> list code, 245
      <ol> ordered list code, 245
      <p> paragraph code, 243
      <strong> code, 246
      <ul> unordered list code, 245
   anchors, 241
   logical codes, 246
   paired codes, 248
   physical codes, 246
   viewing, 247
   conventions, 247
   link text, 241
   resources, 249
   tags, 299
HTTP (HyperText Transfer Protocol), 13, 97, 294
hyperdocuments, 77, 131-133, 295
   creating, 240-241
   see also documents
hyperlinks, 13, 295
hypermedia, 4, 295
HyperTerminal, 26, 28, 31
HyperText Markup Language, see *HTML*
HyperText Transfer Protocol, see *HTTP*
HYTELNET telnet directory, 207, 295

305

I

IDs, handles, 294
image maps, see *maps*
images, see *graphics*
Import command (File menu), 115
Inbox, e-mail, 142
indexes, 101-102
inline images, 77, 295
installing
   Dial-Up Networking, 36-37
   helper applications, 121-122
   Navigator, 73-74
   Netscape Chat, 178-179
interactive programs, 295
Internet, 295
   connections
      configuring, 27-33
      logons, 27-28
      troubleshooting, 32-33
   domain names, 40
   e-mail, 16, 137
   finger command, 20
   FTP (File Transfer Protocol), 17, 70-72, 167-176, 293
   Gopher, 16-17, 191-200, 294
      Jughead, 198-199
      Veronica, 195-198
   history, 10
   hosts, 294
   IRC (Internet Relay Chat), 177-190, 295
   MOOs (MUD Object-Oriented), 297
   MUDs (Multi-User Dimensions), 297
   Navigator, attaining copy of, 66-72
   newbies, 297
   postmasters, 237
   service providers, 23-26, 298
   system requirements, 5-6
   telnetting, 18, 202

Usenet newsgroups, 18, 213-214, 297
users, searches, 233-238
WAIS (Wide Area Information Server), 300
WWW (World Wide Web), 11-13
Internet Mall Web site, 14
Internet Movie Database Browser Web site, 14
Internet Movie Database Web site, 279
Internet news and information Web sites, 273-274
Internet Relay Chat, see *IRC*
Internet Underground Music Archive, 126
introductory offers, service providers, 25
IP addresses, 295
IRC (Internet Relay Chat), 177-190, 295
   see also chat rooms
Item menu commands, Set to New Bookmarks Menu Folder, 113

J-L

Java programming language, 127, 296
JPG (Joint Photograph Group) files, 296
Jughead, 18, 198-199, 296

Kermit protocol, 50
key combinations, 155
Kids Internet Delight (KID) site, 126

legal oriented Web sites, 277-278
link text, 241
links, 95
   anchors, 80, 291
   bookmarks, creating, 108
   Java, 127

multimedia links, playing, 125
nonexisting pages, flagging, 87
parts, 80
red links, 95
references, 80
see hyperlinks
status bar, processing messages, 82
lists, documents, creating, 245-246
literary Web sites, 255-259
local access numbers, service providers, 24
local files, opening, 133
logical codes, 246, 296
logins, 27-28, 296
   scripts, writing, 59-64
   service providers, 28-31
   telnetting, 206
logouts, 33, 296
lurking, newsgroups, 220, 296
Lycos Internet Catalog Web site, 273

M

magazine Web sites, 255-259
Mail and News Preferences command (Options menu), 138
mapping files to helper applications, 122-125
maps (image), 99-100, 296
memory
   caches, 162, 292
   requirements, 22
   virtual memory, 302
menus, separators, 111-113
Message menu commands
   Flag Message, 146
   Post Reply, 220
   Reply, 144
messages (e-mail)
   abbreviations, 151-152
   checking, 143-144
   composing, 141-142

Index

copying, 145-146
deleting, 145-146
emoticons, 150-151
files, attaching, 141
flames, 150
organizing, folders, 145
reading, 142-147
replying, 144-145
selecting, 145-146
sending, 141-142
shouting, 150
sorting, 140, 146-147
status bar, 82
threads, 140, 299
Microsoft Corporation Web site, 261
MIME (Multi-purpose Internet Mail Extensions), 296
mirror sites, 296
misc (miscellaneous) newsgroups, 216
modems, 6
  communications programs, 28
  requirements, 22
  transfer rates, service providers, 25
  troubleshooting, 32-33
money information Web sites, 274-275
Monster FTP Site list, 175
MOOs (MUD Object-Oriented) games, 297
More Bookmarks command (Bookmarks menu), 108
movie Web sites, 279-280
movies, playing, 82-83, 130-131
Moving Pictures Expert Group files, see *MPEG*
Mozilla, sample e-mail message, 143
MPEG (Moving Pictures Expert Group) files, 297
MPEG Movie Archive site, 126
MUDs (Multi-User Dimensions), 297
Multi-purpose Internet Mail Extensions, see *MIME*

Multi-User Dimensions, see *MUDs*
multimedia files, 127, 130-131
multimedia links, playing, helper applications, 125
music oriented Web sites, 278-279

N

N (pulsating) cursor, 78
Nando X Sports Server Web site, 286
navigating
  FTP, 170-171
  Gopher, 194-195
  toolbar, 80-81, 95-96
  WWW, 79-80
Navigator, 5, 297
  connecting to Internet, 7
  customizing, 153-164
  exiting, 8
  helper applications, 8, 82-83
  installing, 73-74
  Internet, attaining copy of, 66-72
  starting, 76
  status bar, 298
  system requirements, 5-6
  versions, 66
  viewers, 300
Navigator screen, 77-78
NCSA Telnet program, 202
Netscape, see *Navigator*
Netscape Chat
  attaining copy of, 178
  chat rooms, connecting to, 181-184
  configuring, 189-190
  installing, 178-179
Netscape Corporation's Home Page, 94-95
Netscape's Home command (Directory menu), 120
networks
  gateways, 40
  proxies, settings, 164

Neuromancer, William Gibson, 292
New command (File menu), 53
New Folder command (File menu), 145
New Web Browser (File menu), 100
newbies, 297
news (general information) newsgroups, 216
news Web sites, 280-282
newsgroup window, 218
newsgroups (Usenet), 18, 213-214, 297
  addresses, 216-217
  articles
    posting, 220, 297
    posting new, 221
    reading, 218-220
    replying, 220
    sorting, 220
    threads, 219
  connections, 215-218
  ettiquette, 220
  files, sending and receiving, 221-222
  flames, 293
  lurking, 220, 296
  searches, 217-218
  spamming, 298
  subscribing to, 214
  threads, 299
NNTP (Network News Transport Protocol), 90
NNTP Server Error message, 90

O-P

On Security command (Help menu), 161
Open Location command (File menu), 98
Open Location dialog boxes, 98
opening
  documents, 98-99
  local files, 133

307

operating systems, 22
Options menu commands
  General Preferences, 94
  Mail and News Preferences, 138
ordered lists, documents, creating, 245

Page Setup command (File menu), 134
paired codes, 248
panes, 297
paragraphs, documents, 243
periodical Web sites, 255-259
permanent direct connections, see *dedicated connections*
Perry-Castaneda Library Map Collection site, 126
personal computer oriented Web sites, 261-263
philosophy and religion Web sites, 282-284
physical codes, 246, 297
Pink Slips, 297
PKZip, 52
plans, 297
Playboy Web site, 257
playing
  movies, 82-83, 130-131
  multimedia files, 123
  multimedia links, 125
  sound clips, 82-83
Point-to-Point Protocol, see *PPP*
political and governmental Web sites, 284-285
ports, 297
posting newsgroup articles, 220-221, 297
postmasters, 237, 297
PPP (Point-to-Point Protocol), 23, 36-40, 298
Print command (File menu), 134
Print Preview command (File menu), 134
printing
  chat room transcripts, 184
  documents, 134-135

private conversations, chat rooms, 185-186
processors, 6
programs
  communications programs, 28
  decompression, 7
  Dial-Up Networking, 36
    binding to TCP/IP, 37-38
    creating dial icons, 40-41
    installing, 36-37
    PPP connections, 38-40
    SLIP connections, 41-43
  helper applications, 8, 82-83, 117-119, 294
    decompressing, 121-122
    downloading, 119-121
    installing, 121-122
    mapping files to, 122-125
    telnetting, 203
    viewers, 300
  interactive, 295
  NCSA Telnet, 202
  Netscape Chat
    attaining copy of, 178
    configuring, 189-190
    installing, 178-179
  PKZip, 52
  shareware, 298
  TCP/IP, 6, 48
  telnet, 202-203
  text editors, 248
  Trumpet Telnet, 203
  Trumpet Winsock, 49-53
  Windows Socket program, 48
  WinQVT Net, 202
  WinZip, 52
protocols, 298
  file transfers, 50-52
  HTTP (HyperText Transport Protocol), 97
  Kermit protocol, 50
  NNTP (Network News Transport Protocol), 90

  XModem protocol, 50
  ZModem, 50
proxies, 298
  settings, 164
  WAIS, 227

Q-R

Quit command (File menu), 83

reading
  e-mail messages, 142-147
  newsgroup articles, 218-220
rec (recreational) newsgroups, 216
recreational and hobby Web sites, 271-273
red links, 95
references, links, 80
relative references, 98, 298
Release Notes command (Help menu), 90
religious Web sites, 282-284
Reload button, 81, 95
Reload command (View menu), 96
renaming bookmarks, 109-110
Reply command (Message menu), 144
replying
  e-mail messages, 144-145
  newsgroup articles, 220
robots (WWW), searches, 101-102, 300

S

Save as command (File menu), 132
saving bookmark lists, 114
sci (science) newsgroups, 216
scores, WAIS searches, 298
screen (main), customizing, 154-155

Index

scripts, logons, writing, 59-60
Seamless WEBsite, 277
Sean's One-Stop Philosophy Shop Web site, 282
searches
    documents, 103
    forms, 102
    HYTELNET telnet directory, 207
    indexes, 101-102
    newsgroups, 217-218
    stop word, 299
    users, 233-236
    WAIS, 224-225
        commands, 226
        hits, 294
        performing, 227-229
        scores, 298
    Web robots, 101-102
Secure Sockets Layer, see *SSL*
security, SSL (Secure Sockets Layer), 298
security options, 160-161
security messages, toggling, 160-161
selecting e-mail messages, 145-146
self-extracting files, 52
sending e-mail messages, 141-142
separators, 111-113
Serial Line Internet Protocol, see *SLIP*
server location errors, 86-88
servers, 298
    anonymous FTP servers, 168-169
    mirror sites, 296
    nonanonymous FTP servers, 168-169
    terminal windows, 44-45
    WAIS, 223-232
    Web servers, 300
    WWW (World Wide Web), 11
service providers, 23-24, 298
    commercial online services, 23

configured TCP/IP programs, attaining, 48
considerations, 24-26
dial-in
    terminal accounts, 25
dial-in-direct
    connections, 24
e-mail only accounts, 25
introductory offers, 25
logons, 28-31
startup fees, 24
stipulations, 26-27
surcharges, 25
transfer rates, modems, 25
Set to New Bookmarks Menu Folder command (Item menu), 113
Setting command (Start menu), 37
Settings menu commands, Binary Transfers, 50
shareware, 298
shopping Web sites, 285-286
shortcuts, documents, creating, 107
shouting, e-mail messages, 150
sites (WWW), 14, 251-252
    art related, 252-254
    business Web sites, 259-261
    classifieds Web sites, 275-276
    computer oriented Web sites, 261-263
    educational Web sites, 264-266
    entertainment Web sites, 266-269
    financial information Web sites, 274-275
    Games Domain, 14
    health and fitness Web sites, 269-271
    hobby and recreational Web sites, 271-273
    Internet Mall, 14
    Internet Movie Database Browser, 14

    Internet news and information Web sites, 273-274
    Internet Underground Music Archive, 126
    Kids Internet Delight (KID), 126
    legal oriented Web sites, 277-278
    literature Web sites, 255-259
    magazine Web sites, 255-259
    movie Web sites, 279-280
    MPEG Movie Archive, 126
    music Web sites, 278-279
    news Web sites, 280-282
    Perry-Castaneda Library Map Collection, 126
    philosophy and religion Web sites, 282-284
    political and governmental Web sites, 284-285
    shopping Web sites, 285-286
    sports Web sites, 286-288
    travel Web sites, 288-289
    weather information Web sites, 289
    Wired Magazine, 14
    Worldwide Web Art Navigator, 14
    Yahoo (a guide to the World Wide Web), 126
sites (FTP), connecting to, 168
sites (Gopher), connecting to, 193-194
SLIP (Serial Line Internet Protocol), 36, 41-43, 298
smileys, see *emoticons*
soc (sociology) newsgroups, 216
sorting
    articles, 220
    e-mail messages, 140, 146-147

309

sound cards, 6, 22, 82-83, 127
sounds, documents, adding, 244-245
spamming, 298
Sports Illustrated Web site, 257
sports Web sites, 286-288
SSL (Secure Sockets Layer), 298
Start menu commands, Setting, 37
starting Navigator, 76
starting page, changing, 94-95
startup fees, service providers, 24
status bar, 80, 82, 298
Stop Loading command (Go menu), 96
stop words, WAIS searches, 226, 299
storage
    caches, 81
    service providers, 25
submenus, bookmarks, adding, 113
subscribing to newsgroups, 214
Super VGA (SVGA) monitors, 6, 22
surcharges, service providers, 25
switches, Veronica, 197-198
system requirements, 5-6, 22, 127

T

tags, see *codes*
talk newsgroups, 216
TCP Error message, 90
TCP/IP (Transmission Control Protocol/Internet Protocol), 299
    Dial-Up Networking, binding, 37-38
    programs, 6

telnetting (networking over the telephone), 18, 202, 299
    Archie servers, 210-211
    commands, 206
    connections, 204-205
    helper applications, setting as, 203
    host computers, 205
    HYTELNET, 207, 295
    logging in, 206
    programs, 202-203
    sessions, running, 203-206
    terminal emulation, 205
    terminal types, 205
    UNIX, 208-210
terminal accounts, FTP services, 70-71
terminal connections, 24, 299
terminal emulation, 26, 205, 299
Terminal program, 48-52, 57-58
terminal types, telnetting, 205
terminal windows, servers, 44-45
text, fonts, changing, 157
text editors, document construction, 248
threads, 301
    e-mail messages, 140
    newsgroup articles, 219
Time Magazine Web site, 280
toll-free (800 number) access, service providers, 24
Too Many Users error message, 90
toolbar, navigational buttons, 80-81
Top 5% Web Sites, 290
trading bookmarks, 115-116
transfer rates, modems, service providers, 25
TRASH folder, e-mail, 146
travel Web sites, 288-289

troubleshooting
    document location errors, 88-89
    error messages, 90
    server location errors, 86-88
Trumpet Telnet, 203
Trumpet Winsock, 49-57

U

Unable to Locate Document error message, 88-89
University of Illinois Weather World Web site, 289
University of Minnesota, Gopher, 16
UNIX operating system
    directories, 208
    files, 209
    Finger command, 234, 293
    programs, running, 210
    shell, 299
    telnetting, 208-210
    Whois command, 236, 300
unordered lists, documents, creating, 245-250
unzipping files, 52-53
uploading, 299
URLs (Uniform Resource Locators), 13, 76, 80, 96-99
    absolute references, 98
    bookmarks, changing, 114
    components, 97-98
    FTP sites, accessing, 170
    HTTP (HyperText Transport Protocol), 97
    relative references, 98
Usenet (user's network), 302
    newsgroups, 18, 213-214, 297
        addresses, 216-217
        ettiquette, 220
        flames, 293
        lurking, 220, 296

310

Index

reading articles, 218-220
searches, 217-218
spamming, 298
subscribing to, 214
threads, 299
see also newsgroups
users
handles, 236
searches, 233-234

V

Veronica, 18, 300
Gopher, searches, 195-198
switches, 197-198
wild cards, 196-197
VGA monitors, 127
View menu commands
Document Info, 161
Document Source, 131
Reload, 96
viewers, 300
virtual memory, 300
visual art Web sites, 252-254

W-Z

WAIS (Wide Area Information Server), 223, 300
gateways, 227
Gopher, accessing, 230-231
proxies, 227
searches, 224-229
commands, 226
hits, 294
scores, 300
stop words, 226
weather information Web sites, 289
Webmasters, 300
Weightlifting Page, 269
White House Web site, 284
Whois command (Unix), 236, 300

Wide Area Information Server, see *WAIS*
wild cards, Veronica, 196-197
Window menu commands
Address Book, 147
History, 106, 294
windows
frames, 79
multiple, viewing, 100-101
Windows 3.1
logon scripts, writing, 60-64
Terminal program, 48-52
Windows 95
Dial-Up Networking, 36, 292
binding to TCP/IP, 37-38
creating dial icons, 40-41
installing, 36-37
PPP connections, 38-40
SLIP connections, 41-43
Windows Socket program, 48
WinQVT Net program, 202
Winsock, 48
WinZip program, 52
Wired Magazine Web site, 14
Word Wrap command (Edit menu), 240
World Wide Arts Resources Web site, 252
World Wide Web, see *WWW*
Worldwide Web Art Navigator Web site, 14
writing
e-mail messages, 141-142
logon scripts, 59-64
WWW (World Wide Web), 11-13, 300
browsers, 300
bugs, 86

encyclopedia, 3-5
forms, 293
home pages, 11
HTTP, 13
navigating, 79-81, 95-96
origin, 13
robots, 300
servers, 11, 300
sites, 14, 251-252
art related, 252-254
business Web sites, 259-261
classifieds Web sites, 275-276
computer oriented Web sites, 261-263
educational Web sites, 264-266
entertainment Web sites, 266-269
financial information Web sites, 274-275
health and fitness Web sites, 269-271
hobby and recreational Web sites, 271-273
Internet news and information Web sites, 273-274
legal oriented Web sites, 277-278
literature Web sites, 255-259
magazine Web sites, 255-259
movie Web sites, 279-280
music Web sites, 278-279
news Web sites, 280-282
philosophy and religion Web sites, 282-284
political and governmental Web sites, 284-285
shopping Web sites, 285-286
sports Web sites, 286-288

travel Web sites, 288-289
weather information Web sites, 289
system requirements, 5-6
URLs (Uniform Resource Locataors), 13, 96-99
Webmasters, 300

XModem protocol, 50

Yahoo (a guide to the World Wide Web), 126
Yahoo's Entertainment Page, 266

zines, 300
zip compression, 300
ZModem protocol, 50

GET CONNECTED
to the ultimate source of computer information!

The MCP Forum on CompuServe

Go online with the world's leading computer book publisher! Macmillan Computer Publishing offers everything you need for computer success!

Find the books that are right for you!
A complete online catalog, plus sample chapters and tables of contents give you an in-depth look at all our books. The best way to shop or browse!

- ➤ Get fast answers and technical support for MCP books and software
- ➤ Join discussion groups on major computer subjects
- ➤ Interact with our expert authors via e-mail and conferences
- ➤ Download software from our immense library:
  - ▷ Source code from books
  - ▷ Demos of hot software
  - ▷ The best shareware and freeware
  - ▷ Graphics files

Join now and get a free CompuServe Starter Kit!

To receive your free CompuServe Introductory Membership, call **1-800-848-8199** and ask for representative #597.

The Starter Kit includes:
- ➤ Personal ID number and password
- ➤ $15 credit on the system
- ➤ Subscription to *CompuServe Magazine*

Once on the CompuServe System, type:

GO MACMILLAN

for the most computer information anywhere!

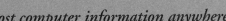

PLUG YOURSELF INTO...

THE MACMILLAN INFORMATION SUPERLIBRARY™

Free information and vast computer resources from the world's leading computer book publisher—online!

FIND THE BOOKS THAT ARE RIGHT FOR YOU!
A complete online catalog, plus sample chapters and tables of contents!

- **STAY INFORMED** with the latest computer industry news through our online newsletter, press releases, and customized Information SuperLibrary Reports.
- **GET FAST ANSWERS** to your questions about QUE books.
- **VISIT** our online bookstore for the latest information and editions!
- **COMMUNICATE** with our expert authors through e-mail and conferences.
- **DOWNLOAD SOFTWARE** from the immense Macmillan Computer Publishing library:
    - Source code, shareware, freeware, and demos
- **DISCOVER HOT SPOTS** on other parts of the Internet.
- **WIN BOOKS** in ongoing contests and giveaways!

TO PLUG INTO QUE:

WORLD WIDE WEB: **http://www.mcp.com/que**

FTP: ftp.mcp.com

Complete and Return this Card for a *FREE* Computer Book Catalog

Thank you for purchasing this book! You have purchased a superior computer book written expressly for your needs. To continue to provide the kind of up-to-date, pertinent coverage you've come to expect from us, we need to hear from you. Please take a minute to complete and return this self-addressed, postage-paid form. In return, we'll send you a free catalog of all our computer books on topics ranging from word processing to programming and the internet.

Mr. ☐ Mrs. ☐ Ms. ☐ Dr. ☐

Name (first) _____ (M.I.) ☐ (last) _____
Address _____
City _____ State ☐☐ Zip _____
Phone _____ Fax _____
Company Name _____
E-mail address _____

1. Please check at least (3) influencing factors for purchasing this book.

Front or back cover information on book .... ☐
Special approach to the content .... ☐
Completeness of content .... ☐
Author's reputation .... ☐
Publisher's reputation .... ☐
Book cover design or layout .... ☐
Index or table of contents of book .... ☐
Price of book .... ☐
Special effects, graphics, illustrations .... ☐
Other (Please specify): _____ ☐

2. How did you first learn about this book?

Saw in Macmillan Computer Publishing catalog .... ☐
Recommended by store personnel .... ☐
Saw the book on bookshelf at store .... ☐
Recommended by a friend .... ☐
Received advertisement in the mail .... ☐
Saw an advertisement in: _____ ☐
Read book review in: _____ ☐
Other (Please specify): _____ ☐

3. How many computer books have you purchased in the last six months?

This book only .... ☐   3 to 5 books .... ☐
2 books .... ☐   More than 5 .... ☐

4. Where did you purchase this book?

Bookstore .... ☐
Computer Store .... ☐
Consumer Electronics Store .... ☐
Department Store .... ☐
Office Club .... ☐
Warehouse Club .... ☐
Mail Order .... ☐
Direct from Publisher .... ☐
Internet site .... ☐
Other (Please specify): _____ ☐

5. How long have you been using a computer?

☐ Less than 6 months   ☐ 6 months to a year
☐ 1 to 3 years   ☐ More than 3 years

6. What is your level of experience with personal computers and with the subject of this book?

	With PCs	With subject of book
New	☐	☐
Casual	☐	☐
Accomplished	☐	☐
Expert	☐	☐

Source Code ISBN: 0-7897-0680-6

7. Which of the following best describes your job title?

- Administrative Assistant ☐
- Coordinator ☐
- Manager/Supervisor ☐
- Director ☐
- Vice President ☐
- President/CEO/COO ☐
- Lawyer/Doctor/Medical Professional ☐
- Teacher/Educator/Trainer ☐
- Engineer/Technician ☐
- Consultant ☐
- Not employed/Student/Retired ☐
- Other (Please specify): _____ ☐

8. Which of the following best describes the area of the company your job title falls under?

- Accounting ☐
- Engineering ☐
- Manufacturing ☐
- Operations ☐
- Marketing ☐
- Sales ☐
- Other (Please specify): _____ ☐

9. What is your age?

- Under 20 ☐
- 21-29 ☐
- 30-39 ☐
- 40-49 ☐
- 50-59 ☐
- 60-over ☐

10. Are you:

- Male ☐
- Female ☐

11. Which computer publications do you read regularly? (Please list)

_____
_____
_____
_____
_____
_____
_____
_____

Comments: _____

Fold here and scotch-tape to mail.

BUSINESS REPLY MAIL
FIRST-CLASS MAIL PERMIT NO. 9918 INDIANAPOLIS IN

POSTAGE WILL BE PAID BY THE ADDRESSEE

ATTN MARKETING
MACMILLAN COMPUTER PUBLISHING
MACMILLAN PUBLISHING USA
201 W 103RD ST
INDIANAPOLIS IN 46290-9042

NO POSTAGE
NECESSARY
IF MAILED
IN THE
UNITED STATES